SUGAR HILL

Where The Sun Rose Over Harlem

Sugar Hill
Where The Sun Rose Over Harlem
By Terry Baker Mulligan

ISBN: 978-0-9846929-0-3

Published by: Impulse Press | U.S.A.
For information, contact:
www.TerryBakerMulligan.com

Printed in the United States of America

Book Design – Sue Sylvia
        www.StaircasePressDesign.com
Cover Photos of Harlem – Jim Cummins
        http://tranquility49.com/blog/2011/05/30/jim-cummins/
Map Art – Anna Sheyko

Publisher's Cataloging-in-Publication Data:

Mulligan, Terry Baker.
Sugar Hill : where the sun rose over Harlem / Terry Baker Mulligan. -
- 1st ed. – St. Louis, Missouri : Impulse Press, c2012.
    p. ; cm.

    ISBN: 978-0-9846929-0-3
    Includes bibliographical references and index.

    1. Harlem (New York, N.Y.)–History. 2. Harlem (New York, N.Y.)–Civilization. 3. African Americans–New York (State)–New York–History. 4. African American arts–New York (State)–New York–History. 5. Harlem Renaissance. I. Title. II. Where the sun rose over Harlem.

F128.68.H3 M85 2012
974.71–dc23   1201

SUGAR HILL

Where The Sun Rose Over Harlem

TERRY BAKER MULLIGAN

IMPULSE PRESS ‡ USA

TO MOTHER
AND MOM

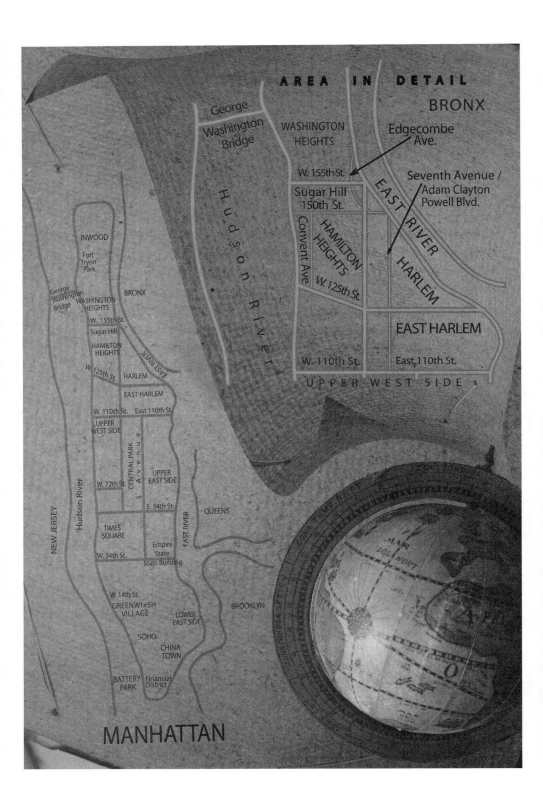

Table of Contents

Introduction

I started writing this book in 1974 when I was still a new bride, in a new city, with a new house and a new baby. Two months before, I'd resigned from teaching. And despite tidily wrapping up the school year and looking forward to raising my son, I couldn't shake the feeling that some part of this transition was incomplete. I had new friends and acquaintances, but too many of them held a monolithic view of Harlem—the place I was from. At the beginning of school, when my department chair learned where I'd come from and previously worked, he immediately changed all my classes, assuming I was an expert with troublemakers.

Three years later, on my last day of work, a student named Darnell helped me carry a heavy box filled with books and papers from my desk. While walking to the parking lot, he asked where I'd go next and what schools I'd worked in before. I told him I was taking a few years off; that I grew up in Harlem, and previously taught in New York. "Mrs. Muggagan," he said, shifting the box to his other shoulder so he could face me, "you couldn't be from Harlem; you too nice." Thus, a book idea was born. That idea was to tell the world about Sugar Hill, Harlem, a scenic 400-year-old chunk of prime New York City real estate that sits on a bluff, atop an island empire. That scrappy community that I love remained as large a "character" in my life as the real characters who helped make me the woman I had become.

The hardest thing about writing a book over half a lifetime, besides getting it to sound right, is getting it right. Fortunately, when I was closer to events on these pages, and before I first put the manuscript aside, I'd already laid out the bones of the story. The mid-20th century was not the best of times for Harlem. I could not ignore the community's problems with drugs and crime, but I didn't dwell on them either. Nor could I write a story about Harlem without replicating some degree of earthy language. Such is the case with the "N" word, which was commonly used, especially among men, but rarely uttered in public as it is today, and never in mixed-race company. My doing so in a book would be anathema to the people whom I quote. I use it sparingly and, for the sake of authenticity, I hope they'll forgive me.

Sugar Hill, Where the Sun Rose Over Harlem is a true story. However, in an effort not to invade privacies, I have changed a few names or blurred identities.

1. The Number Two Bus

Twenty-seven years is a long time between bus rides. I'd ridden other buses in the interim, but twenty-seven years had passed since I last approached this corner, 34th and Fifth Avenue, to wait for the number two. It was March of 1994 and I was thinking again about finishing this book on Harlem. My New York life can be plotted on a timeline of riding the two, three and four bus, so my plan that day was to retrace a once familiar 1950s route uptown, back to 369 Edgecombe Avenue, to the house where I was born.

To some observers of this city, climbing up that transportation grid translated into what might be described as an "improved lifestyle in a better neighborhood." I switched to the number three when we left Edgecombe Avenue and the easy routine of living with my grandmother. It happened the year I turned twelve, when McCarthyism had a grip on the nation, Emmett Till's lynching was a raw wound, and I was in the hormonal throes of starting junior high school. The move occurred after my mother and stepfather, eager to live independently of my grandmother, spent two years searching for their own home. I just never figured on them finding it.

Snow was still on the ground the day Mom informed me we would be moving. I was huddled in the far corner of my bed and she was perched on the edge. "We're not going far, so stop crying," she pleaded for the umpteenth heartbreaking time. "We'll only be twelve blocks from Mother. You'll see how much you like having a large room of your own. It'll make everything better."

"I have my own room. It already makes everything better," I sobbed, trying to prevent the snot dripping down my nose

3

from getting on the quilt. My room was a small cozy one, with enough space for my bed and chest of drawers to hold socks and underwear. Atop the chest, my penny jar almost had enough coins to roll fifty pennies in brown paper and swap them at the candy store for two quarters. Eight-paneled French doors, that I kept shiny with glass wax, allowed the sun to flood my room and on a clear day I could see as far as Connecticut.

Actually, from my front window, the naked eye could just see the tops of downtown skyscrapers and maybe ten blocks into the South Bronx. But at age twelve, when your world is collapsing, drama replaces reason and for some reason, nothing was going right for me that year. Along with a pending move, I'd grown four ungainly inches and broken out in pimples. Even my hair, once soft and curly, had betrayed me by turning coarse and kinky, refusing to flip up or under, like hairstyles in *Seventeen* and other magazines. Completing this new look was a pair of brown, thick-lens glasses that weren't the cat eye frames I wanted.

Ten years later, just out of college, with a job and blessedly beyond the ugly duckling stage, I bought my own damn glasses in the latest style, with gold wire rim frames. Then, after two weeks of training to be a New York City caseworker, I moved into an apartment with a girl named Carol, who became a lifelong friend. This time my preteen mood swings were in check, but America was still in a mess. Our Vietnam War strategy had soured and hoped-for Civil Rights legislation wasn't happening. These events rocked the world and turned my new neighborhood and the Columbia University campus, four blocks away, into its own war zone when protesting students seized Fayerweather Hall.

After watching an ugly student-police confrontation on CBS, Mom called me up on a Friday evening. "Jean, I just watched Walter Cronkite on the news and it's dangerous down there. I think you should consider moving back home."

"Mom, I'm fine," I assured her. "Carol, Lois and I are just talking in the kitchen."

"What did you cook for dinner?"

"We're finishing cheese balls that Carol's mother sent from Jersey," I told her, "and I made a pitcher of Sangria."

"That's no kind of dinner and you never eat cheese, unless it's grilled."

I'd also sampled escargot in a fancy restaurant, but only said, "I'll eat dinner later and I'm just being polite to Carol's mother," neither of which was exactly true, because nibbling and snacking now counted as dinner if I wanted them to. In a louder voice I tried to ease her worries, because kids all over the Upper West Side were hearing from anxious family members, some as far away as the Virgin Islands.

"Lois just walked over from 116th and Riverside," I added, "and earlier when I went out to buy fruit, Broadway was just like on a normal afternoon."

"What kind of fruit are you eating?"

"I bought oranges, Mom, and stop worrying. Even if I wanted to go on campus, where all the trouble is, I couldn't. It's locked down tight as a drum. I promise, the streets are safe. Everyone's just going about their business and there're ten cops at every intersection. All kinds of people my age live around here; it's exciting."

"Say whatever you like, but I predict you'll be back home in a week."

A few months earlier, she watched me pack my pink plastic Emerson clock radio and cherrywood jewelry box, a gift that her cousin Leamon brought back from Japan. I was only moving thirty blocks away, but we were playing out a variation of the theme from ten years ago, when Mom needed to move from Gram's house, because it meant independence and ultimately, an "improved lifestyle in a better neighborhood."

Unlike my mother, my girlfriends said living near all those Chinese restaurants and university men was pretty cool and if we ever needed a third roommate to let them know. Despite anti-war and family protests, proximity to Columbia turned out fine, because I married one of those college boys. But the blueprint of my life—those cunning early years when you develop into who you will become—was drawn in Harlem, my first home—the community and the people that this book is about. The place I was headed on the bus.

I thought a wait for the number two would work in my favor, because right now I needed to be a New Yorker again. However, in my eagerness to get going, I'd forgotten that Fifth Avenue had long been changed to a one-way street in the downtown direction. My options were to head over to Madison to find the bus, or start walking, which was clearly the better plan.

At street level, the lavishness of Fifth Avenue is more apparent than when viewing it from a bus, the way I had usually navigated this section of Fifth. Gorgeous boutiques I'd never seen before were lined up next to empty storefronts with FOR LEASE signs beckoning new tenants. High-end clothiers such as Altmans, Best, Russeks and Bonwit Teller were gone, replaced by retail flagship stores, like F.A.O Schwarz.

One thing that hadn't changed was Fifth Avenue's cast of thousands: dog walkers, tourists speaking unfamiliar languages, scurrying business execs, ordinary people in boots and barn coats, and those frightening females who carry $1,000 handbags and Emilio Pucci or Gucci shopping bags. Striding up the Avenue, they act like they own it, or are on a mission to buy it up.

Like the retail stretch of Fifth, the residential area between 59th and 72nd Street never seems to change, unless you consider current fashion trends, and whether investment bankers or dot-com millionaires occupy the penthouses. This is Manhattan's version of a gated community, where doormen guard turf while rocking back and forth to relieve legs that ache and backs that hurt, all while managing to look majestic in their own $500 overcoats. These gatekeepers snap to attention when one of those beautiful Gucci women marches in with a dog on a leash or an armful of Armani. And despite all the cute, curly haired poodles who must have pooped somewhere, the sidewalks remain manicured. By 72nd Street, I'd seen enough and had enough walking in my unlined raincoat and too-new shoes, so I headed over to Madison to find the bus.

Today, as in the past, the Harlem portion of this trip would unofficially begin at 110th Street and Seventh Avenue, and end at 155th Street, where I would get off. I like to think of Seventh Avenue as Harlem's center hall because the famous boulevard runs through the middle of the community, starting at 110th Street, and extends all forty-five blocks north. Taking the analogy a step further, the first blocks of Seventh were, at one time, the hall's foyer because it held the select architectural "furnishings" that a hostess would want visitors to see when first entering her home. Though now a bit shabby, two of those landmarks remain: the Graham Court apartment building with its landscaped garden and arched, drive-through entrance and the Regent Theater, once a grand movie palace that is now a Baptist church.

With a few exceptions, by 125th, housing along Seventh Avenue becomes less opulent, with fewer tall or stately structures, and the avenue takes on a commercial quality, notable for small businesses in low rise apartment buildings. When I was a child, Harlem was the undisputed heartbeat of Negro America, and 125th Street at Seventh Avenue was its crossroads and gathering spot for singles, families, beautiful people, numbers bankers, pimps, soapbox orators and newcomers, arriving by bus, train and car from Southern states or flying on bargain shuttles from islands like Jamaica and Trinidad.

Whenever I rode the bus with Mom and it reached Hotel Theresa at 125th Street, she perked up like a birdwatcher, hoping to add a colorful species to her list of celebrity sightings. Acting like the young star-struck twenty-something she was, if Mom spotted her quarry, I got poked in the ribs. Entertainers, athletes and high profile figures hung out in front of the hotel. Sometimes Mom got lucky. "Look, Jean, there's Duke Ellington," she might say, or we'd catch a glimpse of Sammy Davis, Jr., or spot Sugar Ray, standing next to his pink Cadillac.

Then there was Adam Clayton Powell, Jr., our United States Congressman. A Negro of means who could pass for white, Powell was the epitome of cigar smoking, playboy cool. He also had a bent for radical politics and was the pastor of Abyssinian Baptist, the church many still consider to be Harlem's most influential.

When Powell left Washington, or his summer home on Cape Cod, or Bimini, his island in the Bahamas, to visit our district or preach on Sunday, the service was packed with Baptists, Presbyterians, beautiful women and everybody else. Despite his scandals and arrogance, Powell was a crowd pleaser; the kind of educated, good-looking elegant man who rubbed shoulders with kings and queens, or shot the breeze at Jock's, Red Rooster or the Baby Grand, uptown hot spots known for cool jazz, tall drinks and a bevy of pretty young fans.

But Harlem also had a thriving underground economy, so not everyone got a paycheck from the government, a congregation or the boss. Plenty of financially successful men were hustlers, con artists and numbers bankers. Poor people in Harlem, who routinely dodged bill collectors and dispossess notices, were often in awe of fellow citizens with power or money and they didn't always care how it was acquired. At Smalls Paradise and a few other night spots, my mother remembers seeing a thin, light-skinned, shady character with freckles and the nickname Detroit Red, who waited tables in the clubs for awhile, but mostly hustled in the streets. Red ended up in prison and when he got out, he had found religion, given up drinking, hustling numbers and women, and had a new name, Malcolm X. So Seventh Avenue, the tree-lined boulevard of legend and mystique, had all types to revere or revile.

Manhattan has a complex topography. Downtown, at the island's flat southern end, skyscrapers rise at the rim of the water, their front doors awash in overflow when mean nor'easters whip through and stir up New York Harbor. Much of Harlem sits on cliffs and jagged rock formations at steep elevations. My favorite view from the number two was when the bus reached Dunbar Apartments, at 150th and Seventh. Off to the left, high above the apartment complex, I could see my house perched on the cliff. In the 1600s the Dutch settled in Harlem and years later, when the British arrived, the island was organized into grids. Our street was named Edgecombe because it sits at the edge of the combe, which is the Old English word for a basin or valley.

I assigned great value to my sweet, lovely place on the hill. Harlem had culture and character, but it also had deep pockets of poverty and little children with haunted eyes, wild hair and parents who struggled to care for them. Something prayerful stirred within me when I passed run-down tenements I didn't have to live in.

I still pick at the scab of a 1950s slight that enraged me. Patsy, the daughter of my mother's childhood friend, invited me over for the weekend. She and her family were the first blacks on their block in Queens. Later, when I reciprocated and invited Patsy to spend the night with me before my birthday party, she whispered over the phone, "I can't, Jeanie. My mother won't let me."

"But it'll be fun. We're going to play pin the tail on the donkey and I'm going help make my cake. We can lick the bowl. Why can't you come?" I asked, thinking it might be her birthday, too.

"My mother said you live in Harlem and she doesn't want me to come over there."

I'd heard grownups say our community was changing and they worried about drug addicts and increased purse snatchings, but I'd never known a black person who wouldn't come to Harlem. Uttering a confused, "Oh, okay," I passed the phone to my mother, but I understood we'd been insulted. I could hear Patsy's mother, Helen, hemming and hawing and still refusing to come "into the city," even after being assured, "Very nice children will be at the party, Helen." Then Mom pulled out her trump card. "This new little boy in Jean's class will be there. His father is a lawyer." That didn't work, and maybe name dropping was uncalled for, but back then the world didn't have many black lawyers, so we were proud of the ones in Harlem.

For days, weeks, years, I thought of this family, remembering the weekend I'd spent in their paper thin-walled house in Queens; them subtly, insistently showing off white GE appliances and a pink-tiled bathroom. Me, falling for the bait, saying all the right-wrong little girl things. "Ooh, what a pretty washing machine. When the machine in our basement works, Mommy washes our clothes down there." Where did these boastful, former Brooklyn residents with the tacky paneled living room, who lived one house away from a noisy highway think I lived? In the ghetto?

Like everyone in Harlem during the 1990s, I knew the community was trying to get its swagger back, but that March day in 1994, when I rode up Seventh Avenue, what I saw didn't look too promising. A renovated apartment building stood next to one whose burned-out, windowless top floors were yet to be boarded up; ugly black scorch marks marred the tan bricks. Idle young men and a few women, seemingly unemployed or skipping school, loitered on street corners and in front of graffiti-scrawled front stoops. Just off the avenue, in an elementary schoolyard, I glimpsed three teenagers who should have been across town in a high school classroom. Instead, they were shooting hoops and even from the bus, I glimpsed athleticism and undisciplined natural grace that could break the heart of any high school coach looking to build a team.

Further along, the "new" Adam Clayton Powell State Office Building sat diagonally across from the Hotel Theresa, which had also been converted into an office building. Powell's namesake structure had anchored the northeast corner of 125th Street for over twenty years, but other hoped-for construction was still in the talking stage. Around the year 2000, with the opening of a multi-screen movie theater, this main commercial zone would begin to rise again. Then, in 2001, when President Clinton opted to locate his New York office in the Powell building, that further jump-started a resurgence that just keeps getting stronger.

As the bus neared my stop, all remaining passengers were black, except a white, or perhaps Hispanic, couple talking animatedly in their seat. Sleepers, their heads drooping, still catnapped their way home, magically awakened by some internal alarm that alerted them to an approaching departure point. The lady across from me, who was no longer young, had boarded the bus around Madison and 86th Street. In her shapeless camel coat, scarf tied resolutely under her chin, she cradled the day's essentials in a well-worn tote bag. Years of hard work showed in the strength of her jaw and in roughened brown hands. I'd been with her on other buses, too. A veteran rider, she was one of the people who left home early and passed through several culture zones before arriving safely back to Harlem in time to cook a second dinner. In houses at both ends of the city, she was the glue that held things together; indispensable, faithful and tired.

A different sort of woman sat in a wheelchair, encouraging intelligent talk from a girl and her older brother who did not seem happy when the woman pointed at the instrument case resting between his knees and asked, "Jason, are you practicing your violin?" The little sister eagerly answered for him. "He wants to quit, but Mama won't let him. He has to stick it out for the rest of the year."

The engaging, soft-spoken, honey-colored woman showed a new kind of strength. She was a teacher and the two children attended her school. Conceding nothing to her disability, she'd draped a fringed black shawl over stylish shoulders and wore freshly painted nails. After a brief ride, as if by prearrangement, the boy and girl set down their backpacks, and with the driver's assistance, helped lock the chair's wheels into a drop-down lift to depart the back of the bus, the way she entered. The woman showed grace under the other passengers' scrutiny and confidence in a system that must, at times, have failed her.

About ten blocks back, a suspect passenger had gotten off, taking with him pent-up tension that sometimes rides public transportation in big cities. The young man, with his aggressive stare, straddled two seats, had eyes scattershot with red from heavy drinking. Despite that, he still snuck sips from a tall bottle of malt liquor—something he must have been doing for most of the day, by the lit-up look of him. His uniform shirt made me wonder where he worked that allowed such furtive drinking. Maybe in the Mt. Sinai Hospital complex, around 103rd Street, where he'd gotten on with the afternoon shift change.

Also gone were two young hip hop teens with their bad language and baggy jeans, crotches down to their knees. They'd been standing close to me and I'd wanted to see how their pants stayed up, but prudently kept my eyes straight ahead as they jived and jostled, intentionally trying to bump other passengers. The boys talked big and showed off, peppering their conversation with vulgarity, everyone hoping they'd just get off before the driver called a cop, causing a delay or a worse scene. I wondered if these young kids were just wannabes, or already the seriously bad little "gangsta dudes" they were trying so hard to be. In the past, I knew who to watch out for. Not any more.

Despite nostalgia and the good times rolling on this ride, I was glad my mother wasn't with me. I could just hear her saying to one of those boys, "Young man, you mustn't call our women hos and bitches. It demeans us all." Or she would have admonished, "Son, pull your pants up. Take some pride in your appearance." Perhaps, before I could stop her, the grandmotherly palm of her hand might have settled on one of their shoulders.

Witnessing her city and its people change was also altering my mother, making her angry. When I was last home, I heard her sidewalk drill in front of our house. She'd gone up to a young teenager with a boom box and told him to turn it down and it hadn't even been loud. Surprised and a little embarrassed, I said, "Mom, that's what kids do now; they carry around their music. You're going to be labeled 'the mean old lady who lives in 302.'"

"Mean old lady? I'd take that in a minute. You should hear how these children talk to adults. But they're not going to blast that rap music on this street when I'm around. Somebody has to speak up." Apparently others agreed with her and when Mayor Giuliani took office, he wrestled New York into a semblance of civility that had been sorely lacking. His strategy was to reduce serious offenses by first attacking nuisance crimes, such as panhandling and noise. Both that approach, and the sudden proliferation of earphones, helped bring things under control.

When my seatmate stood up to leave, I wished her a good day. At 143rd Street, while we idled at a light, she had spoken to me as strangers in New York often do. "Well, if that isn't something," she said, pointing out the window. "Just look at that crying child. Do you think it's the mama or daddy that's holed up in there?"

It would have been easy to miss on a busy sidewalk. Just another corner tavern and a small crying child, sitting cross-legged and alone on the cold ground, in front of the bar's mirrored-glass door. The little boy's heartbreak didn't approach that seen in H.S. Wong's iconic wartime photo of a similar-aged child in Shanghai, after Japanese bombs flattened the city, but the tableau of a distraught toddler alone amid the ruins of his life was eerily similar. The woman didn't expect an answer to her question, but we shook our heads in unison, as strangers in New York often do while observing the human condition from the seat of a bus.

Just before our last turn onto the 155th Street viaduct, the McCombs Dam Bridge caught my eye. When I last saw the old swing bridge it was rust colored. Today it was gussied up in a bright blue. In 1895, the McCombs Dam Bridge replaced a dam on the river and, despite the passing of a hundred years, the bridge remains a reliable connection between Manhattan and the Bronx. Yankee Stadium sits just over the water from Manhattan, but the ballpark I saw that day was replaced in 2009, by the new billion-dollar Yankee Stadium.

With the Harlem River flowing right outside the bus window, I thought how limited my interaction had been with this thing of wonder, considering its power to amaze me when I was a child. Today a large tree branch floated through the channel and, in the blink of the eye, shadows from the bridge changed the water's color from glittery silver to blue black. Manhattan is surrounded by two beautiful rivers, but all anyone in Harlem ever wanted from these rivers was a 10th floor apartment with a view.

In the early 1940s, my grandmother worked in Edgewater, New Jersey. Edgewater is across from Harlem on the other side of the Hudson and to get there, she commuted by ferry. Most of my river crossings were done underground, in subway tunnels. Up to that point, I had never been to North Jersey or crossed the George Washington Bridge, despite its nearness to our house. When our family visited Jersey, we traveled via Lincoln Tunnel, then headed south to an area whose name, thanks to reality TV, has become ubiquitous in American pop culture, the Jersey Shore.

My grandmother told me about her Edgewater job soon after we returned from a trip to Norfolk, Virginia, where I fell in love with trains and ferryboats.

Peppering her with questions, I asked, "What was the Jersey boat like?"

"Very convenient," she told me. "Today it would be hard to take that job without a car and it would take three times longer to get there."

"Does Edgewater have beaches like Norfolk?"

"No, it's on the river, not the ocean, but in some ways it reminded me of Norfolk because people over there depend on the water to make a living."

"Like what?"

"Well, you know, fishermen, tugboat captains," she answered, which didn't make much of an impression at the time, since I'd never been on a fishing boat or tug.

Getting to the crux of the matter, I asked, "Was your Edgewater ferryboat big and beautiful like the one we rode to Norfolk?"

"No honey, it was just a small commuter line."

"Wasn't it fun to ride it every day? No one else takes a boat to work. Why don't you work there any more?"

"They discontinued service, but plenty of people commute by ferry. Besides," she added, reaching over to engulf me in her soft, sweet smelling bosom, "that was before you were born and now I take care of you."

The summer before, Gram and I had traveled to Norfolk in a Pullman car sleeper, where our porter pampered us like royalty, repeatedly swabbing out our sink, bringing fresh towels and over-demonstrating how to turn on and off the lights. Later, while the train was traveling through Pennsylvania, we ate dinner in the dining car and got served all kinds of extra butter and rolls because Gram—who would have done well to get out of the house more—was acting like a flirt. She kept flashing her dimples and dipping her wide-brimmed, Sunday-go-to-meeting hat in our grinning waiter's face, and he fell all over himself doing her bidding. I didn't know much then, but I knew a few railroad men and I can tell you, not many passengers got better treatment than we did on that train. Back in our sleeping car, I climbed to the top bunk feeling like I'd been sprinkled with angel dust. Then, it was either the angels or God who tucked me in, and sang me to sleep with their clickity-clack lullaby.

In the morning, at Cape Charles, Virginia, when fog and mist lifted, the beauty waiting to sail us across Chesapeake Bay was a sleek, two-story white ferry, as majestic as the Queen Mary docked back home at Chelsea Pier. So, my idea of both train travel and ferryboats remained inflated until I started riding the Staten Island Ferry. And although those plain, serviceable boats didn't have dining rooms with fawning waiters or porters to carry luggage, there really wasn't anything shabby, either, about standing on the deck of a Staten Island Ferry and having a flock of laughing seagulls escort you across New York Harbor.

Once, after my trip to Norfolk, to get a better look at the Harlem River, Mark Wright, a cute boy on my block who, like me, got a new pint-sized Schwinn for Christmas, persuaded me to sneak down to the McCombs Bridge with him on our bikes. The only other kid our age with a two-wheeler was wild and crazy Albert, who fell down the elevator shaft in his building and only ended up with a scar on his head. Another time, when riding his bike, Albert plowed so hard into Angela that his father took the bike away, because Albert caused Angela to spend all summer in a heavy leg cast and a wheelchair.

I'm sure I got a nifty blue and white girl's two-wheeler because my parents never imagined me doing anything like what I was about to do with Mark. My girlfriends were content to jump rope or play hopscotch, which I liked, too. But Mark was a nice boy with dimples and shiny black hair like Mowgli's in *The Jungle Book*, only Mark's was curlier, plus he lived in 409 where all the rich, dignified people on our street lived, so I decided it was okay to venture out with him.

I knew a few safety rules of the sidewalk, like don't stomp on my brakes to slow down, and since I navigated two tricky corners on the way to school, I figured crossing a busy inter-section would be a cinch. But, just to be sure, I asked Mark, "When we get down there, how do we cross the street?"

In a perfectly polite tone of voice, he said, "When the light turns green." Yes, of course, I thought, obviously already nervous as I watched his Keds pedal away at a wild and crazy pace. Standing up to pump harder, he then coasted recklessly at breakneck speed, like Albert might have done. I could have found my way home blindfolded, but for some unknown reason, I was suddenly terrified to be left behind. Making this bad idea worse, the viaduct we were on was 1600 feet long, on a straight downhill slope towards the bridge. It also had prop-erties similar to a suspension bridge; heavy traffic bounced it up and down and it swayed in the wind. But the stiff breeze coming from the river wasn't the only thing blowing off my repeated yells to "Wait up, wait up."

Pedaling furiously to close the distance, I saw him reach the bottom and spin his bike around with a fancy flourish. By the grace of God and mercifully minus the pubescent testo-sterone leading this folly, I braked to a stop before catapulting into traffic. It was cold, but I felt hot disapproval from real and imagined eyes watching me ride too fast and dash across heavy traffic onto the swaying McCombs Dam Bridge that made me dizzy with dread and nausea.

Today, while getting off at my bus stop, I remembered how Ralph, my grandmother's boarder, also her sometime boyfriend, used to say, "Great day in the morning" when he felt good about something. That's how I'd felt about this corner. It once hummed with a great day, good golly, morning glory excitement. 155th Street is a major intersection roughly shaped like a pinwheel, its arms pointing in six directions. The arms lead to the Bronx, Upstate New York, the Harlem Valley, New Jersey, Queens and highways that go beyond. The smallest section winds down Edgecombe Avenue to the secluded block where I'd lived.

Men constructed the street's pinwheel, but nature made our corner. Up here, Manhattan is about a third as wide as Midtown. On a map, the island loosely resembles a plucked duck on a poultry chart, its sections conveniently labeled. The Battery is the bird's pouty little mouth (with the beak removed); the fat tummy protrudes at what we call Midtown, although technically, the Times Square-Theater District in the 40s and 50s should be relabeled Quartertown, because Manhattan's numbered streets end in the 220s. But anyway, the bird's stubby webbed feet hang over the island's northern edge in Inwood. The skinniest part, a bend in the duck's slender knees is the Sugar Hill area, where I stood.

The intersection hadn't changed, but the stores on my corner had. Once, ten of them formed a vibrant enterprise zone run by Mom, Pop, Harry and Bud, honest merchants who sold groceries, fresh meat, produce, dry goods and fish at fair prices. This day, those stores were inhospitable and boarded up, with weeds growing in front of the neglected, cracked sidewalk. Two open stores with no signage had plywood covering the glass, and I couldn't tell if renovation or desolation was causing their state of disrepair. Under a cloud of disappointment, I did not enter any of the stores.

I used to know this street so intimately I could tell you there were 63, 67 or maybe it was 73, sidewalk squares between my house and the corner. Turning the bend and crossing to the parkside of Edgecombe, I remembered the old herky-jerky way I used to walk to avoid "stepping on a crack and breaking my mother's back." Staring at my feet, I suppressed a grin and silly impulse to stutter-step.

With a sense of melancholy, I looked down at the sloping parkland that separated this hill and valley. In 1894, the city purchased these twelve-and-eight-tenths acres from Dr. Samuel Bradhurst's estate for the sum of $1,473.01.[1] As children, we were told to stay away, not just because bad guys might be lurking in the park—although they occasionally did—but because the foliage was so dense, no one could find us through the trees. What had been a dangerous thing of beauty was now a pale dirt floor pitted with little gullies of erosion, sprouting crooked little junk trees. Some of the trees looked sickly; others would have benefited from pruning before their canopy completely blocked the eastern view. To the East, large apartment complexes now cluttered the once wide-open horizon. To my left, four twenty-five story-tall buildings that someone had bravely named Polo Ground Towers occupied sacred baseball ground.

A man dressed in a suit walked out the front door of 409 and watched me huddled in the collar of my raincoat. My prop, an important-looking briefcase that suddenly weighed a ton, must have signaled I had purpose and connection to this place because he turned and walked in the direction I had just come. I wondered if this side of the street was still the summer domain of old men on benches who read the racing news, watched cars drive by or dozed in the sun. As kids, we rushed outside after dinner to claim our favorite bench and talk about what happened since lunchtime.

Occasionally on warm evenings, someone's mother joined us on the parkside. She'd leave her dinner dishes in the sink, put a sundress back on and come outside wearing stockings rolled down to the ankles. She was there to relax and cool off, but ended up saying the usual things. "Tuck in your shirt. Tie your shoe. Stop running. Child, you're making a mess with that popsicle. Isn't it almost time for you kids to go in?" Most women avoided the park. It was a Sugar Hill thing: no hanging out of windows and no hanging out on park benches. An Edgecombe Avenue woman's place was in her home taking care of family, even if she didn't have one.

Bradhurst is the avenue below Edgecombe. Today, the flagstone and concrete stairway leading down to Bradhurst was boarded up. I surmised the stairs, like the neglected soil they rested on, had deteriorated. Later I learned the blockade of boards was there to eliminate an escape route for purse snatchers and other miscreants. Some things never change; that staircase had always been their escape route.

19

In the late 1950s, Mrs. Thurgood Marshall, the woman married to the lawyer who was often in the news and would end up on the United States Supreme Court, sometimes sat on the bench I now approached. Mrs. Marshall lived in 409 and she was always alone, except for her baby and his shiny dark gray, hard-sided carriage, the kind my mother called the Cadillac of perambulators. Being new to the neighborhood and all, I guessed she hadn't met any other mommies who could tell her how things worked, so her only company was a pretty round-faced boy swaddled in blue bunting, who had thick black hair like his father. Since I was always running to the store for one thing or another, I got to see more than just how many cracks lined the sidewalk. I figured Mrs. Marshall's leisure stemmed from living in 409 among rich people, who didn't even have to open their own front door because doormen did it for them.

It was 4:45 p.m. and I was meeting with Jean Beverly anytime after 5:00 o'clock. A half century ago, Jean was my grandmother's neighbor and still lived in the apartment next to our old one. My mother had advised that Jean watched a favorite TV show and wouldn't want to be disturbed before the appointed hour.

The universal reaction, when I asked to interview old friends and elderly family members, was caution. Their veil of wariness and suspicion disappointed, but did not surprise me. Anyone my age can tell you how good this older generation was at holding onto secrets and putting the past behind them. For so long, the past and the secrets were safe because no one was interested in them, or in Harlem. Now, all these questions.

I crossed back to the building side of the street. I knew my pending visit was causing Jean some anxiety. I'd explained I wasn't looking for negatives; they were easily documented. What I wanted was help in recapturing the soft nuances of our past, when life was so big and full we didn't know it could get any better. Or any worse.

My problem was how to use fifteen minutes to walk five houses down the street; not a simple matter in this complex city. It would not be dark for another hour, but it was windy and cold, and as I approached number 375, I was running out of ways to dally.

On the stoop of 373, I passed a group of teenage boys having a heated discussion in Spanish, a new language on an old block. Across on the parkside, a young woman sat leaning over the edge of a bench, alone and ignored by the boys. She was nodding out in that loose-limbed way that a heroin high allows a body to slacken like a marionette on a string. Crack was the new street drug; I knew heroin was making a comeback, although I hadn't seen a strung-out heroin addict in a long time. When I was a kid, the junkies were our street people. Rarely violent, stealing was their thing and they apologized when they robbed you. The only shooting up they did was into their own veins. I knew the tortured soul on the bench posed no danger, but the boys had stopped talking and were watching me watch her. I moved along and rang Jean's bell at 4:53 p.m.

North view of Harlem River, at 155th Street. Jumel Mansion can be seen on hill at left (circa 1890). Photo courtesy of NY Public Library.

2. Harlem Vista: An Ice Age Beauty

Throughout New York City—and mostly ignored—are the roots and remnants of an ancient mountain range created some 250 million years ago, when Africa and Europe crashed into North America. The collision crumpled the earth's rock and granite interior, resulting in a mighty chain of mountains. Those large chunks of molten material support upper Manhattan's steep hillsides. From the Bronx to the Battery, smaller remnants sprout randomly around parks and playgrounds, and these perfect child-sized mountains have delighted generations of kids with imaginative rough and tumble play. This geologic mass is the bedrock of the city.[1] It harbors skyscraper foundations and bears the weight of an underground subway system that brushes the edge of the ocean.

In upper Manhattan and neighboring New Jersey near the George Washington Bridge, nature left a more ornamental legacy, the Hudson River Palisades. The Palisades are smooth white bluffs, rising 550 feet from the water's edge on the Jersey side of the river. These stately formations begin the Southern anchor of the 50,000 acre Palisades Interstate Park, a hilly wooded recreational chain that meanders north up both shorelines. If you follow the chain fifty miles upriver on the New York side, folks start calling this configuration the Catskill Mountains.

The Manhattan side of this shore lacks the dramatic beauty of Jersey. Over here, glaciers pushed the mountain back a thousand yards, providing a scenic drive and spare rocky beach along the water's edge. This is where New Yorkers walk, bike or sit and watch the sun roll behind the mountain

23

as it runs out of daylight. In 1938, the Metropolitan Museum of Art used four acres on the New York side of the river to build The Cloisters in Fort Tryon Park, atop the prettiest spot and highest point of Manhattan. The Cloisters is home to the Metropolitan's collection of medieval religious art. In the middle of the complex, a landscaped courtyard and well-tended gardens are surrounded by connecting arched cloisters. Indoors, beneath a wall of tapestries, statuary and 14th century stained glass, the hushed atmosphere is church-like. When walking through the museum, it's easy to imagine you're in a French monastery, where around the next corner you'll stumble upon a chapel where a hooded monk is sitting in the front pew, praying and clicking his rosary beads.

I was born in this hilly part of the city when black and white New Yorkers were recovering from a world war. Whatever their differences, and there were many, both races were united in prayer and hope for a better world. My neighborhood was a reflection of this post-war optimism and blacks lucky enough to live here embraced the sweet life on Sugar Hill.

In a crowded city, stingy with space and light, Edge-combe was Harlem's big sky country; a street blessed with a wide-open view, where the sun rose over Harlem and bathed our front windows in a three-season glow. Each year, by mid-September, deep green leaves began changing into orangey-yellows, then muted browns before dropping off when hurricanes swooped in, preceding the colder weather. Once, a line of dangerous hurricanes brushed the city. With one named Hazel bearing down, even fortress-like Manhattan with its nailed-down benches and concrete canyons took notice. Superintendents stowed away garbage cans, office workers hurried home, and in our house, the old oil lamp came off the shelf—ready if needed in a blackout. Before satellite weather technology and 24-hour talking heads did all our thinking for us, it was exciting for city residents to anticipate the unknown of a hurricane.

Outside, with evening well advanced, heavy rain fell, some of it leaking under the window sill and with Mom still not home, Gram nervously twisted her dish towel into a tight knot and decided she needed to worry about something besides the clock. "Jean," she said targeting me, "depending on whether the brunt of this storm arrives tonight or tomorrow, you might have to stay home from school."

I didn't want to stay home. Because of Jewish holidays, we'd just returned after the usual late start that always made the final draggy weeks of September's chilly nights seem like anything but summer vacation. I thought about my blue savings book back at school. Last time I saw it, someone had stamped $1.31, reflecting my giant life savings. That bankroll came from change I got to keep after running errands at the store.

"I don't want to stay home," I said more forcefully than usual when trying to get my way with Gram. "It's only rain, Gram. School just opened and Mommy said I have to learn how to multiply interest. I need to go tomorrow. I'll stay dry in my slicker and boots."

"First of all," she snapped, "school didn't just open and arithmetic is one thing, but I'm not talking about keeping your clothes and feet dry."

A new learning tool that year at P.S. 46 was for our class to open classroom savings accounts since the closest banks, on 125th Street and 181st Street, were both more than a mile away. When World War II ended, the savings bug spread across the country. Popularity of piggy banks grew and many homes, including ours, also started keeping dimes in cardboard March of Dimes coin savers. When a card filled with a few dollars in dimes, the donation went towards finding a cure for polio and caring for the sick. Besides convenience, our school's in-house banking system was a variation of this national thriftiness. We were also saving because our teacher, Mrs. McWhorter, told us interest rates were at an all time high, which somehow meant that a little bit of money could grow into a big pile. Multiplication had gone pretty well for me, until decimal points intruded. So far, about all I understood about decimal points was they kept changing places and giving me a hard time.

With no intention of backing off her desire to keep me home with her, Gram said, "A hurricane's nothing to mess with. Didn't you see the wind whipping around out there? Little as you are, just let one of these hurricanes get ahold of you, and you might end up in kingdom come."

At least she didn't say Mississippi, the bogeyman badland of all things terrible for black people. When I was young enough to believe her every word, she threatened to send me to a Mississippi boarding school if I disobeyed her. All things being relative, even a wised-up third grader didn't stand much chance of winning an argument with her because she didn't argue fair. Confrontation was her sport and she zeroed-in on a dispute, like a torpedo locking on its target, and refused to let go until her opponent was dead in the water, or died laughing because she could be infuriating, but also funny.

Gram may have been born ornery, but I think she lashed out because something deep in her soul, some past insult, injury to her pride or harsh treatment of indifference was never forgotten. Knowing she'd likely win a fight, she was quick to pick one, and maybe her best victory was getting safely out of the South, despite having that big mouth and a tendency to sass white people.

One morning, earlier that summer, I answered the doorbell and a white man in a baggy brown suit stood there holding a black book in his hand, a satchel resting on the floor. Door-to-door salesmen peddled everything from Hoover vacuums to four-piece bedroom suites. This one was selling Bibles and when Gram trundled to the door on her achy knees, he asked if she'd like to buy one. Instead of just saying, "No," even without tacking on the "thank you," she challengingly asked, "Mister, do I look like a fool who doesn't already own a Bible?"

I guess the sight of a dimple-faced, roly-poly grandma standing there with an attitude at 11 a.m., wearing a fresh layer of face powder, dab of Pompeii pink rouge, pearls strung around her neck, nylons held up with garters under her usual calf-length rayon print dress that concealed rickets-diseased bow legs, failed to get him all flummoxed and red faced, as usually happened when she dressed-down salesmen.

"No Ma'am," he politely replied, "you don't look like anybody's fool."

Sizing him up for a few seconds, she must have liked something about him. "Well then," she said with less edge, and in a lower register, "for your troubles, try ringing their bell." She pointed across the hall. "That poor family's daughter is cursed with that evil heroin and they could use any help the Lord might give them."

Beyond loving her raggedy black Bible, the one in question being an old King James version with a torn back cover, my grandmother wasn't partial to religion anyway. Her worst sarcasms and insults spewed forth when Kingdom Hall sent a "Jehovah" to apartment twenty-two, which happened regularly since many Harlemites were receptive to religious persuasion. Proselytizers might have done better jumping on the back of a saddled-up Iberian bull and waving lunch under his nose, than trying to convince my grandmother that Jesus Christ had anything to do with "a bunch of fools whose main mission," as far as she knew, "is being a pain in my ass."

This woman with the chip on her shoulder was barely five feet tall, light complexioned and vain enough to think she still resembled the beautiful young woman in a 20 x 13-inch portrait that hung on our living room wall above the mantel. In the painting, she's wearing a pensive look and a lilac blue sweater, fingers delicately intertwined at chest level. Currently, she was a soft, round 18 dress size, who moved with a tortoise-like slowness I attributed to every grandmother's need not to be rushed. Besides wearing XL dresses and enormous flesh colored bloomers that she insisted on calling drawers, the only other outsized part of her was personality.

On the evening of the hurricane, Gram sat fidgeting in a high wingback chair, as if she was the child in the room. Checking the clock again, she put aside the twisted dish towel.

"Olivia should have been home by now," she said again.

Just as I dealt out a game of solitaire, Mom put her key in the door. Gram yelled down the hall, "Olivia, what took so long on a night like this?" I followed with, "Mommy do I have to stay home tomorrow?"

"I stopped at the store. Let me put this milk in the refrigerator and get out of these rubbers. Did Jack call yet?"

"No," we both answered.

Jack was her boyfriend and would soon become my stepfather. He lived nearby on St. Nicholas Avenue and tended bar up on the corner at Bowman's, and after dinner, she sometimes went up for a drink since he worked long hours and weekend nights, only getting Thursdays and Sundays off.

Mom came in the living room, kissed us both, kicked off her high heels that had gotten wet, despite the rubbers, took a deep pull of Chesterfield and eyed my homework, a single notebook page with a few multiplication problems.

"Did you check for careless errors?"

"Yes, but I didn't find any."

"We'll see. Go set the table and I'll look it over after we eat."

We were having meatloaf for dinner and, after a raw rainy day, heat from the still-warm oven felt good. I laid out plates and silverware and put ketchup on the table. From the front room I heard Mom say, "Mother, they pay me little enough already. I can't just leave early because it's raining." I didn't hear school being discussed but outside, the wind was already easing up.

Lying in bed that night, rain tapping at the window, I felt safe in my tiny front room, but I fell asleep thinking about second chances. Six weeks before, on a weekday in August, we had ridden Upstate on a bus outing to a place my aunt called a private black country club that the Masons owned. Typically, no other kids came on these all-day picnics sponsored by Aunt Annette's Eastern Star church-lady friends.

The weather was perfect: hot, sunny and windless with low humidity. The "club" was nestled deep within a country road on a few open acres of weedy grass that badly needed mowing. Thick woods shrouded three sides of the property, blanketing it in a silence I might have expected if we'd traveled to the far end of nowhere, instead of somewhere up Route 87. Standing in the gravel parking lot, I saw a two-story white farm house with peeling paint that looked abandoned, but probably contained the bathroom that would be crawling with spiders.

For the first twenty minutes after we arrived, I helped tote straw food baskets, giant ice tea thermoses, towels and changes of clothes to the picnic area. Then, with little else to do, I watched two dozen women swat mosquitoes and circle tables like boys choosing up sides before a stickball game. No one wanted to sit in too much sun or shade, on too steep a slant, or at a splintery picnic table or bench, which was what all of them were. Mom and my Aunt Cee weren't there. Mom had to work and Aunt Cee knew better than to spend a whole day with a bunch of silly looking grandmothers wearing pedal pushers and muumuus.

The day's prospects improved considerably when I spotted the blue water of a swimming pool down a ravine. Just as I cried out, "Look," Aunt Annette, fed up with all the indecision, said, "Mother, just stop worrying about which table. We'll use these," and dumped our towels on the nearest table.

"I didn't come all the way up here to spend half the morning finding a damn seat. I'm not planning to get wet anyway," she said, spreading the table and both benches with what looked like every last towel we brought.

"Wait." I grabbed a small hand towel with Pennsylvania Railroad stamped down the middle. "I'm going to change to go swimming. It's hot. The pool's right down there," I pointed.

Without looking, Aunt Annette snapped at me, "I know where it is," as if it was my idea to come up here.

"Jean, Annette, stop rushing me," Gram said. "Just hold on a minute."

I held on for a second, then took off towards the peely-paint house I hoped had a bathroom, even with spiders.

"Come straight back and don't go wandering anywhere," Gram said distractedly.

"I won't."

"And stay away from any poison ivy."

I didn't know what it looked like, but said, "I will."

Five minutes later, dressed in my orange daisy two-piece, I detoured down the hill, out of sight of the grownups, and slid in the water. They took me on these long, dawn-to-dusk trips because I was an easy child to take places. I might fidget and ask, "When can we leave?" but normally I didn't stray or go near deep water. The water wasn't deep; it came to my waist. But someone had left a pair of swim fins by the side of the pool. If you weigh next to nothing and can't swim, you learn in a bad way that fins will flip you upside down if you don't know how to use them. Surprised and panicked by water up my nose and unable to stand, I felt a stab of certainty that I wouldn't be coming on any more picnics when they found me in the pool. Choking and flailing on instinct against weight pulling my feet, I managed to rescue myself and thrashed back to the side. It all happened in a flash.

Back at the tables, Gram, sorting waxed paper-wrapped food, stopped rummaging and straightened up. Eyeing my wet hair and suit, she looked over her shoulder, only now registering that I told her I was going swimming. At first all she said was, "Dry off." Then she told me to sit down and eat lunch, but remained uncharacteristically quiet fixing a plate of potato salad and a baloney sandwich that I managed to nibble at without throwing up. Next time she spoke it was to say, "Now stay put." It sounded like the word of God giving me a second chance.

Unlike me, my family didn't always operate in a state of bliss about were we lived. No one tried altering my high-toned feeling about the rightness of living on the hill. However, Mom insisted Strivers' Row on 138th and 139th Streets, down in the Valley, was a posher area where famous black New Yorkers and big wheel musicians, like W. C. Handy and Fletcher Henderson, owned homes. I knew posh meant rich, but I thought those big shots who I never heard of had nothing on our spacious six room apartment with a view that looked down on the world, including the posh people who thought they were better than us. If kids down there wanted to play in the shade of a tree, or see what a real wooded park looked like, they practically had to come up to our neighborhood.

My cocksure, eight-year-old self hadn't learned that every dreamer's vision of a sweet life in Harlem didn't begin and end on Edgecombe Avenue, or on Sugar Hill. Nor did I know about the area's glory days in the 1920s and '30s, during the Harlem Renaissance, when the Jazz Age reigned. Back then, New Yorkers, both black and white who wanted a good time, headed uptown to one of Harlem's speakeasies, or to private parties with the beautiful people who lived in the soon-to-be historic district of Strivers' Row. My mother's fixation on the neighborhood mostly puzzled, but sometimes alarmed me. I thought she and Jack might be thinking of moving down there.

In 1942, with his Pullman porter earnings, my Uncle Smitty and Aunt Annette bought one of the nearby, more traditional muddy-colored brownstones that uniformly line streets throughout Manhattan and Brooklyn. Then they did what most colored owners did with sprawling townhouses—rented the upper floors so they could afford to live in the bottom half. In Harlem, after achieving the American dream of home ownership, renting out spare rooms was commonly how one held onto it. Annette managed the property and was hard on tenants if they didn't hold up their end of the rental agreement. Early in life, kids know who they can butter up or

31

joke around with, and I quickly learned that Aunt Annette was not reliably malleable like my other aunt, Cecelia, nor was Annette blessed with an abundant sense of humor.

My aunt and uncle only rented rooms to men, and during years that Uncle Smitty was away on the railroad, Annette wasn't afraid to challenge men who lived under her roof, including the gentleman who was supposed to move because he hadn't paid several weeks' rent. One day, Gram and I happened to be with her in the upstairs parlor, when he returned home, entering through the tenant's second floor door. My aunt must have recognized his walk, because she made a beeline towards the hallway, and with no prelude asked if he was packed and ready to go.

"Not yet, I'm waiting for Mr. Smith."

"Waiting? What for? Smitty won't be home 'til Sunday. Your rent's late and you've been drinking in your room. You know perfectly well tenants aren't allowed to drink in my house. I've already told you to get your behind moving."

I couldn't see him behind the door, but from his tone, he seemed to bristle at her choice of words. "Ma'am, Mr. Smith's the one found me the room. I'm beholden and I take orders from him." She was the wrong woman, or perhaps he was the wrong man to take that approach, because Aunt Annette started launching F-bombs like grenades. She bleeped his mother and whole sorry-ass family, then stomped past us into the bedroom, not saying a word, just high-stepping her giraffe walk that sort of matched her exotic, long eyelash, bent-neck Egyptian-Ethopian-African looks. Grabbing a pistol from her nightstand, she scared Gram enough that she didn't even have to struggle out of her chair.

"Annette, what are you doing? Where did you get that gun?"

"Mother I won't hurt him much, but I want that M-fer outta here."

The tenant was gone when she got back to the hallway and thank God she didn't follow him upstairs, where he may have rushed to pack, or maybe he just left.

This was the aunt who, as a teenager, attended Palmer Memorial, a pioneering North Carolina prep school for Negro girls, where they were taught formal character education and manual training. Aunt Annette did graduate with excellent beautician skills. She also dressed elegantly in signature dark wool suits, with pearls, and cream or white silk blouses from Bonwit Teller or Lord and Taylor, high-end Fifth Avenue stores my mother couldn't afford to patronize. Annette didn't look like a hell-raising, foul-mouthed, ghetto chick.

If a reader asked, where exactly did the gum chewing, smack-talking, ungirdled, slum dwelling women live, if Sugar Hill on the bluff, Strivers' Row and other charming Valley enclaves didn't claim them? I'd tell the inquirer, the ghetto and its inhabitants were on my aunt and uncle's block and others nearby, often in brownstones with absentee landlords. The truth is, Harlem has always sheltered poor people and housed an underclass who often resort to crime or antisocial behavior. They, too, must live somewhere and usually it's among their own kind. The world has opened up, providing opportunity for minorities to move around. But in the past, whether you were good, bad or indifferent, Harlem was always there waiting for you because that's what it was—the home of black America.

Smitty and Annette didn't let destitute or unsavory neighbors prevent them from living their dream. Besides her gun that we hadn't heard about, we learned she also carried a switchblade in her pocket. About six months after the gun incident, Annette told my grandmother that late one night, when rounding her corner, an addict tried stripping away her pocketbook, "But, he didn't get it," she added, "because I stuck the F-er."

Rather than dwelling on the negative, Annette and Smitty's homeowning success rippled through the family. Mom wanted a house; Aunt Cee did, too, and she got hers ten years later. For me, whose previous exposure to daily living was the apartment variety, the brownstone's grand parlor, gilded mirrors, old house smell and off-limits top floors, held all the fascination of a world that needed exploring. The five-floor, 19th century house contained a small fortune's worth of woodwork in the form of paneling, crown molding, ornate mantels, floors and stairs, most of which squeaked. A few times when I was young enough to test Aunt Annette, I tried slipping away, but the third or fourth step caught me as surely as if I'd ridden horseback across a guarded moat. Annette didn't allow locks on tenant's doors and kept her own second floor rooms open when she was downstairs, but still on the premises. Her ears knew every moan and groan between point A and B, and even my slight weight on a loose board caught her attention because sure enough, I'd hear, "Jean, where are you?"

"On the stairs," I mumbled.

"Why? Did you leave something upstairs?"

"No. I want to look around. There's nothing to do down here."

"I don't want you bothering my tenants. Just come back here and stay in the kitchen."

"Okay," I sighed, longing for a break from long hours when she, my mother or grandmother, and sometimes Aunt Cee, convened around the white porcelain table, or over on the beauty parlor side of the kitchen. If someone, or maybe all of them was getting her hair washed, hennaed, straightened or curled, it turned into a marathon. Compared to our cramped, odd-angled kitchen with the building's chimney hogging up a third of the space, Aunt Annette's kitchen was approximately 18 x 25 feet. Besides two sinks, built-in cabinetry, a pantry about the size of my room, and the usual appliances, she had an antique wooden ice box that came with the house when they bought it. A professional beautician's chair sat on the other side of the room, next to a silver floor-model hair dryer and a pie safe, where she stored curling irons and other hair paraphernalia. The supplies were hers and Gram's—both licensed

34

beauticians—from years before when they owned their salon, The Beauty Box, on Lenox Avenue and 138th Street.

While I was restricted to the kitchen, just outside its double windows, her lucky dog Chen, a fluffy white chow, was either asleep in the shade or looking in at me, with his big weepy eyes, as if he needed a playmate as badly as I did. As far as yards went, her weed-filled enclosure wasn't much, but I equated it with picture books where children picked flowers, romped with the puppy or did anything but be bored in the kitchen.

"Aunt Annette, may I please play in the yard today?"

"No, maybe next time. I need to clean it up and Chen might get snappish."

"Can I look in the basement, then?"

"Don't be ridiculous. There's nothing but coal dust down there. Why do you ask such silly questions?"

"Because Uncle Smitty said you have a bicycle built for two."

"That old thing is nothing but a piece of junk."

Eventually, the entire gang of four jumped in, telling me to play with my doll, get my coloring book or read the funny pages. The first time Aunt Annette saw me reach for the newspaper, she asked, "Jean, when did you learn to read?"

"In first grade."

"What grade are you in now?"

"Fourth."

"Olivia," she looked over at my mother with a grin that should have warned me she was about to say something else I didn't want to hear. Besides her weird, high-stepping dromedary walk, Aunt Annette had about as much tact as a camel. "Jean's really growing up," she said to Mom. "Next thing you know, she'll be menstruating."

So far, an explanation of puberty or of how my body would change had never been broached, beyond Gram's dis-informational outlays on relationships, including "Jean, I'm here to tell you, some men are no good." I was not blind and I lived with a menstruating mother, so I knew "it" was coming, but I certainly didn't want to hear about that stuff from Aunt Annette.

When my friend Mary Jo's mother had a hysterectomy, requiring what was then a routine ten-day stay in the hospital, Mom told me she hurt herself "down there" by falling off the kitchen table onto the back of a chair when hanging her venetian blinds. Ouch. That cockamamie story, evoking images of extreme pain was preferable to something simpler, like, "She had a female operation." The way they chose not to tell me I had a baby brother bordered on child abuse. My girlfriends at school and on the block were shyly beginning to talk "around," rather than about, puberty. Not too long before Mary Jo's mother went into the hospital, I told Mary Jo I hated when Mom sent me to the store to buy her Kotex.

"Girl," she said, "I know what you mean. That man up there might think those things are for me."

On the bus ride home, after leaving my aunt's, I whispered to Mom, "That was so embarrassing. She said that in front of everybody."

"Just me and Mother, that's not everybody."

"It's boring at Aunt Annette's. She won't let me do anything in that house and she thinks I'm a baby who can't even read. She's just old and fussy; I don't like it down there."

"Watch your mouth, and don't let her hear you calling her old, because she's not. And if you want to be treated like a young lady, then you can't get embarrassed to hear your aunt saying you'll soon be one."

"Mommy, you know that's not what she said."

"Well, that's what she meant. You can say something in different ways. Annette's not used to children or in mincing her words, but she certainly didn't intend to embarrass you. And when it comes to her home, you have to do what she says. She's afraid you'll get lost or hurt in that big house or end up where you don't belong, like in somebody's room."

Aunt Cecelia didn't have kids either, but her heart was kid-like and we spoke the same language, only she talked funnier. Unlike Annette, who was sixteen years older than my mom, Cee was close in age and lived with Uncle Harry in a one-bedroom apartment on St. Nicholas Terrace across from St. Nicholas Park. Cee had a curvy Marilyn Monroe figure, dagger-like fingernails lacquered in Chinese red and she smelled of Shalimar. Cee wore a gold ankle bracelet and owned a sexy white lace suit that I inherited when I grew up and she gained weight. She was even left-handed; the only lefty I knew. Part of her cool factor was calling me darling or sweetie and she proved that nowhere in the Bible, or in the *Book of Arbitrary Grownup Rules* is it written that aunts have to say no to everything nieces want, even if it's asking, "Aunt Cee, can I have another sip?"

"Oh what the hell," she reasoned, handing me a red and white label can, the brand with a catchy "My beer is Rheingold, the dry beer" jingle that played endlessly on radio.

"Your mother will get on me if she finds out, but here, just one sip. Beer is healthier than that orange Nehi she lets you drink. You know the difference between a sip and a slurp, right?"

"Uh huh," I assured her, slurping icy liquid as fast as I could before she grabbed it. Telling someone not to enjoy herself wasn't her way, but there was a line to cross. If I stepped over it, like asking for too many sips, instead of saying no, I got her hand-on-the-hip, wide-eyed stare-down that clearly meant, I hope you don't take me for a complete fool and no, you cannot have another sip.

I spent many evenings in her home on St. Nicholas Terrace and I can't remember if I was there because Mom needed a sitter or my aunt wanted the company of a daughter she and Uncle Harry never had. One day I was playing in one of the jewelry drawers of her new bedroom dresser. I had on a pair of her shell earrings, the only clip-ons I could find, plus a couple of long pendants and some pop beads strung around my neck.

Aunt Cee's good gold jewelry was tucked away in velvet cases and her signature pieces, six chunky silver bangles, rarely left her right arm. Her vast, three-drawer collection of beads and rhinestone doodads would have sent many wardrobe mistresses into a state of euphoria.

"What's this?" I asked, holding up a matching rhinestone set I couldn't figure out. Aunt Cee squeezed in next to me, onto the vanity stool where I sat.

"You wear those on shoes. They're shoe buckles."

"Like the Pilgrims?"

"No, not like Pilgrims. I've wore them in the past, and so did your mother when we dressed up. They used to be popular. They jazz up plain shoes. That pair belonged to Harry's mother when she was a flapper."

"What's a flapper?"

She thought a minute. "A glamour girl. In the Roaring Twenties, around the time I was born, that's what they called good looking, stylish girls."

"How do they work? Can I try them on my shoes?"

"They may not fit on those," she said. "Take off your shoes and slip mine on." She was wearing high heels and had on her rust-colored straight skirt; the kind of grownup skirt I liked. I had on Mary Janes and thin socks, but my feet were slightly larger than her size fives. She kicked off her black pumps and bent over to clip her mother-in-law's buckles on the front.

I stepped into shoes that were too tight. Looking down, I said, "They look like Dorothy's shoes in *The Wizard of Oz*."

"What?"

"She wore red high heels, but these hurt. The buckles dig in."

"Well, take them off now, before you stretch them."

She helped me step out, then examined the clasp. "One's bent in the back, but buckles aren't the most comfortable jewelry to wear. That's probably why I don't see them around much anymore."

Sometimes I talked to her in ways I hesitated to do with Mom. "Aunt Cee, I want pierced ears. Mom said I have to wait because I'm too young and Gram said only eight-year-old

38

hussies have pierced ears. If that's true, how come babies wear tiny gold dots like the kind I want?"

She laughed, but wouldn't take the bait. "Sweetie," she sighed, "Just wait. Someday you'll have pierced ears and jewelry, too. You'll be a beauty like your mother and have to fight the boys off." A few years later, I saw the movie *Auntie Mame*, about a permissive, fun-loving aunt and I started calling Cee, my Auntie Mame. Despite her frank femininity and liberal ways, it should be noted, her leniency didn't always carry over in group settings, if all the women formed a united front against what I wanted to do, or to wear.

My mother Olivia, the tall, sweet-natured, last-born, bookish sister, had wanted to attend a good secretarial school or maybe even college. She was a whiz at solving algebraic equations, at least any pesky ones I struggled with in high school. Mom was also the only female in our family who had to work outside the home and she always resented it. When she retired forty years later, the disappointments and what-ifs still gnawed at her. Ironically, some of her frustration occurred in one of her most stimulating jobs at the *Amsterdam News*, while working among other young colleagues who frequently had college degrees and were on a career path that was out of her league.

Under the stewardship of Dr. Powell and Dr. Savory, two genteel West Indians who owned the paper, its prestige and circulation skyrocketed. They heavily featured Negro cotillions, weddings and society news before it was the norm in black journalism. Business also flourished when the 1950s Civil Rights machine cranked up in Harlem. The newsroom was on Eighth Avenue, just around the corner from 125th Street and the atmosphere was alive with Traditionalists, Black Nationalists, Black Muslims and officials from CORE, SNCC, NAACP and other civil rights organizations. My mother loved working in a high-profile office with breaking news. She remained at the newspaper about six years. She'd already taught herself shorthand, but while studying at home in the evenings from an old book she bought second-hand, she also learned the basics of balance sheets, taxes, accounts receivable and other bookkeeping skills before leaving the newspaper for a better paying, but less glamorous, job as a bookkeeper for a coal company.

In the long term, Mom found satisfaction in her working life. I don't know how much she brooded over her failed relationship with my father, who never married her. Because Daddy didn't live with us, I was raised by committee. My mother was chairman, but Gram held the seat of power. Daddy was an ex-officio member at large, just showing up on weekends. This grouping afforded my still-young mother opportunities to slip back into her youth. But my grandmother's endless love and white glove, iron-fisted manner of assuming primary care of me, kept the door open for her. It was an arrangement that worked for all of us.

A chronically harried working woman, Mom hurried through life, coping with disorganization and single motherdom. During morning makeup-time, after Gram fixed breakfast, which Mom routinely skipped to iron a blouse or find a stocking without a run that matched the intact sable brown nylon that she'd dug up from a jumbled mass of scarves, belts and gloves in her top drawer.

"Jean?" she routinely called to me in the kitchen where I was sitting with Gram, "quick, run into the bathroom and see if I left my compact on the sink. Oh, Lord, it's almost nine and I can't be late again, but I can't leave the house looking like this."

Returning empty handed, I told her "I didn't see it, but you already have goo on." Her pretty face was framed on the sides by long hair. A puckish nose sat in the middle of smooth cheeks that were smeared in a rushed-job of brown pancake-overkill that definitely didn't look better than before she started.

"Foundation. I need my powder puff to tamp down the shine."

"Use Gram's powder. I'll get it."

Giving up on powder and muttering through pursed lips, "Way too light; too light for me," she struggled to eke out a dab of lipstick from a near-empty tube.

"Bye, baby. Gotta run." Grabbing her pocketbook from chaos on the dresser, I watched as she tottered down the hall on spiked heels. Her lipstick tubes were often overdue for replacement, like the ones she applied with the aid of a toothpick. Organizationally, it didn't help that she had about thirty tiny lipsticks rolling around on a large glass cosmetic tray, among perfume bottles, loose change and odd earrings that needed a mate. Most of Mom's lipsticks were leftover miniature Avon samples in unpopular colors, like Peaches 'n Cream, preferred by white customers, of which she had none. The tubes were from when Mom was an Avon Lady. She hadn't done well at what was supposed to be a side job, but was more like a none job. A few girlfriends at the office, two sisters, a mother, and an interested daughter who would have loved to wear Peaches 'n Cream, but had a snowball's chance in hell of doing so, weren't enough of a customer base to get her Avon business off the ground.

Besides a beautiful face, my mother's affirmation of loveliness was lustrous ebony-colored hair. Sometimes she wore it piled towards the front of her head in one of those lingering vampish styles from the 1930s. The pompadour was secured with a human hair rat, that ugly black blob on her dressing table that wasn't called a rat without reason.

For all the times she didn't bother with details, a formal night out was a rhinestone spectacle in our house, with Mom draped in satin or chiffon whimsy, elbow-length kid gloves and fox-faced stone martens draped around her shoulders. In the 1950s, glamour was in and she was a knockout. Our albums are filled with pictures of her at tables or on dance floors, taken by nightclub photographers at places like Smalls and the Savoy. They immortalized my young mother's cool, serene confidence in her looks, captured her wearing upsweeps or cascades of curls, with a wrist corsage or an orchid in her hair, and bathed in the glow of flawless skin.

A PAL sponsored "loadies" game in Central Harlem, circa 1950. Loadies were loaded or weighted bottle caps. (Photo courtesy of New York Public Library)

3. Sidewalks of New York

In the 1950s, the City's population hovered around eight million. But with the steady stream of blacks abandoning the Jim Crow South, Harlem had a disproportionately high number of residents, and many of them lived in hot, overcrowded tenements. In summer, to help entertain some of the children in these crowded neighborhoods, settlement workers and the Police Athletic League sponsored mini camps and play sessions. These programs sprung up like mushrooms inside church basements and on vacated schoolyards. If a block lacked the right facility, a safe area was created by cordoning off parts of the street with PAL sawhorses. Do-gooders swarmed around high crime areas that, by the 1960s, were acquiring nicknames like Junkie Haven and Needle Alley. Elvira and Melvin, my grandmother's friends from Norfolk, lived near one of those streets and each summer they babysat their grandson, James, who was about my age.

James and I were both in similar situations, since our grandmothers took care of us. When she could still get around on public transportation, Gram and I rode the bus one day to Elvira's house on 112th Street, near Manhattan Avenue. The name on the downstairs bell showed she lived on the top floor, and before we reached the second level, Gram was puffing and complaining. "If I knew we'd be climbing damn near to the roof, I wouldn't have come. I can't imagine why, at our age, Melvin and Elvira would be living up there."

The thin, gray haired-lady in a freshly starched house-dress, who was waiting at the door, had a face full of wrinkles and eyes that danced at the sight of me. "Come in, come in," Elvira gushed, hugging Gram then fussing over me. "Little

Jeanne, turn around, let me look at you. You're just what James needs to break up the long day before my son Arthur picks him up this evening." Then she shoved an elfin-sized boy forward, as if we didn't already see each other.

The apartment was a shotgun, as were others in that neighborhood—all the rooms connected like a subway train. To get to her living room, the only one with windows, we passed through the kitchen and two bedrooms. Besides a shotgun floor plan that I'd never seen before, Elvira favored modern furniture and decorated her end tables with family photos, instead of tall porcelain vases filled with gladiolas, or schefflera leaves that Gram put on her tables.

While Gram was still catching her breath, Elvira did all the talking, launching into a long scary story about James coming home crying from the community center. "Out of pure meanness," she emphasized, "a boy tore up his construc-tion paper chain. I'd been wracking my brain about what to do with him this summer. He's not content to spend all day in these four rooms with me and Melvin, so I signed him up at the church program. But children are so rough these days and James, bless his heart, is not a fighter."

James didn't seem like a fighter to me, either. In neatly ironed pants and oxford shoes, he looked like a boy kids picked on precisely because he was quiet and didn't know how to be mean. While the grandmothers talked about Norfolk, James asked, "Wanna to go sit outside on the fire escape?"

Glancing over my shoulder, I said "Okay," fully expect-ing to be called back. On Edgecombe, sitting on fire escapes was considered uncouth and no one did it. Gram, still fanning herself, hardly noticed me climb out the window behind James, who wasn't at all uncouth. He just needed to sit where his art project wouldn't be torn up, and his sandwich stolen, which had also happened to him at that day camp.

Within minutes, I thought maybe Gram had a point about fire escapes, because I didn't like it out there. We weren't near the ladder and wouldn't fall through, but we were five dizzying floors above the ground. Safely tucking my bottom against the brick, I said, "My friends and I play outside."

"Me too, but only at my house, not here."

"Where's your house?"

"On Riverside Drive."

I understood Riverside Drive. It was a safe neighborhood where people didn't sit on fire escapes. "My grammy won't let me sit on our fire escape."

"Mine wouldn't either," he explained, "but now I can, because I can't sit on the stoop anymore."

"Sometimes my friend Mary Jo and I play on our stoops. We turn them into our doll house and keep the jump rope and Bazooka comics inside the columns."

Not interested in doll houses or jump ropes, James said, "See down there," and pointed beneath us. "That's why I can't go outside."

Peering straight down, I searched for a reason Elvira and Gram were allowing us to sit out here, but it was hard to see through five floors of iron slats. My shifting right or left only made the metal grids shift with me. "What are you looking at down there?"

"Those men sitting on the stoop."

Two guys had partly blocked the door when Gram and I entered the building, and I was glad she hadn't told them to move or kicked them when we steered around them. On the subway a few weeks before, we were riding downtown to Centre Street to meet the lawyer handling her negligence suit and Gram punched a *New York Times*. The man in the seat next to her kept letting the pages billow into her face. My grandmother didn't always make the best decisions when it came to interpersonal relationships, but I think she punched the paper because the man reading it had on a suit and didn't look like the two thugs on the stoop.

"Last summer," James explained, "my grandmother asked a couple of men she knew to do her a favor and not let anyone bother me when I played out front, but my daddy said 'uhn

uhn' and told her she couldn't do that, because they were dope heads."

Elvira's belief in the goodness of her dissolute young neighbors partly explained why she continued living there. She didn't harass or call the cops on the junkies and in return, their job was to keep bullies away from James and prevent their friends from knocking her and Melvin in the head when they came home after dark. It was a practical ghetto relationship that eventually soured when more heroin and worse times ended the fragile peace.

On our hilltop enclave, parents didn't have to make deals with the devil to survive summer. My friends and I were lucky to live on a safe street with loving parents and extended family who sheltered us from the harsher realities in Harlem. While my mom worked at the newspaper, my grandmother Jean, for whom I was partly named, loved me just about to death.

My caregiver was a complex woman. She had that quarrelsome side to her nature, but she was also old-fashioned, traditional and full of contradiction. For instance, on the topic of independent women, Gram was a progressive and would have bitten her tongue off before admitting she was trying to shape me into little Princess Jean who might someday marry Prince Charming. Nevertheless, we went through years of dress rehearsals.

Gram taught me how to baste a roast and thin-peel potatoes with an eight-inch butcher knife. She was better at cooking and styling hair than doing needlework, but she showed me anyway how to crochet, cross-stitch, embroider and sew a hem, and she didn't care that my stitches came out crooked. I knew to place a fork on the left side of the plate, learned that bluing made clothes white, not blue, and in my first baking experiment proved her right about cakes not needing a whole bottle of vanilla.

Our morning breakfast routine took on mythic proportions. "Go ahead, eat some," she said from across the table,
patiently waiting me out while I eyed a runny soft boiled egg.
Why she didn't just scramble the egg in bacon grease, the way
I liked it, I don't know because there certainly wasn't any fear
of frying in that kitchen.

"Olivia," she went on to complain about Mom sleeping
late, "ought to be up early fixing you a hot breakfast. A good
day's start keeps you healthy and beautiful. All I have to
do is look in the mirror to see that rising early hasn't done
me any harm."

"Mommy likes to sleep. She said you fix breakfast better
than her cornflakes."

"That's just an excuse. No one needs as much sleep as
Olivia thinks she does. Here," she picked up the fork, trying
to feed me like a baby, "take another bite of egg."

"I'm full; I don't like the egg. Can't I just finish my toast
and bacon and drink the orange juice?"

"Eat a little more and I'll wear bells at your wedding," she
said, then sang a little ditty, like she did every morning, if she
wanted me to eat something.

> Honey, marry money
> and all your dreams will come true.
> Your days will be sunny
> and never blue.

Despite tender loving care, a child couldn't live on Sugar
Hill without sensing poverty nipping at the heels of Edgecombe just as it did in other parts of Harlem. Still, there was
something almost holy about living on the Hill. Heaven would
come, but Edgecombe Avenue was God's country, a tree-lined
street where residents wanted white people to drive through
so they could see how well Negroes lived. Whites did come
to Edgecombe, but most of them were salesmen or New York
Giant fans looking for a parking spot and rarely ventured past
409. However, there were enough worthy attractions in our
part of Harlem that didn't need a pint-sized girl with an out-

sized sense of tribalism to get whites and other outsiders to appreciate this community.

One of those popular venues was Lewisohn Stadium, the athletic field at City College, a massive structure resembling the Roman Colosseum, built on Convent Avenue and 139th Street. The college held sporting events, plays and graduations in the stadium, but for several weeks each summer, its concrete viewing terraces were used as seating for classical music lovers who poured into Harlem from all parts of the city. For a small sum, patrons could sit up in the cheap seats under the stars and listen to New York Metropolitan Opera singers, like Marian Anderson, or hear the Philharmonic Symphony play classics such as *Porgy and Bess*, which is how I discovered Gershwin's music. *Porgy and Bess* will last forever, but the college demolished Lewisohn Stadium in 1973.

North of the stadium, another treasure, the American Indian Museum sat a block away from my school on land donated by descendants of the naturalist, John James Audubon. Audubon, as well as Alfred Tennyson Dickens, son of novelist Charles Dickens and Clement Clarke Moore, author of *The Night Before Christmas*, are among notables buried in Trinity Cemetery, just across the street from the museum. History and decades of tense uptown politics hover over this famous location where black Harlem and once-all-white Washington Heights have, for years, tried maintaining individuality while glaring uneasily at each other from across Broadway.

It should be noted that fifty years ago, America was a half-century closer to when great Indian tribes roamed the Plains. The 1950s was also the decade when Native Americans filed lawsuits and reparation claims, frequently making front page news. Indian culture and vocabulary was more deeply embedded in daily life than today. When someone uttered the word "Indians," no one asked the speaker to clarify if he meant East Indians (whose presence in New York was minimal) or American Indians.

In grade school, Indian lingo was everywhere: the classroom drum was our tom-tom, Miss Ballack ordered us to line up against the wall, Indian-style, housewives cooked succotash, not mixed vegetables, my stepfather called his friend's new baby daughter a pretty papoose, and so it went. It was not uncommon to hear the Midwest referred to as Indian Territory, and when I married twenty-five years later and moved to St. Louis, a friend made a snotty, New York-centric joke, "Oh, yeah, St. Louis; that's where Indians roam."

But in my childhood, when an Indian was spotted in New York, wearing long braids, a pair of moccasins (in the 1950s, moccasins were not commonly worn by other groups) or a fringed leather jacket, kids wanted to touch him to see if he was real. Both children and adults stared the way they might today if a bearded Amish man walked through Central Park Zoo wearing his odd black hat and homemade woolen suit. Indians lived on Upstate or Long Island reservations and came in town to visit or do business, which was sometimes carried out in Harlem, and if they married outside their tribe or race, it might be to a Negro.

Lorraine, Mom's cousin, married a handsome, sloe-eyed Sioux named Sonny High Elk who was born on the Standing Rock Reservation in North Dakota. Several years before, his mother Ginny had moved to Harlem and married Gram's brother, my great Uncle Herbert. Sonny got out of the service, came to New York, fell in love—much like his mother had—and then married Herbert's niece, Lorraine. I don't remember Ginny, but Sonny fit right into our family. A snazzy dresser, he was built like an NFL lineman and worked as a sandhog, building the Lincoln Tunnel. He partied hard, got bright red in the face when he drank too much—which was often—and he not only became citified, but also Negrified. As a young, good-looking, good time guy, Sonny was one of America's full-blooded Indians anxious to leave his traditions back on the reservation in North Dakota. I don't think he cared that much of his people's ancestral wealth rested in the hands of private collectors and museums like the one on 155th Street, a block away from my school.

I first discovered the American Indian Museum with twenty-five other curious, wide-eyed third graders when we filed through its carved front door, into a gallery smelling of mold, rotting wood and an unforgettable first glimpse of what was nearly impossible to describe, but I'll try calling it a cross between "This Old Attic," Santa's Workshop and Toys R Us—all on steroids. Besides all that, our class was standing across from a fully assembled animal skin teepee that stood about fifteen feet tall, with an open flap for its front door. Mrs. Mac delayed my gratification by snapping her fingers, a signal for us to turn and listen to her give the same speech on field trip deportment that we'd heard at our desks, fifteen minutes earlier.

"Children, what they have here is old and valuable. These are not toys," our teacher reiterated. "All this belonged to the Indians. Now it is property of the museum. We want to be invited back, so keep your hands at your sides. We will start in the corner, looking at wampum and beads so you can see what the Indians used for money. Remember our stories about them sharing with the newcomers from England. Look around for tools or weapons what might have been useful in helping the Pilgrims survive cold weather or dangerous animals. And remember, do not touch anything. Malcolm," she added, "that means you."

The small museum sat among a five building plaza with its famous totem pole gracing the courtyard. Inside, the building was crammed with artifacts, some as small and finely crafted as a topaz ring and a little girl's deerskin dress that was about my size. There were rifles, tomahawks, saddles, dolls, sleds. A child can be told a dozen times that Indians who once lived near New York City navigated rivers in dugout canoes. But it doesn't make the same impression as standing six inches from a forty-foot dugout that still retains properties of the mighty cedar it used to be.

Three years later, when my friend Michele and I were eleven, we tried visiting on our own, but the haughty over-dressed snob who opened the door, took one look and wouldn't let us in. By museum standards, the building was small (about 15,000 square feet) and only open a few days a week for limited hours. For two sixth graders from the neighborhood, trying to learn exactly what those hours were was like getting a straight answer from Pinocchio. The museum's owner, George Gustav Heye, was still alive and director when I attended elementary school and may have been the man who turned us away.

Art lovers admired his prolific collection, but just as many had misgivings on how he acquired it, a question that may still be rattling around museum circles today. Besides teachers, their pupils, researchers and Heye's society friends, I don't know who was permitted inside. With its air of secrecy and exclusivity, I'm fortunate to have seen the museum at all, and certainly before controversial displays were removed from public viewing.

In the 1950s, voyeurism was an acceptable pastime. Examples could be seen in doctor's offices and medical buildings, where mongoloid and deformed fetuses floated inside jars of formaldehyde. Each year at Madison Square Garden, families brought small children to stare and point at the "freaks" in Ringling Brothers' sideshow. Attractions varied from year to year, but typically they included midgets, a giant, a morbidly obese fat lady or one disfigured with tattoos over 90% of her body.

Buying into the public's appetite for grotesquery, Mr. Heye's most compelling oddities we saw that day at the museum were shrunken heads. Behind a glass enclosure (many items were openly displayed), they looked like three brown doll's heads, the size of medium oranges. Long black hair grew from the heads, the same way an overripe onion sprouts green tendrils. Several years later, in eighth grade, I had the opportunity to hold a shrunken head in my hand because my classmate's globe-trotting older brother brought one back from South

America as a souvenir. The head I handled once belonged to a man, and I'm sure it was real because of the nature of the eyes, ears, nose, mouth and hair. The head was lightweight and felt strangely familiar, like paper mache before completely hardening.

In 2003, to refresh my memory about the museum, I called the new National Museum of the American Indian at the Smithsonian in Washington and spoke with Ellen Jamieson, who verified the shrunken head's existence. She then asked me, "Did you see Heye's shrunken body?!"

I hadn't, so she gave me a primer on how and why shrinking was done. South American Jivaro Indians (Jivaro means savage in Spanish), killed and shrunk bodies of their enemies. To get shrinkage, normally all skeleton and skull bones were removed. However, the victim kept his foot bones, meaning a twenty-four inch body of a human man who was once full size, stood in the display case on his own two, normal-sized feet. Ms. Jamieson further explained that exhibits were frequently switched out. Heye's collection was also vast, so when I toured the museum, the body may have been stored elsewhere, or permanently removed from viewing because of its controversial nature.[1]

The Indian Museum is no longer an upper Manhattan fixture, although the building remains part of Audubon Terrace complex and now houses the Hispanic Society. It took another generation, but word of this under-utilized gem on 155th Street finally spread to the greater world. In 1989, Congress enacted legislation to make the Indian Museum part of the Smithsonian complex in Washington and renamed it the National American Indian Museum. Only a small branch remains in Manhattan, now located downtown on the second floor of the refurbished Alexander Hamilton Customs House at One Bowling Green, near Battery Park.

Curious to see what the City had done to replicate a sacred collection, I visited the Customs House, which in its own right, is a massive 1907 Beaux Arts wonder. To say the least, the collection and display space has been downsized, but there is an educational center on site. As for art, what I found that day were a few permanent pieces and a special exhibit of twelve contemporary Native American painters.

Ultimately, incorporating the Indian Museum into the Smithsonian, in Washington, provides enormous display space and a more prominent location for a million plus artifacts. If Indian spirits could speak, and perhaps they chat regularly among themselves, they might agree that preserving invaluable heirlooms in one safe site is a laudable accomplishment. It's a shame, though, that just when Harlem has rebounded with tourism and development, it couldn't build its own world class art center and keep the museum there.

New Yorkers did protest the government's decision to build the new facility in Washington. Worthy arguments were waged against the move, and one that I thought relevant was offered by Walter A. Fairservis, Jr., an anthropologist, who on February 3, 1989 wrote a letter to the editor of *The New York Times*:

> ...Barring the possibility that these objects might be returned [from Washington, D.C.], the alternative of sending the Heye collections to Washington is another insensitive act in the white man's relations with native Americans. The record of broken treaties, land appropriations, genocide and forced migration is an indelible black mark on the United States. To know that the collections that represent so much of what Indians have lost would be going to Washington, the font of their destruction, is intolerable....[2]

Sugar Hill had its picture postcard view, access to museums (in time I'll tell you of others) and a popular outdoor concert facility. But if you ask anyone from fifty years ago about the sweetness of living there, a museum or public institution is the last thing they'd point to. Sugar Hill was more about satisfaction and quality of life than snobbishness. There were other prime locations, such as Striver's Row, but even rich people didn't strut with the swagger and attitude as everyday folks on the Hill. Sugar Hill had its share of the well-to-do, but Central Harlem was the business district where the majority of affluent undertakers, insurance men, landlords, dentists, doctors and lawyers worked, often living in brownstones with their offices located at ground level. Sugar Hill residents paid homage to Valley mucky-mucks with a L.L.B, M.D, CLU or Inc. behind their names. They owned property, had money and brains, but we had the beauty. If you can't have wealth and power, looking good is the next best thing.

Every neighborhood is as good as its people, and one of the best was Mary Jo, my good friend, who lived across the courtyard. She was a little sprite, who could jump through the sweeping arc of a double-dutch crossover with natural grace and the elegance of a moonbeam. I was tall and lanky with long arms and legs that outlasted hers when we bounced spauldeens in A-My-Name-is-Alice. Once, I bounced the ball all the way to H without missing a beat, name, city or what we sold, as in Hazel, Harry, Harrisburg, harps.

In summer, my pigtails were pinned into a tiara on top of my head, held up with giant three-inch hairpins. The sharp edge of a desk at school forever branded me with a weepy white shin scar that grew bigger than a quarter. I didn't think I slouched or tried to look shorter, but must have, because Mom was always telling me to stand up straight.

Mary Jo, who only reached my shoulder, wore teeny skirts above skinny legs with knobby knees full of shiny little scars. A ribbon of bangs sat in front of her pulled-back hair clipped together with baby barrettes and, unlike the rest of us, Mary Jo was likely to carry her tiny plastic pocketbook when she came out to play. A busybody gifted with mother wit at age eight, she was precocious, judgmental, and for the longest time was the only one of us with siblings.

She learned how to handle big-sistering two younger brothers about as easily as the rest of our circle took to being pampered only children. Hands on her hips, tapping her foot, pocketbook swinging on her wrist, she mimicked her mother's, I'm-not-pleased-with-you look, reprimanding Ronnie, the three-year-old. "Boy, didn't I tell you to stop that? Get down from there and quit putting every last thing in your mouth. Take that thumb outta your mouth before you suck another sore on it. And don't even think of wetting your pants," she ordered, "you're too big for that nonsense."

I scrambled to my feet one day after she aimed her little laser beam voice on me. "Girrrl, you'd better get your butt off that stoop in that good Easter dress, or your grandmother will be on you in a minute. You know Mrs. Luacau don't play."

Deidre Pinkney, my quiet, serious friend with long, thick plaits was a worrier. She didn't say much unless it was important, like when Ronnie ate our chalk. "Hey y'all. Look at Ronnie! His lips and mouth are turning blue. He's sucking all over the chalk and I'm not drawing hopscotch squares with that!"

"Mary Jo, you run upstairs and get more chalk."

"If I do," she said, forcing Ronnie to spit out the chalk, "I have to drag these boys up with me."

"I'll watch 'em," I offered.

"Girl," my younger, pint-size best friend informed me, "you don't know the first thing about taking care of kids. Besides, Mommy said not to let them out of my sight. You go get a piece of chalk."

"I don't have any," I tell her, "besides, you know if I did, Gram would make me stay upstairs, period."

"Shoot. We need a ball or something. There's nothing else to do."

I looked at Dedi. She lived on the top floor in 371 and sometimes wouldn't even come out at all, because she was afraid of her hallway. I knew what she meant. After playing outside in bright sun, it was pitch black on those stairs during daytime hours. Her hallway had pretty colored stained glass windows blocking all the light. The darkness reminded me of the old days, when we were little kids and afraid of the boogey-man, which wasn't all that long ago.

"Dedi, your grandmother's not strict," I nudged, "if you go upstairs, I'll walk with you."

"Uh uh. I'm not doing that. Grandfather might be sleeping."

Dedi's household resembled mine, with a young working mommy and doting grandmother, Mrs. Pinkney, a gentle fine-boned dressmaker, who always wore a tape measure around her neck and walked around with straight pins in her bodice or in her mouth. She tailored suits and sewed beautiful clothes, adding details like bound buttonholes, even on Dedi's dresses, but she was a completely different kind of grandmother from mine. I think the women in that family were timid because Mr. Pinkney lived there, too, and was the sort of grandfather who gave old men a bad reputation. Tall, crotchety and white-haired, he had a phlegmy rumble in his cough and couldn't tolerate noise, even though that house was quiet as a tomb. Worst of all, Mr. P. drank both buttermilk and garlic water.

I accidentally came across buttermilk down in Virginia. After I spit it out, and until I met Dedi's grandpa, I thought all traces of the stuff remained in the South. I was afraid to ask Mr. Pinkney anything, but Mrs. P. said he drank butter-milk because he liked it, as if he wasn't already scary enough, and that garlic water helped control his high blood pressure. That, at least, made some sense because Gram said garlic made good medicine and I saw her mushing it into a paste to salve on cuts and sores.

My third good friend, Ellen, was emotional and subject to having hissy fits over nothing. Now that I can reflect on such things, I think she went through puberty before the rest of us even knew it was coming. Compared to our stick figures, she had a soft curvy body, cried easily and struggled with feelings. We couldn't ask much of Ellen. Sometimes she just preferred staying upstairs with her mother, listening to *Helen Trent* or some radio soap opera, rather than playing with us. Ellen was a good quiet day friend, when we didn't feel like playing high water-low water, hot-spit or double dutch, which you didn't want to play with her anyway because she couldn't keep up. I think we didn't know she had asthma.

It was almost noon the day Ronnie brought our morning to a standstill, but the fun was about to end anyway. Without being told, kids were programmed to go in at lunchtime. If I lost track of time, within minutes, Gram's head popped out the window and I heard, "Jean, come on up, you've been out long enough and the sun's too hot." Hauling kids out of the sun was a carryover for families who once lived in hot Southern states along the Atlantic coastline. My family came from Virginia, Mary Jo's from Florida, and Jackie's mother, next door, grew up in Waycross, Georgia. I can't remember where Ellen and Dedi's folks originated. Despite everyone's home base having shifted twenty temperate degrees North, to New York City, all the grownups retained memories of someone who died from sunstroke.

Latchkey kids, whose parents worked, also went upstairs when everyone else disappeared indoors. Working parents, who couldn't be home at lunchtime or at three o'clock when school dismissed, relied on what black people called home training. Home training meant saying please, thank you and respecting yourself enough to keep your shirt tucked in and zipper zipped, even if your mother was at work all day. If you were an older girl, you better not be sneaking on makeup or sitting on a park bench in a pair of hussy-looking ride-up shorts, because somebody was sure to tell your mother.

The four Goodwins were poster boys for the art of home training. They not only went in during lunch, they started dinner, cleaned the house, ironed their clothes for the next day, and knew not to flood the basement washing machine with too much Tide down the soap hole. Juanita, their mother, was highly respected for raising four industrious, mannerly boys. She disciplined with a killer look that could freeze your scalp and, when necessary, her strap, or she lowered her voice instead of raising it. For Juanita, screeching like an ordinary mother would have been tantamount to admitting she was no longer the law, or at war, two ways she approached child rearing. I couldn't imagine anyone looking into her bullet hole eyes and getting away with lying to Juanita. She was sturdy like a bantam rooster—squat, plump, cocky and ready to fight. Even her skin was a creamy chicken-colored light yellow, like a tough little bird after plucking. With Juanita, you got the whole nine yards, because on top of all that, she was really pretty.

The Goodwins were a group of four and everyone watched their classy operation which managed to minimize screw ups, brotherly brawls and the hard-edged fatigue of single parenting. If Juanita Goodwin could manage, then by God, anyone with just one or two kids had better find a way. Hard times was no excuse because it sort of went along with being black, having kids and stretching your budget to live on Sugar Hill in the first place. People struggled, coped and kept money troubles quiet or moved someplace cheaper.

Once when I was about ten, Billy, the oldest Goodwin brother, looked over to where I sat watching their stickball game. "Hey Jeanie," he yelled, "come on, we need another player. You be the catcher."

Being asked to play with Billy was better than getting picked as the first girl for coed dodgeball. That was hot stuff, even if boys on the other team were going to try to kill me. I caught the first few balls bouncing to the plate, but sure enough, intent on not letting any get by, I didn't see the stick or hear someone say, "Watch out," until after I got whacked up side the head. No sweat. I just wobbled off to a bench, acting like these things happened all the time. I probably had a concussion, but never mentioned the tender spot and knot hidden under my hairline. Luckily, the batter was Jackie instead of Billy, our big man in the neighborhood who routinely crushed spauldeens and might have killed me worse than the dodgeball bullies. Billy was a strong, strapping kid—taller, more muscular than his brothers and the most skilled stick ballplayer on the street. He pulled his hits towards left field, aiming for the buildings instead of right field which was over the park fence and down in the Valley.

The niftiest thing about stickball was watching Billy organize a fishing expedition with a tin can on a string, if a ball rolled down the sewer. He had power-packed arms, a bull neck and was strong enough to get leverage on a 200-pound manhole cover and pry it up. Everybody gathered around, staring into a thirty-inch diameter that led down to the devil's house, we thought. Little kids looked on with wonder, asking questions, breaking Billy's concentration, "Ooh, it's deep. How're you gonna get it out?"

Sidewalk superintendents appeared, with older men chiming in. "You have to bob the can up and down. Man, put some weight in the can. That's how we used do it."

"You're blocking the sun, I can't see. I almost had it."

A few times when the water ran high, Billie and Philip or Wallace dangled Ronald, their youngest brother, headfirst into the manhole so he could grab the ball by hand. Fishing was the best entertainment of the summer and if the Goodwins had thought to charge, we would have gladly paid.

The only time boys acted terrible to girls was when they had ash fights and we got caught in the crossfire. Ash came in ugly, fist-sized chunks of brown and tan-speckled spent coal. Most of my scar has faded where Albert Hawkins nailed me between the eyes with a chunk of ashes. Blood squirted everywhere, and although it looked worse than it turned out, it must have looked bad. I can't remember much except getting stitches in Dr. Gold's office and blood stains that never came out of my blouse. He got me on the way to school, in front of their favorite free-for-all spot, the block-long garage with frosted windows that you couldn't see through. Ash fights didn't usually draw blood, but Albert packed the chunk that hit me in a tin can.

When we were thirteen and I had moved and everyone was in different schools, Albert came by my new house, sat on the couch sweating and stammering before finally spitting out an apology. "I'm sorry for putting a scar on your face," he blurted out. "I won't do it again."

"I know. It's okay. It doesn't hurt anymore."

Rushing ahead, he asked, "Can you go to the movies with me on Saturday?"

It was my first request for a date, but it felt more like a dilemma. I had to decide if I wanted to sit with him or Michele, who I usually sat next to.

"I have to ask my mother."

He blushed an "Okay," then put me on the spot. "Ask her then."

Without thinking, I yelled, "Mommy, can I go with Albert to the movies on Saturday?"

Since she wasn't walking up and down the hall, or popping in the living room pretending to look for her cigarettes, it meant Albert was back in her good graces. When she came in from the kitchen, Albert jumped up like a gentleman, securing his status. Mom was all smiles when she said, "The RKO is fine, but come straight home before it gets dark."

Albert had grown six inches and was kind of cute. But when Mom went back in the kitchen, he started blushing again and I thought I'd just made a big mistake, because he tried to put his arm around my shoulder, but I wouldn't let him.

Around 1962, the city finally got rid of coal, ashes and the sooty residue they left behind. When oil tankers replaced rumbling coal trucks, the upgrade set off a chain reaction. Other long-standing, though better loved, city systems disappeared, including what was then an ancient form of New York City street theater—peddlers. When I was very young, the knife grinder trolled through the streets and alleys intoning, "Grinder, grinder." His plaintive cry sounding like a muezzin calling from the minaret. Most peddlers were taciturn older European immigrants of unknown origin like Abe, the vegetable man, who was the last vendor to clip-clop down our street in a horse-drawn wagon. Gram, whose bowed, arthritic legs restricted her from going many places, was one of Abe's best customers and I think that's why he always parked under our window. That allowed Gram to do what she did best, focus on food and give orders from her throne—a kitchen chair she kept by the window.

"I'll take two melons, eight ears of your corn and five pounds of mustards and five of collards, but I want tender greens. Abe, do you hear me?" she hollered down to the sidewalk, as though Abe and everyone within eight car-lengths of his wagon didn't hear which vegetables we'd be eating the next several days. "Last week, the collards were too tough," she told him. "You can get away with selling stalky greens down on Eighth Avenue where those Negroes just up from the country don't know any better, but I don't want any more in my kitchen."

Abe's buckskin horse was swaybacked and barrel-bellied. He looked like a working class version of Dale Evans' Quarter Horse, Buttermilk, on the *Roy Rogers* television show. The horse (whose name we didn't know because Abe never spoke a word) sometimes dropped piles of steamy yellow poop that looked like corn muffins, and he could pee for a full minute without stopping. Abe outfitted him in blinders and a wide, dinged-up straw hat with holes punched out for his ears. Kids thought the hayseed hat was funny, but Abe was serious as heartache about that animal and every boy knew he better watch out when Abe threatened (by flicking his whip) to horsewhip the first one who messed with his animal.

For some boys, the lure of the street or making mischief was never a problem. That's how Jimmy was. His parents were quiet, private people from Trinidad. Among Harlem's largely homogenized Southern population, neighbors with thick island accents were frequently labeled different or standoffish, which was double talk for saying they were stuck up and too good to let their kids play with us, and that's what some folks said about Jimmy's parents.

Jimmy was a tall, intelligent, athletic-looking boy who played tennis, an oddity in itself because there were no tennis courts in our neighborhood. He may not have needed exercise, but running and bike riding with us might have changed his stay-at-home, mama-boy image. While his parents worked, I pictured him upstairs reading *Hardy Boys* books or playing with an erector set, because he didn't seem like a kid whose mother would put him in charge of anything physical, like cleaning the house. One reason was his clothes; no sneakers or dungarees, just dark chinos, white shirts and ties. I got to know Jimmy because we lived on the same courtyard and I caught him spying on us from up above, when Mary Jo and I were in our kitchen windows playing dolls across the distance. Jimmy lived in a back apartment, two floors above Mary Jo, whose windows were beneath and to the left of his. They couldn't see each other, but from my kitchen, I saw both of them.

"I see you up there. How come you never come out to play?" I asked.

"Cause I go to art school." I thought about that for a minute. At regular school, we'd just made tinfoil pictures with glass, black paint and green tape, so art sounded okay, even if he was missing playtime with us.

"How long've you lived over there?"

"I don't know. Forever."

"Why don't you go to our school?"

"Cause I go to Resurrection."

"Is that some kind of school for smart kids?"

"It's in another neighborhood and it's Catholic"

"Is that why you wear church clothes everyday?"

"They're not church clothes; that's my uniform."

I made a mental note to tell everybody why Jimmy wore church clothes, then asked him "Do you want to come to my birthday party? My mother and grandmother think you're a nice boy."

That's how I remember Jimmy meeting the kids. He and a dozen other children came to play pin the tail on the donkey and eat ice cream and cake. It was my first large birthday party, and the living room tables and chairs were piled on Grammy's big bed to make space for us to bump and spin in a blindfold. Although he's not in it, I have a black and white snapshot of the snaggletoothed, grinning group of kids that day who were standing around our gate-leg table. The girls have on organdy party dresses with ribbons in their hair. The boys wear crooked little bow ties and paper birthday hats. Everyone's mugging for the camera.

Holding a balloon at my birthday party. Billy, Jackie and Philip in back row, left.
Wallace is at my right shoulder. Claudette Sterrett is behind my left shoulder.

4. On Being Rich

Sometimes I wondered if we were rich, but after meeting Colleen, I knew we were. She was my new best friend at school and she was white and poor. I asked Grammy, "Do you think it would be okay to start bringing Colleen home with me for lunch?"

"You might as well," she said. "That child is all you've been talking about lately, so go ahead, bring her on over here."

Colleen was skinnier and littler than the rest of us and had slumpy bad posture that made her look like she was already defeated by eight years of living. Her hair stuck up in funny places and she had delicate see-through skin, the kind with tiny blue lines under the surface that made me almost believe blood inside the body was blue and not red.

I knew Colleen had a difficult life. Everyone in third grade could tell. On good days you noticed her big blue eyes and pasted-on smile. On bad days, those eyes were like her smile, empty. Colleen's dresses were too large and slid off her bony shoulders, but the worst times were when kids started snickering and holding their noses because she smelled like pee, which truthfully, was most every day. Mrs. McWhorter did not comfort her when she couldn't answer a question. Instead of moving on, the teacher made her stand up, then asked the same question in a different way like, "Why don't you know $5 \times 4 = 20$?" I guess Colleen didn't want to fall into the "I don't know" trap, because Mrs. McWhorter would've asked why she hadn't memorized 5×4, or when she planned on learning it. So, Colleen just stood drooped over, wearing her bad day, stupid-looking grin and making us all glad we weren't Colleen.

By springtime of that third grade year, she became a lunchtime regular in our kitchen, but on her first visit, Gram studied her a split second before blurting out, "Lord Jesus have mercy on my soul." She didn't even talk to door-to-door salesmen like that, but at least she didn't say anything else mean before sending us in the bathroom to wash our hands.

Later, when I came home at three o'clock, she gave me a glass of milk and some leftover vanilla wafers from lunch, then she started in on Colleen. "Your new friend is poor white trash and she smells. If you bring her back into this house, I'm going to give her a bath."

My first thought was the time I played bathtub-beach with Beverly Green, when we were in first grade. That was fun on a hot day and we wore our bathing suits in the tub. Now it was March and still cool outside, so I knew Gram wasn't talking the same game. She was just being mean, as if she and Mrs. McWhorter were in cahoots when it came to embarrassing my friend. But Grammy had embarrassed people older than Colleen, so I knew she was capable of carrying out threats.

"Why do you have to spoil my fun? She won't come anymore if you make her take her clothes off."

"She smells like a piss pot, that's why and she probably has lice, to boot. Fun! You think it would be fun to have to sit and pick nits out of your hair if you catch lice from that dirty child?"

I didn't know what "lice" was, but I didn't want to catch it or have any more of Gram's sickroom treatments. I'd recently had the measles and chicken pox. With the measles she closed the blinds and I couldn't look out the window or at sunlight until the scabs formed. Her chicken pox treatment was worse because I itched everywhere and she tied my hands in a pair of socks, then ordered me to leave the itches alone every time she caught me scratching. When I ran a temperature she tied smelly onion slices to my wrists to draw out the fever.

Her most lethal treatment was a regular dose of Father John's Tonic, a thick, foul smelling diarrhea-colored concoction that was her first line of defense against whatever might be festering, like a sore throat. Just the bottle, with its picture of Father John, who looked about as old and dead as Moses, was enough to make me sick. Castor Oil and Milk of Magnesia were heaven compared to Father John's. My first act of willful defiance was hiding the tonic inside the white porcelain bedpan, a freakish looking thing in its own right, on top of our toilet tank. It was an old fashioned model, with a brown wooden water tank that flushed with a pull-chain. The tank sat near the ceiling and I knew the bottle was at least five feet above my grandmother's reach, because I had to stand on the edge of the sink to reach it myself.

Until we moved several years later, I'd walk in the bathroom, look up and cringe at the thought of ever swallowing another spoonful of brown crude. In 1967, after my grandmother died and we were downsizing her full life into an assortment of cardboard boxes, about the only light moment during that week was when I remembered the tonic and climbed up to get it.

Mom was in the kitchen, wrapping Gram's last pieces of unbroken green depression stemware in newspaper and I walked in to show her what I found. Recalling the loathsome taste as if it had been yesterday, I asked, "Do you remember when Gram used to give me this?"

"Of course I do. You can hardly find that stuff anymore," she said, smiling nostalgically, as though hard-to-find Father John's might be a loss to medical science.

"You probably can't find it," I reminded her, "because it nearly killed everyone who had to choke it down. Didn't you ever wonder why Gram stopped giving it to me? I hid it in this bedpan years ago and, until we moved, I worried she might find it and start dosing it out again."

"Well, her memory wasn't that good those last years, but you also got through a string of childhood illnesses, so Mother relaxed her vigilance. But I bet she was on to your little trick and took pity on you. She would have just sent you to buy another bottle if she thought you needed it."

"Yep, you're probably right. Like a lamb to slaughter, I would have marched right up to the drug store and bought it."

So, during the discussion with Grammy about Colleen's health and hygiene, she had my attention when she got to the lice part. "What's lice?" I asked.

"It's what dirty people get," she said, hard-rolling the "r" in dirty for better effect.

"Well, she's not dirty or sick, so I can't catch anything," I defended my friend. "She's just quiet and wears funny clothes."

"I'm not talking about sickness. I'm talking about these people treating this child like a common street urchin. Did they just get off the boat, or something?"

"Which boat?"

"Never mind. Does your teacher check the children's heads each morning?"

"I don't know," I said. "She checks for clean fingernails and brushed teeth. But anyway, you're being mean, just like Mrs. McWhorter."

For some reason, fingernails and teeth were magic words. Because our teacher did a morning hygiene check, in the curious logic of adulthood, it was now okay for my friend to come over without submitting to the indignity of a bath. Once or twice a week until school ended, Gram responded to this pale waif of a child in the way she knew best, by feeding both of us with baloney or grilled cheese sandwiches and overflowing bowls of vegetable beef soup.

Colleen's school attendance was spotty, but when she showed up, I was a reliable friend. She wasn't responsive enough to pump high on a swing with me, play hopscotch or even dolls. Colleen was like a doll, insubstantial and silent; a phantom child hovering in a corner of the playground. I felt a flush of satisfaction in befriending this quiet, unfulfilled girl whose fragility was so apparent. Being Colleen's partner in line or sharing my Tootsie Rolls with her were little kindnesses that sustained her, but they also nourished me. My brush against her gentle spirit was a look into that dark place where adults don't know we children can see. From her, I learned the texture of poverty, saw its little girl outline, breathed its sour smell. She made me feel rich. In September of the following year, no one was surprised when she didn't return for fourth grade.

150 years before the U.S. Constitution was signed, the Dutch had already settled Harlem, calling it New Haarlem, a name that stuck. Three hundred years later when baby boomers like myself nervously entered Mrs. Rubens' afternoon kindergarten, young GIs were flooding classrooms across American and millions of high school and college texts flew off printing presses. But by then, Harlem was becoming America's new war zone, and despite its glorious history, publishers had little interest in documenting urban ills, so it got left out of textbooks.

For sixteen years, all my schooling, except four years of college in another borough, took place in Harlem classrooms, but only Mrs. Katz directly linked history's larger picture to our community. She didn't exactly say we'd be studying Harlem, but first she reviewed lessons we had learned from Mrs. McWhorter. Then, to help us picture Indians as the first inhabitants of Harlem, she pulled out a large library book she'd borrowed, with drawings of seventeenth century New York City. They were antique black and white sketches with little visual appeal for a ten-year-old, but one illustration caught my attention. It showed a group of Indians standing on the banks of the Hudson, wearing nothing but loincloths and headbands with single feathers. Three Dutchmen next to them were dressed in formal black, thigh-length coats, ruffled shirts and Pilgrim-styled hats.

I never forgot that page because it depicted the Indians getting snookered into selling Manhattan to the Dutch for a few trinkets and twenty-four dollars, in what was perhaps the first and largest fraud perpetuated on Indians. The contrast of clothing in the picture troubled me. Even though I was a little kid, I sensed that any businessman who showed up at the meeting looking half naked wouldn't be dealing from a position of strength. If the Indians had dressed in dazzling buckskin shirts with fringe on the sleeves, worn leggings and intimidating full-feathered headdresses, they might have fared better. I've always imagined this summit taking place somewhere around 145th Street, where the river is most majestic, as it flows past Harlem, beneath the Palisades. If the meeting had taken place in some swampy marshland that once permeated parts of the shore, the Dutch might not have been so eager to get their greedy little hands on Manhattan. Whether the transaction was hard fact, or apocryphal anecdote, that picture was a powerful example of how things can fall apart.

Despite the Indians getting snookered, Mrs. Katz said we lived in a great country. She and her family had emigrated from Germany shortly before World War II broke out, and she never missed an opportunity to champion her adopted country. She wasn't shy about praising Harlem, either, especially its parks and free resources. When she discovered everyone didn't have a library card, we started making regular visits to the Washington Heights Library on 160th Street.

After one visit, I stumbled back to class, fully absorbed in *The Sunken Garden*, my first Nancy Drew mystery, and kept sneak-reading in the back of the room behind my composition notebook. Until then, I'd been laboring through Mom's *Encyclopedia of Classics* containing novels like *The Hunchback of Notre Dame*, an unintelligible translation written in tiny print. Finally discovering age-appropriate fiction was liberating.

Later that summer, Mom unearthed her old, battered-up copy of *A Tree Grows in Brooklyn* and I immediately clicked with Francie Nolan, the main character. We were about the same age, both loved books and library visits and her mother was planning to get married, just as mine was. But Francie's life also mirrored Colleen's, my third grade friend, because they were both poor Irish girls who got picked on by teachers, who seemingly favored better-off kids in the class.

After learning of Francie's positive attitude, despite humiliations at school, I felt better about Colleen and hoped she was somewhere with a kind, pretty mother like Katie Nolan to reassure her about the future and maybe do a better job of keeping Colleen from smelling.

Colleen would have liked Mrs. Katz, who knew about suffering and would never have belittled anyone less fortunate than herself. Mrs. Katz was also an avid bird watcher and member of the Audubon Society, and it appalled her that city kids knew so little about nature. That fall, while the weather was still decent, she took us over to Edgecombe Avenue a few times to become better acquainted with "the vorld of nature."

Walking over, she didn't care who led the line and by then, I don't think we did either, but she was a neat freak, so we couldn't straggle and had to pay attention when she bellowed, "This is an elm," in her cheerleader voice. "You should familiarize yourself with this North American variety that does not grow in all parts of the vorld," she once said with red-faced passion about a behemoth near my friend Michele's house. Then, purposefully kicking through a tall leaf pile, she bore down on a tree I'd passed dozens of times, without ever noticing.

"And, what ist this?" She waved dramatically at a tree near the elm. Like a lot of the class, I was good at identifying Christmas trees. I knew oaks, because my friends and I used to collect acorns to decorate mud pies. That day, acorns were scattered over the sidewalk and street, but mostly I marveled at how Mrs. Katz kept plowing through leaf piles without worrying about stepping in dog poo.

"An oak?" someone offered timidly to, "Vhat ist this?"

"No, no. It is not an oak," she said in sweaty exasperation. It was hot and humid for early October and her thin blonde bangs were stuck to her shiny forehead. "Does that leaf look like an oak leaf? Every tree in New York is not an oak, children. It's an elm, just like the one over there."

Mrs. Katz never allowed our scientific ignorance to dampen her enthusiasm. Later in spring, when the trees budded, we explored the miracle of rebirth and had to look for birds that weren't pigeons, and it was then that I discovered robins aren't really red-breasted, but more like orange.

In my youth, all American kids were well acquainted with George Washington. We knew he was a great president who wore wooden teeth. We could retell the story of him confessing to chopping down the cherry tree, as if it had happened last week. Mrs. Katz also used Washington's temporary stay in our neighborhood, as a way to connect the dots between past and present.

When I was in college, I watched a Harlem night club act featuring a standup comedian who cracked jokes about George Washington. "Man, I'm telling you, that old white-haired cat was efficient. He slept his way all up and down the Northeast coast. Seriously," he emphasized to a skeptical audience, who didn't get it.

"Last month I was Upstate," the comic continued, "driving to a small town gig when I saw this sign, big as day, telling the president's private bizness. 'George Washington Slept Here,' it said. No shit," he added, attempting to garner more laughs. "And damn if I didn't go another fifty miles and spot the same sign, in front of the Ye Old Inn. And you didn't think old George had it in him, did you?"

In Harlem, the joke's on us. Too many people never heard and still don't know about Washington's former headquarters, Jumel Mansion. The beautiful two-hundred-plus-year-old house on 162nd Street and Edgecombe Avenue was formerly

Washington's headquarters and one of the places he slept while his army marched up and down the Atlantic coast.

With our country's tear-down, pave-over mentality, few surviving buildings date back to 1765, the year Jumel Mansion was erected. The original owner was Roger Morris (the home's official name is Morris-Jumel mansion), a lieutenant-colonel in the British army, who abandoned the dwelling to American troops in 1776, the year Washington commandeered it.[1]

This magnificent Palladian house sits on a high point of Manhattan, on the next block of Edgecombe, up from my house, that was sometimes called Coogan's Bluff when I was a child. James Coogan, along with a Dr. Samuel Bradhurst, were large real estate investors in the neighborhood. When blacks arrived in the 1930s and 40s, they discarded the Coogan moniker and started calling the area Sugar Hill.

Because this section of Manhattan island is both narrow and steep—rising approximately 250 feet above sea level, the mansion's rooftop widow's walk once provided unobstructed and panoramic views of New York's and neighboring state's shorelines. It was a strategic location for Washington's struggling army that badly needed to regroup and reconnoiter before the Battle of Harlem Heights, their next engagement, a skirmish the Americans won.

After the war, the government confiscated Mr. Morris' property. Over the years it reverted to a private residence; also a public house and a banquet hall where President Washington returned in 1790 for a nostalgic dinner with several members of his cabinet. In 1810, a widow named Eliza Jumel, who was briefly married to ex-Vice President Aaron Burr, owned the house and lived there until her death in 1865. Then in 1906, the Washington Headquarters Association and four chapters of the Daughters of the American Revolution opened the Morris-Jumel Mansion as a museum.[2]

I visited the 8,000-square-foot Jumel Mansion a year after I fell in love with the Indian Museum, which sits ten blocks away. What I remember of Jumel Mansion was a very large, shabby house with tall ceilings, tilting floors, and a few pieces of upholstered furniture in faded blue fabric. I've since returned to the house, which has received some much needed attention, but there is still work to be done on the old building.

By contrast, Thomas Jefferson's residence, Monticello, a large plantation arguably situated in the middle of nowhere—on a mountaintop just outside of Charlottesville, Virginia—was built three years after Jumel Mansion. Monticello retains not just land, but gardens, outbuildings and original household furnishings. It's a tourist mecca, raking in millions of dollars and busloads of visitors who wait hours in long lines, baking in the hot Virginia sunshine, to get inside.

The half-block Jumel compound sits in a densely populated urban center with easy access. Unfortunately, on my most recent visit, the house was closed, but I walked a perimeter of paths and meticulously cared-for gardens; quiet shady spots to sit and nurse my disappointment at not seeing the inside. Crossing over to Sylvan Terrace, a narrow cobblestoned lane next to the mansion, I was heartened by the colorful refurbishing of these once derelict, 19th century wooden houses. This picturesque setting is reminiscent of a stroll through a Disney-staged town, or a recreated early American village. But nothing here is fake. It's beautiful, it's original, it's Harlem.

Today, many local people still don't know about this home or the area's past. But there is also a new faction who knows, but dismisses Colonial history as anathema to the black experience, especially in light of our first president having owned slaves. I wonder if such thinking occurred in the late 1970s, when Colonial Park (between 145th and 155th Streets) was renamed for Jackie Robinson. Great man that he was, Jackie Robinson played third base for the Brooklyn Dodgers. A spot in Brooklyn should be named after him and perhaps one or more has been. If our park needed renaming, my choice would have been Willie Mays.

When Willie landed in New York, his man-size athleticism and boyish behavior galvanized the New York Giants,
the National League and our neighborhood. As a rookie, he
lived on St. Nicholas Place, cattycorner across the street from
the team's stadium, and almost every boy I knew wanted to
grow up and catch fly balls or hit home runs like number
twenty-four. Willie Mays got his Major League start in this
neighborhood and he spent his glory days at the Polo Grounds.
That achievement should be worth something, but as far as I
know, nothing in Harlem is named after him.

Benzinger House. (Jim Cummins)

5. The Way It Was

Despite its distinguished history, Harlem is a lightning rod for contention, and has been for more than a century. Until the late 1800s, the area remained rural and few people of means were interested in leaving midtown's cosmopolitan social and business scene. As roads and transportation improved, wealthy townspeople were drawn to Sugar Hill's scenic location on the bluff. One prominent resident, Nicholas Benzinger, built an estate at 345 Edgecombe Avenue, five houses from where our apartment would later stand. Mr. Benzinger's wealth came from publishing popular Catholic materials, including the Baltimore Catechism that I used in 1952 to prepare for my first communion.

Shortly after beautiful homes like Mr. Benzinger's were constructed, the area's demographics changed when subway service was extended to upper Manhattan, allowing ordinary citizens to move uptown, and thus creating a land rush. Vacant lots were gobbled up, but established Sugar Hill mansions were also torn down to make way for apartment buildings.

The Benzinger house survived because their descendants didn't move until the 1930s, when they sold it to Dr. Henry Lloyd to use as an annex for his larger existing Lloyd's Sanitarium, across 150th Street. When I came along, the Benzinger home had been converted to the Edgecombe Avenue Hotel. Some kids on the block thought the old-fashioned and by then, out-of-favor word, "sanitarium," had referred to a mental asylum, so we sometimes also called it the old crazy house.

345 Edgecombe is a large three-story reddish brown brick building with multiple dormers forming a beautiful roof line

that the New York Landmarks Conservancy recently helped replace with red tile.[1] As was the custom around Harlem, this mansion was graded above street level and surrounded by a black rock wall that, on its south side, stands taller than five feet, concealing the house from prying eyes like mine. That wall was a psychological and physical barrier that contributed to the home's sinister reputation and as a kid, the place gave me the willies.

About ten years ago I was in the neighborhood, again visiting with Jean Beverly, my friend Jackie's mother, and while talking with her, decided after decades of rumor and innuendo, I'd try to visit the hotel.

"It's a halfway house," Jean informed me. "Sometimes one of their representatives attends our association meetings. The residents are quiet people who never bother anyone around here."

"What kind of halfway house?" I asked. "I'd like to call before just marching up there and ringing the bell, possibly disturbing them at meal or rest time."

"I'm not sure what all they do, but look under AIDS or Alcoholism. Maybe Halfway Houses," she suggested, offering her Yellow and White Pages directories.

I also checked Rehabilitation, Clinics, Drug Centers, Social Services, New York City, but no Edgecombe Avenue address popped up. The anonymity suggested a community that valued its privacy, as 345 always had. My plan was to introduce myself, make a few inquiries about the past, share what information I could and maybe get a tour of public rooms.

The house has a wrought iron fence above the rock wall and at that time, it was topped with barbed wire; whether to keep folks in or out, I couldn't tell. The building looked as solid as ever as I walked up steps to a glassed-in porch and rang the doorbell. Within seconds I was buzzed in, without hearing the intercom ask "Who's there?"

Thrilled by such easy access, I stepped into a busy vestibule where fifteen or so people, several severely obese, shuffled around the room ignoring me. I could picture this square, high-ceiling foyer having once been a reception area for a small hotel or hospital. A registration desk might have filled the empty space across the floor, now occupied by a woman in street clothes holding a tray stacked with four ounce paper cups that she had just used to distribute snacks or medications.

Trying not to be obvious, I glanced down at bare spots in the cracked brown linoleum and up at patched pink walls marred by a century of bad plastering. Assorted paint colors bled through chipped and cracked plaster. I'd seen other vintage Harlem mansions with worse histories of abuse that had been loved better than this one.

Keeping my smile in place, I got a good look, but minutes ticked by and I wondered how this lack of urgency justified a buzzer and barbed wire. Searching for the paper cup lady, I turned around and bumped into a large woman who had planted herself inches from my left side. Some part of me knew a manic-grin looking down from a massive body in a flowered housecoat posed no harm, but my heart wasn't the part because it thumped so hard it hurt.

The big woman's movements caught the supervisor's attention because she came over to draw the patient away. Someone, possibly me, said hello, but I couldn't hear because my ears were ringing. I also couldn't remember my good neighbor speech, or what to ask about a past that stood madly raving at me as I fumbled for the door knob and backed out of the crazy house with my neck hair standing on end.

The property behind the hotel, 10 St. Nicholas Place, tells a different story. It belonged to James A. Bailey, of Barnum & Bailey Circus fame. The entertainer moved in around 1888, two years before Benzinger came along. An old photo of Bailey's backyard gazebo, long since torn down, showed makeshift steps descending to a vacant site that would become Mr. Benzinger's home.

Bailey's house is the sort of vision you expect to see on a tour of Great European Homes. It's an ornate, three-story, 18th century limestone castle with an engraved coat of arms, elongated peaks, arches, towers, a turret, moldings, stone carvings and extravagance that only great wealth and a sense of the theatrical could create. Land has always been valuable in New York, so it's startling to see photos and drawings of other grand homes like the Benzinger's and Bailey's that were demolished in the name of progress.

In a *New York Times* article about the Bailey mansion, reporter Christopher Gray stated that the family of Franz Koempel, a German doctor, lived there from approximately 1910 until 1950.[2] The German angle corresponded with information my mother gave me a few years ago when I asked her to tell me what she could about this house.

"For one thing, we knew James Bailey built it" she recalled, "because he was prominently attached to the circus, and everyone loved the circus. When we first moved here, I assumed his place was a boarding house, because that's what most of the big houses in the area had become.

"Even Benzinger's was nothing more than a boarding house. They fancied-up the name, calling it Edgecombe Avenue Hotel, but long-term boarders lived there. Back then, rooming houses didn't carry the stigma they do today. Residents were mostly respectable owners, like your aunt and uncle who lived on the premises of their brownstone. No one needed permission from the Housing Authority to get rid of problem tenants if they damaged property or didn't pay rent. That's how things used to work.

"The people in Bailey's house were very private. Sometimes I saw a light, but after a while I assumed everyone had moved out, until they arrested the Germans."

"Germans? Which Germans?" I asked, thinking there'd been some international sex or financial scandal. "Why were they arrested?"

"They were spies," she said.

Seeing my astonishment, Mom warmed to her story. "It was during the war, and the FBI was ferreting out spies all over New York. Every day you read something, or heard on the radio that more spies had been captured."

"Why would German spies hide in Harlem?" I asked, trying to picture our neighbors hearing police sirens, thinking it was a mugging or car accident, then coming outside to see German spies led away in handcuffs.

"I don't know why they were here, or if they were guilty of anything other than spy hysteria. They probably always lived here. After all," she added, in her don't-you-know-anything-tone, "white people don't all head for the hills when someone with a black face moves next door. When you were a little girl, white folks still lived around here. They didn't bother anybody and nobody bothered them, until drugs and hoodlums started scaring everybody off. When the last whites left Harlem, your Aunt Cecelia and Uncle Harry were right behind them because their neighborhood had gotten so bad."

After our conversation, I scoured newspaper archives, searching for spy arrests during the 1940s. As my mother stated, on some days, arrests and detentions numbered in the hundreds, but reporters only wrote articles about the sensational cases. More often I found printed lists, sometimes several columns long, of suspects' names. Since addresses weren't included with names, I couldn't find anything specific to the Bailey house.

In 1951, 10 St. Nicholas Place was sold to Warren and Marguerite Blake, who lived on the premises and operated M. Marshall Blake Funeral Home, until a fire in the 1990s forced them to move. On a recent walk by the house, I noticed repairmen standing out front looking at something on the second floor, so it appears that the house is in the process of being renovated.

In 1967 I met the Blakes when we arranged to have my grandmother's funeral in the home, but I did not get beyond the front rooms. Since then, Harlem real estate has skyrocketed in value, tourists pour in from around the world, and 10 St. Nicholas Place is a designated landmark. It is part of a broader area beyond the Edgecombe Avenue section that is increasingly being referred to as Harlem Heights, and less so as Sugar Hill.

When we moved to Convent Avenue from Edgecombe, the new apartment sat cattycorner across the street from Hamilton Grange, Alexander Hamilton's mansion, another 18th century house that had fallen into deplorable condition. During my first autumn in the new neighborhood, I also started a new school and waited for the downtown number three bus in front of the Grange. One morning Roxanne, a high school girl who rode the same bus, jutted her chin at the Grange and asked, "Do you know about that house?"

"Yeah," I answered, glad to be up-to date, since before moving here, I'd never paid any attention to it. "Alexander Hamilton used to live there, didn't he?"

"Yes, but that's not what I'm talking about. Do you know not to go inside?"

Looking across at the building's dirty siding, out of plumb windows and lopsided porch was a little like Edgecombe-Avenue-déjà-vu, with me again living a stone's throw from another rundown relic.

"I wouldn't go in that old dump," I assured her. "It's not even open to the public, is it? The only person I ever see is some creepy man."

"Oh, it's open," she said, acting like she knew all about it. "That man is the caretaker and he's supposed to let visitors in. But never go inside if you want to graduate from college."

"What does college have to do with it? Don't you mean it's haunted or something, because it looks like it could be?"

"No, not haunted. There's a hex on the house. I'm going to college next year and I've never been in the Grange," she added, like that was supposed to make sense to me. "Seriously, just don't go in there is all I know. Something bad will happen."

My new friend was seventeen, wore penny loafers and sweater sets, had a page boy flip and was the only girl in this neighborhood who had spoken to me. So if she'd said the moon was made of chicken fat, I would have given it some thought.

Roxanne should have been on the cover of *Seventeen*, and down the line, she did some modeling. She was one of our race's blond, doe-skinned, green-eyed beauties that genetically are hard to figure out because their parents, like hers, are often brown-skinned with dark hair and eyes.

Roxanne wasn't kidding about the hex. Fourteen years later when I went to grad school at City College, a block away, students there had been spreading stories of a hex for years, probably generations. No one knew how it started and no one actually believed it, but they also wouldn't go inside the Grange.

A hex, for all its silliness and superstition, is symbolic of the bad luck that parallels this house and its first owner. The Grange was completed around 1802, shortly before Alexander Hamilton's death in a duel with Aaron Burr. Before he passed away, his personal and professional life took a messy turn because of mistress problems and accusations that he misappropriated government money. If he were alive today, or if more Harlem residents knew his story, I believe they would dismiss the unproven accusations and consider him an American hero who helped black people achieve equal rights, much as they felt about President Clinton when he opened his office on 125th Street, after a not dissimilar sex scandal.

As for Hamilton, despite his great intellect and immeasurable contribution towards shaping our country's monetary and banking systems, other founders and statesmen frequently snubbed him for being a bastard outsider who had the audacity to try to end slavery. Because he was born to an unwed mother on the West Indies island of Nevis, some detractors, trying to further damage his reputation, insisted he was of mixed heritage—meaning part black. Hamilton's formative years were spent on nearby St. Croix, where he took an immediate dislike to slavery after witnessing plantation owners and overseers brutalize blacks.[3]

Years later, as a prominent New York politician, he was active in the Manumission Society, an early civil rights organization that espoused justice for people of African descent. Throughout his political life, Hamilton labored to protect freed black men and denounced slavery, pointing out to his colleagues that slaves (despite their state of degradation) were men and not subhumans, as many Southerners professed to believe.[4]

Although he, better than most, understood that laws and sentiments varied from state to state, he still urged Southern friends, like Thomas Jefferson, to free their slaves, insisting that they were entitled to live under the same state laws as everyone else, as well as live within the laws of nature and human decency.[5]

Jefferson, a savvier politician and more temperate personality, deservedly received much glory for writing the Declaration of Independence, especially the famous words that state: "All men are created equal." However, there is a huge disconnect between what Jefferson said and what he did. He never supported legislation to free America's slaves, nor did he ever grant freedom to his many personal slaves, including his alleged paramour, Sally Hemings. He was unyielding on the subject and, despite his love for all things French, he also declined to join the French organization that proposed to free slaves in the French West Indies. When asked to do so, his slightly indignant and obtuse reply was that he would not free them because, after all, he was an American from the state of Virginia.[6] Had Hamilton not been killed, and had Jefferson embraced his moral obligation, this country might have had a happier 200 year history. With Hamilton's death, the founding fathers had one less anti-slave voice urging them do the right thing, and it's too bad more Americans don't know that about Hamilton.

The Hamilton Grange originally sat a few blocks north of its current location, in a lush grove that included thirteen gum trees, gifts from George Washington, that were a reward for Hamilton's leadership in the Colonial War, and during his later nation-building years. The gum trees, like the hundred-year-old homes that once graced the street, were destroyed by 19th century development. However, the Grange was saved, although moved twice, stripped of its original wraparound porches and finally squeezed into an inappropriate spot between St. Luke's Episcopal Church and 287 Convent, an encroaching five-story apartment building.

For 200 years, the Grange had a succession of overseers but only the National Park Service, who currently owns it, bothered fixing it up. In the late 1990s, after minimal remodeling, I visited the house and was welcomed by Douglas, a young Ranger in a crisp new uniform, who seemed pleased to see me. Two German-speaking tourists were also in the building, but they only wanted to look at old photographs. Douglas had my undivided attention and eagerly launched into a history on Hamilton. When he finished, I thanked him, then asked, "What do you think of the plan to move the Grange down the street to St. Nicholas Park?"

"This location is too crowded," he happily stated the obvious. "The park is a great idea."

"Can such a fragile old building be moved from this tight spot without falling apart, or damaging the church?"

"Oh sure," he said, "it's just a matter of raising enough money. The decision to relocate has been made; now it depends on government financing and finding the right people for the job. That'll take time, probably years, but it will happen. Then the outside restorations can continue."

This would have been news to my mother, who was under the impression that her faction, the "Don't touch the Grange" group was winning the neighborhood tug-of-war over what to do about this house.

"Did you know," I asked him, "that some old timers are against moving the house to the park? They worry that it can't be protected, because the city can't keep drug users from gathering down there, or stop kids from vandalizing trees and playground equipment. Will the house be patrolled or gated?"

"I guess it will have to be," he said uncertainly. I don't think Douglas was used to such questions and I didn't want to make him uncomfortable. After years of neglect, this facility was fortunate to have such a fresh-faced, enthusiastic young official manning the door.

"I think putting it in the park is a great idea," I said, deciding there on the spot that my mother's view was understandable, but maybe not best for the long term. Mom and others who'd lived here for decades, both applauded and resented Washington bureaucrats and newer residents with money and modern ideas, who were suddenly throwing around their weight, know-how and connections to dictate what should happen in the area. For forty years, neighborhood pleas to spruce up Harlem and save the Grange fell on deaf ears. Now everyone had their ears cocked, mouth running and an opinion about what was best for Harlem Heights.

But spacious grounds with walking paths, shade trees and landscaping, like Jumel Mansion's site, would enhance the Grange, I thought. The Park Service would likely reproduce two large porches that appear in old photographs. If the Grange moved, St. Luke's Church would also have breathing room, opening a view of its lovely arches and curved porch that now sit practically in the Grange's lap.

Before ending my visit, I asked, "What'll they do with the empty space once the house is moved?"

"They plan on converting it into a vest pocket park." Good use for a small urban space, I thought, but I also knew this neighborhood. I pictured a new line drawn in the sand and heard the yeas and nays squaring off at another community meeting.

"If we put a park there, those crack heads will show up, or rowdy kids will take it over," Louise, Gladys, or my mom Olivia might say.

"Olivia, how can you even think like that?" someone else would ask. "We've worked too long and hard preserving this stretch of Convent Avenue to let drug addicts take it over now. As for kids, all of them—my sons included—need more safe places to gather and play."

"Yes, but not next to my first floor window," says Mr. Williams, who lives in 289. "We'll have no peace if kids start playing loud boomboxes right under our windows. It's bad enough now, the way youngsters stay out all hours of the night. Besides, the kids already have fifteen blocks of St. Nicholas Park to carry on in."

And so it might go, as it has since my childhood. These meetings can center on the merits of having a block party, or whether the flowerbeds look better with purple petunias or red impatiens. People have always cared deeply about this neighborhood, but now stakes are higher because real estate values have soared.

In the 1990s, when I took my bus ride, the price of brown-stones and townhouses around here were inching into six figures; now they cost several million. Two bedroom co-ops then cost approximately $70,000 to buy; now they have more than doubled. Prices for these spacious, high-ceiling apartments are still artificially low because 1980s agreements with the City Housing Authority specify that they be sold to low and lower-middle income buyers. When co-ops go on the market, high rollers with six figure salaries use subterfuge to buy one, claiming disabilities or layoffs have forced them into part-time work with reduced income. They're disappointed when documentation is required and they can't prove their claims.

My mother, then treasurer of her co-op board, said current tenants were also disappointed when good prospects had to be turned away. One gentleman, who would have been a welcome newcomer, claimed his elderly mother as a dependent. "It wouldn't have mattered," Mom said, "if he was supporting both parents, because he owned two lucrative restaurants and made too much money."

But this wouldn't be Harlem if housing or anything else was perfect. This is also New York, with its shortage of affordable apartments and array of rent laws that either control, stabilize, regulate, reform, or shoot for the moon when it comes to what to charge for an apartment.

And as for the Grange, it took ten additional years to arrange, but the yeas who wanted to move it won the battle and, in a spectacular engineering feat, Alexander Hamilton's home was relocated to St. Nicholas Park in June, 2009.

FRAN

THIS BOOK WAS WRITTEN BY A CLASSMATE
OF MINE FROM WHSHFER. WE NEVER KNEW
EACH OTHER. UNTIL THEN BUT FOUND OUT WE
HAD A NUMBER OF MUTUAL FRIENDS FROM
THE HOOD.
    IT BROUGHT BACK A LOT OF GOOD
MEMORIES FOR ME.
        ENJOY THE READ!

6. World War II, Polio and Puberty

In the 1950s, the Broadway RKO on 145th Street and other theaters across America played a major role in helping children conceptualize a world at war and instilling us with a sense of patriotism. Each Saturday, before screening the week's cartoon or cowboy movie, the RKO first showed old war footage. I loved those newsreels, looked forward to their patriotic drum-rolling music with the narrator whose voice sounded like Uncle Sam. He rat-a-tatted his delivery, hammered the D's, boomed out B's, reassured us with cadence. I held my breath at Dunkirk and on D-Day, places and events where good triumphed over evil, and Allied forces stormed the beaches and won battles—of Britain or the Bulge.

Skipping a few Saturdays didn't matter since every weekend, for at least ten years after the war, cameras zoomed in on what looked like the same convoy of chisel-faced, chain smoking tough guys hunkering in foxholes with M-1 carbines, or standing by howitzers and threading billy club-sized bullets into thundering guns. When soldiers were on the move, they rumbled along in jeeps, trudged down miles of road strewn with shot-up vehicles, or they hitched rides on armored tanks, and despite cold and snow, the men just kept smiling and marching from one ravished European country to the next.

What the films didn't show were wet socks, frostbitten toes, or young men who looked sick because they had tonsillitis or strep throat. And the movie screen never flashed to any of the nearly one million colored soldiers, like the ones from Harlem, who had also been in Europe. I learned about them during family gatherings, when Jack and my uncles reminisced. They laughed or joked about sailing overseas on crowded troop ships, enduring seasickness, or eating bad food, and they made fun of commanding officers. But like the men in the movies, they smiled a lot and never got around to discussing the horrors of war.

Mom's cousin, Leamon, Jr., was twenty-four years old and unlike the veterans in our living room, was still on active military duty. The day after he returned from his deployment in the Pacific, he dropped by with a duffle bag full of GI gifts stamped "Occupied Japan." I was proud of him and my other relatives for helping liberate Europe and making Japan act right, although I didn't know exactly what went wrong in Japan because the newsreels mostly focused on Europe. The filmmakers seemed intent on assuring audiences that a bad guy named Hitler, who caused most of the problems over there, was going to lose the war.

My stepfather Jack was a playful mimic, even impersonating my grandmother a few times when she was safely out of the house. When he depicted the hell of war, it was with hand gestures he'd picked up in Europe, along with a sprinkling of Italian words like *belissima*, *signorina* and *si, si, si*. He told the funniest stories, but World War II had enough spectacle for ex-soldiers and civilians alike, to chronicle what happened during those six long years.

"One thing we didn't have enough of was sugar for making cakes," Aunt Cee groused one night, when everyone was sitting around our dinner table. Despite her comment, I couldn't remember Aunt Cee making too many cakes now that the war was over, either. Then Mom, who totally didn't bake because Gram did it for her, agreed. "Yeah," she said, "and, don't forget Spam. We ate so much Spam that if you gave it to me today, I know I couldn't choke it down."

I knew that Spam cans had dangerously sharp edges because they opened with a key, but as far as taste, Spam wasn't so bad, especially compared to Father John's Tonic or brussels sprouts. The talk about Spam made me think of one of the saddest RKO newsreels. It showed a soldier sitting in a foxhole and he didn't look much older than the boys on my street. Mom probably didn't know about that guy in his foxhole, because she rarely went to the movies. Wherever he was, it was cold and snowy, and the soldier's face and hands were smeared with mud. His hood was up and he was missing a front tooth, but he was wearing one of those brave soldier smiles for the camera, while eating a frozen chunk of food that he had speared with his knife.

When the adults talked about the war, I took into account how much Johnnie Walker had been imbibed. I was old enough to know they exaggerated, but one night, before I had much fashion sense, when the topic of wartime stockings came up for the umpteenth time, I asked, somewhat indignantly, "What's the big deal about wearing cotton stockings? They sound like a good way to keep warm on a freezing day. They couldn't have been that bad."

Mom laughed, "Yes they could," she said. "Most of the nylon was diverted to the military to make parachutes, so we had to settle for pink or flesh-color cotton stockings." Wrinkling her nose, Aunt Cee chimed in, "Yeah, pig-ugly pink, about the color of a sow's flesh. Even the white girls wouldn't wear them."

Watching my mother and aunt sitting and laughing on the couch, wearing high heels and sheer nylons, showing off shapely legs, I couldn't imagine either being caught dead in what sounded like nun's stockings. I hadn't yet had much contact with nuns, but occasionally I got a glimpse of ankle under their long skirts, when they glided past on the sidewalk. There was really no way to exaggerate how awful those stockings were. Still, temperatures in New York sometimes dipped into single digits, so I asked "Mom, if you didn't have nice stockings, what did you do when it was freezing and snowy outside? Didn't you have to wear the cotton ones then?"

"I wouldn't wear them at all. If I couldn't get a pair of stockings I wore socks, like many women did. Nylons were for special occasions and if I didn't have any, I went bare-legged."

Years later, when Jack was an old man, I visited him in a Bronx retirement home. By then, he and Mom were divorced, but better friends because of it. He was still handsome and his mind sharp enough to make me laugh again by impersonating my grandmother. But that day, he mostly wanted to talk about the war, when he traveled through ravished towns in Europe: "A place," he reminded me, "that's mostly populated by white people."

"In one spot," he remembered, "everybody came out their houses to see us, and I mean the kids, their mothers, grandfathers and grandmamas; old ladies in black dresses who all looked like they were in mourning for the dead. You could tell these villages had once been beautiful, but by then, everything was broken down or shot-up and the streets and roads were a muddy mess from heavy truck traffic. That day, the local people didn't seem to care, because they stood outside, or waved from second floor balconies, welcoming and staring at the dark-skinned Americans marching through their town.

"Oh la la," he added with a twinkle, "I never thought I'd live to see the day when a town full of lovely, brown-eyed white girls would stand by the road blowing kisses and acting the fool at the sight of bunch of grinning niggers."

"There was a fella in my outfit named Cornelius," he continued, "a nice quiet guy. He was a barber and used to give us haircuts. He came from somewhere around here, but I never saw him after the war. Man, talk about love at first sight. He spotted this little gal, and good God Almighty. After meeting her, that boy wasn't much use. It's a good thing they sent us home soon after that. You could kind of tell she felt the same way about him. I don't know what happened to them after the war, but a few guys sent for European girlfriends that they ended up marrying."

I mention World War II in a book about 1950s Harlem, because the stories struck a chord then, and reverberate now, as male members of my family and others I grew to love, like

92

my father-in-law who fought that war, die off. History never sleeps and Aunt Cecelia recently put a little bug in my ear as she recalled the conversation we had a few years ago. She'd turned eighty-five by then and as we reminisced while looking through old photo albums, I couldn't help sidetracking for a minute, because I wanted to ask about her hair.

"Aunt Cee, you've been a redhead for a long time. You look great," I added cautiously because she was vain as ever about her appearance, "but when did you go natural (gray) and stop dying it?"

"Honey, I had to let that go," she answered without taking offense. "You have to know when to hold 'em and when to fold 'em and at my age, it was time to close that deal. Besides all the time and expense, it was hard on my hair. You remember how my teeth broke off, don't you? Well, I don't want that happening up here," she said, patting the top of her head.

Three years earlier, Cee had absentmindedly bitten down on an ice cube and broken two front teeth. It happened after she had tentatively agreed to let me treat her to a St. Louis visit for my birthday party. "There is no way," she declared after the mishap. "I'm sorry, but I can't go anywhere looking like this. I have to wait until the dentist makes a new bridge."

That made sense, and it wouldn't feel right having my friends meet this old glamour girl if she had a sunken top lip and big hole in her mouth. The gap had been obvious, and even with me, she mostly talked while holding her right hand in front of her mouth.

"But yes," she steered us back. "Those were wonderful family days. We were all so young and now so many of us are gone. Giggling a little, she pointed to the giant fat and sodium-laced pastrami sandwich sitting in front of us; the one she'd asked me to get from the Kosher deli. "I'm bad," she said, taking a bite of her pickle. "I still eat too much salt, but I'm here."

After lunch, she rewrapped half her sandwich to save for later and we turned back to the old days. Before she got too tired and I had to head back to the city, I said, "Aunt Cee, those family gatherings in Gram's living room were the closest thing we had to a storytelling tradition. But tell me something. Is my memory correct that Jack, Uncle Harry and the other men, never mentioned bad things that happened to them during the war? They made war sound like fun and I know it wasn't."

My question touched a nerve. "Honey," she answered, "Harry and all of them weren't going to tell us all that happened to them over there. And after the war, not much changed. The white boys were treated like heroes. The black ones got a pat on the head, but they still had to scuffle to find decent housing and better paying jobs."

If any bitter GI memories marred those magical occasions, I didn't detect them. But perhaps by then, I wasn't listening as carefully. As happens with a growing preteen, even at favorite family events, the day came when my own personal dramas took precedence over stories about air raid sirens and ration books. I'd turned eleven and a few weeks before, I'd gotten my first period.

"You're a young lady now," Mom informed me, "and you can't do some of the things little girls do." We were sitting on Gram's bed and I sniffed, trying not to cry because it was the Fourth of July. All the kids were outside lighting sparklers and stepping on caps to make them pop, and I had come inside to find out why my underpants felt wet. I heard pop, pop, pop echoing from the street and looked at my box of sparklers. I was only allowed to play with them on this one day in the year, and now they were sitting on top of the dresser going to waste because I had to stay in and listen to Mom tell me that growing up meant I could do even less than when I was a little kid.

"It's a time when you start liking boys," she said.

What was she talking about? I'd always liked boys. Some of the nicer ones were my best friends and outside waiting for me.

"You're growing up and young ladies can't roughhouse with the boys or even get too close to them." She sounded like Gram.

"I don't roughhouse. It's arm wrestling, and sometimes I almost win."

"When you become a young lady," she continued, ignoring the fact that I didn't roughhouse, "your body starts changing."

Already, barely detectable nubs on my chest had generated one boy's rude comment. Then Mom said the word I hated. "We're going to have to buy you a training brassiere."

Why do you alway say it like that, I wanted to yell? It's a bra, a bra, not a stupid brassiere. I will never wear a stupid old-fashioned brassiere. Instead of yelling, I did what I was doing a lot of then—started crying.

Mom still spent some early evenings up at Bowman's Bar with Jack, before the crowd picked up. That left me at home with Gram, who spent her summer evenings by the window watching everything that went on, and for some good-news, bad-news reason, everything went on under our window. I didn't appreciate the power of raging hormones, or under-stand why my grandmother was suddenly as interested in teenage boys as I was. And to this day, I'd swear those days, with the boys and girls laughing and talking on park benches, were nothing other than good clean fun. But in Harlem, there was always something to worry about. Boys. Polio. Gangs. Poverty. Polio was finally under control, but my grandmother still paraded-out her list of polio horrifics—wheel chairs, crutches, crippled children withering away in little hospital beds, and her scariest image, iron lungs—if I even suggested going swimming with my friends.

The pool down the street, Colonial Park Pool, was a turquoise jewel that would have made the country club set envious, if they'd ever seen it. It was nestled into the bottom of the 145-146th Street hillside, in the Valley, and despite its Olympic proportions and picturesque setting, parents on Edgecombe had an uneasy relationship with it.

Some of Harlem's most destitute families were crowded into Eighth Avenue slums that were just a block from the pool's Bradhurst Avenue entrance. In the 1950s, a shameful number of buildings were coldwater flats with one bathroom per floor, and the buildings rarely had laundry facilities. Whether right or wrong, people on Edgecombe assumed Colonial Pool attracted the unwashed masses. If that wasn't enough to keep skittish folks, who already thought living on the hill made them superior, from swimming in the pool, add lingering jitters over polio germs, plus frequent reports that a gang of trouble-making Valley kids had beaten someone up.

Sugar Hill swimmers preferred High Bridge on 173rd Street in Washington Heights, or a smaller pool on 137th Street near Riverside Drive, in the Puerto Rican and Cuban neighborhood. A few times when Mom and I walked over to 137th Street, we passed Broadway markets whose colorful assortment of apparel hung from racks set up on the sidewalk. From inside the bodegas, the sounds of *"Eye yi yi te amo,"* and other moaning Spanish lyrics drifted out onto the street. Pretty Cuban girls chattered in their foreign language and swayed to the music. They wore clashing-color dresses in a dizzying mix of chartreuse ruffles or a mish-mash of red, green, aqua and yellow frills and flounces.

Back on Edgecombe, my girlfriends and I made fun of the Spanish girls' clothes and felt superior to them, but we also felt safe entering their space. Most Spanish kids around there hadn't turned territorial yet. Many were new arrivals who'd just gotten off what Gram provocatively called banana boats, even though Cubans and Puerto Ricans flew on planes from Havana, San Juan or Ponce, and were as scared of Negroes as we were of Valley hooligans.

Hooligans, gangs and packs were interchangeable terms for tough kids who roamed in groups. Occasionally, girl or boy packs from Bradhurst or Eighth Avenue swaggered up the park stairs and postured down our street. They may have been looking for trouble or just looking, since the first time

I witnessed this, I only saw a cocky group of Valley boys strutting their stupid, diddy bop roll. The diddy bop is that bee-bopping, rolling-ship-on-a-rough-sea walk that generations of Negro boys have used to silently scream, "Hey look at me, I'm tough."

The second time Valley kids showed up, it was more tragedy than comedy. A pack of raggedy, dirty-looking wild girls, their hair standing up every which way, ran down our block, crazily darting back and forth on both sides of the street. One of them flew by, seemingly too afraid to slow down, or else she was running from something.

I don't know how it happened so fast, but the littlest girl, pulling up the rear, who shouldn't have been so far from home anyway, darted in front of one of the few cars that came down our street and it tossed her butt naked into the air. The thump made all of us freeze, then my first thought was I'd never seen another girl's bare behind, or known anyone too poor to wear panties. Within seconds, kids who'd been sitting on the bench moved at once. The driver jumped out, we ran over and all but one of her friends took off. Several mothers, fearing their child was the one under the screeching tires they'd heard, rushed from their apartments.

The little girl was lying wide-eyed in the middle of the street, a tiny broken thing, either in shock or bravely fighting back tears while twenty strangers stared at her. The women comforted her hurts, softly cooing over raw scrapes that oozed bright blood, marring her delicate black skin.

"It'll be all right sweetheart; tell us your name." Eloise knelt down and tried coaxing her into talking. After the ambulance pulled away, we were silent, listening to some woman I didn't know say, "I wonder where she came from and how they'll contact her people if they don't have a phone?"

After witnessing that accident, my friends and I decided fear of girl gangs was more imagined than real. Our street was safe as long as you looked both ways before crossing, and polio had been wiped off the list of what could kill or cripple us.

97

But then Jack started coming home with stories about teenage junkies wandering into the bar with their arms full of stolen goods. One guy, he said, was trying to fence a pocketbook, possibly snatched within the hour.

This was a new breed of young and desperate heroin addicts; not Harlem's cool cat musicians in dark glasses who were cut plenty of slack. The cool cats' music fans didn't much care if they were strung out, as long as they kept playing those crazy far-out riffs. For years, the press and public followed Billie Holiday's path to self-destruction. Yet, heroin, negative publicity and the crush of fame didn't destroy her voice, as friends feared and critics predicted. If anything, her white stardust seemed to give Billie some degree of peace from a real world she couldn't handle. After hearing her edgy songs about stormy weather or morning heartache, listeners begged for more.

Before uptown fully grasped what was going on, heroin became an epidemic of fear and terror that mostly ravaged young people, wiping out some of the best and brightest. Nervous, twitchy hopheads invaded the streets and started hanging out in what had previously been wino parks. Hanging out, however, was where comparisons ended. Drunks sobered up, and if they didn't, fifty cents for a bottle of happy juice made them mellow. Heroin users quickly built $100-a-day habits. They snatched purses, mugged strangers and broke their parents' hearts.

Misery and secrecy surrounded heroin's sinister appeal and users weren't just the misbegotten or from lower classes. Young people who had everything going for them got sucked in and under. Pretty, gray-eyed Gloria, who used to take me to the playground, the pride of her junior high graduating class; she was engaged to be married. Bobby, a young man with the tip of his thumb missing, lived on St. Nicholas and was apprenticing in a butcher shop. Gloria got scarred up with needle tracks, became glassy-eyed and started turning tricks to support her habit. The butcher boy changed into a scabbed-over thief.

Families with a heroin user closed ranks, kept quiet in their desperation and denial. Few people knew where to seek help for a child or loved one on drugs. Some young addicts were saved when parents shipped them off to relatives in the South. That plan worked in a few instances, but the pull of heroin sometimes landed them back in New York. Then one day, as though it was part of the long-range plan for Harlem, Bunky died.

He lived up the street, was a few years older than me, and already in junior high. I'd known him since day one and he wasn't the type to get my grandmother all riled up and suspicious. He was just starting to notice girls. Small for his age and goofy acting, he was a frequent strikeout victim when batting in stickball, making him the butt of jokes. He didn't join in when the other boys made wooden scooters, and he had a narrow, lumpy-shaped head, which somehow tagged him with the nickname Bunky.

Neatly groomed, with closely clipped hair, Bunky always tucked his shirt in and he carried a handkerchief, the way men did, but his was for spreading on stoops before sitting down, so his pants wouldn't get dirty. Shortly before he died, Bunky was the boy who asked me, "How come girls have mountains growing on their chests?" It was the sort of stupid question a little girl with budding breasts was not good at answering, so first I told him to shut up, then tried hitting him with my jump rope, but he was faster and ran away.

Bunky's mother had considered sending him to Catholic school, but he wanted to follow his sixth grade class to Stitt Junior High. Emboldened at the big school, he switched his awkward adolescent silliness into a swagger that caught the attention of JDs—that crowd of juvenile delinquents that urban schools are often burdened with, and parents hope their child will avoid. New friends at the junior high complimented his meticulous appearance, instead of teasing him for being so fussy. They weren't into stickball or scooter making, either.

The police discovered Bunky's body on a roof near school. No one was ever charged or blamed in his death. Bunky became another statistic among the rising number of youth who were dying, going to jail or living in hell in Harlem.

At his funeral—the first I attended—there was shock and a church full of slack-jawed grief, although there was plenty of the screaming, moaning kind, too. So many kids were there, hanging our heads, leaning against our parents, scared, not having seen enough sorrow to show emotion like adults did. Someone had dressed Bunky up, but he still looked all wrong; not the way he'd want to be. He was skinnier, grayer, dead. I hadn't wanted to come, but Mom said I had to and I knew she was right.

It was hard to understand how Bunky's mother, Dolores, could stand to be there. I'd heard people found the will to carry on and Dolores must have found it, because a bunch of other mothers were falling apart and carrying on in a louder, different way from Dolores who sat quietly, probably sedated, heavily veiled. After the service, she could still put one foot in front of the other and follow the coffin out to the street to accompany her son to the graveyard. We filed out behind her, kids quiet and teary, adults blowing their noses, shaking their heads, talking that talk that had become a dirge—Bunky, of all kids. Too young. Why him? This can't happen again.

7. A Numbers Game and Twelve Planets

While drugs were damaging thousands of kids and young adults, another mob-controlled enterprise—the numbers racket—had a firm hold on a different Harlem demographic: gamblers. The community had and continues to have a complicated relationship with the numbers. When I was growing up, Sugar Hill residents wagged their snooty fingers in the rest of Harlem's face, but like black folks in every nook and cranny north of 110th Street, people living on the hill savored the bet.

The description of a typical Harlem numbers player defied definition. Teachers, undertakers, athletes, police officers, entertainers and dentists claimed forty-year playing streaks. Citizens of more modest means boasted similar records and our old neighborhood was filled with such people. Players were superstitious. They asked friends or relatives to place their bet if they went to Chicago for a week, or underwent anesthesia for an appendix operation, because they feared that one elusive number would pop up while they were away. For devotees like my stepfather, who was one of those forty year-ers, missing his hot number because of a trip to Atlantic City, or the VA Hospital would be akin to St. Peter sleeping through the Second Coming; it just didn't happen.

Numbers money bought some of the Buicks and Volkswagens parked on Harlem streets. It put food on family tables, and it helped parents winnow down their daughters' nursing school debts. Gambling dreams did come true, but the game didn't always serve our citizens well. For its most vulnerable victims, of which there were thousands, numbers playing ate

101

rent money, fostered gambling addiction and all too often erupted into repossession and ruin.

In high school when I rode the bus home each afternoon, traffic on Convent Avenue was light and the driver always stopped on 128th Street, at a tailor shop along our route. It wasn't uncommon to see a driver park and dash into a corner market while everybody on the bus watched him. Usually he came out a minute later with a can of Coke or a Snickers bar, but our guy came out with the day's number. Softly, not fooling anyone, he whispered his findings to the overdressed blind lady in dark glasses, who carried a white cane and sat ramrod straight in the seat directly behind him. Mr. Roosevelt, her German shepherd guide dog, quietly rested at the woman's feet.

The driver was kindly, and the two of them chatted along Morningside Avenue and up Convent. She and the driver talked about religious radio shows, the kind of programming my grandmother made fun of. But Gram and the blind woman had one thing in common; both hoped today was the day they'd hit the number.

In Harlem, women socialized in beauty parlors, got their hair straightened or curled while talking over life's problems. Men met on the street, or in barber shops, to brag about women or talk about the Giants or Dodgers. But if you watched closely at certain times of day, you might see the men and the women silently mouthing 0's or 2's, or subtly finger-flashing 4's, 9's or 6's. This was Harlem's sign language—the daily number—a vernacular everyone, whether they played or not, was fluent in.

The commercial hub of my neighborhood was a five-block length of St. Nicholas Avenue, a street just west of Edgecombe. Two bus lines passed through and so did Harlem's last express "A" train before it switched to a local. Near the subway station, there was also a dimly lit and noticeably uninviting general goods/hardware/junk/plumbing parts store that I never entered. Men who did "shop" there always walked out empty-handed. Instinctively I knew the store wouldn't have the white ribbon I wanted or the eggbeater Gram sent me to buy at the real hardware store. I can't swear on a Bible, but I'm sure that the store's true business had something to do with the numbers syndicate.

In the 1970s, New York State muscled-in on this thriving underground economy by legalizing gambling and establishing Off-Track Betting parlors. Technology keeps improving this government-sanctioned pastime, enabling people to gamble at these parlors. There, they can wager on horses, buy lottery tickets, or play three-pick Lotto games that mimic the illegal numbers game played on the street; the one that lives on and refuses to die.

I grew up in the laps of numbers players. My mother's neighbor Buddy, who was near eighty and in poor health when I spoke to him, had played since the 1930s. He gave me a primer on how the illegal and complex street game works, and I hope I can do it justice. Players bet with "someone they know," he explained, by placing money on three digits, typically their house number. That bettor often stays with that number through a lifetime, as though it's part of his DNA.

The daily number is generated from winning horses at thoroughbred race tracks. After money from the first two or three races comes in, a calculation from those figures generates the day's first digit, which is the first number left of the decimal point. Totals from the fourth and fifth race generate the second number, and the last races determine the day's third and final number.

At the end of our lesson, Buddy told me if I wanted to, I could legally phone in and get the day's racing results and also hear the daily number. In the old days, the only place to get such news was on the street, when word of 257, 589 or whatever number spread through neighborhoods as reliably as a mail delivery. Friends, family, maybe ex-wives who did not play themselves, still listened for results because they knew a friend or former partner's pet number. Before the generous glow of success faded, hangers-on, and those who felt entitled to a portion of the money, approached the winner, requesting loans, cash gifts, or back alimony they might be owed.

I later called the information line Buddy gave me, but didn't understand the system, resulting in confusion, plus I couldn't shake the feeling of doing something criminal and the sense that I should hurry off the phone before the authorities showed up at my mother's apartment door.

Technical gambling doesn't suit everyone, especially folks who don't like automation, don't live or work near betting centers, or view gambling as a private, even social, exchange between the bettor and his or her connection. The worst knock against legalization is having to share winnings with Uncle Sam, and thousands of gamblers refuse to do it (in December 2010, New York City closed its Off-Track Betting parlors).

It's true that street betting avoids state and city taxes, although winners, especially of large jackpots, often cough up generous tips for their runner, even though runners and others in the hierarchy get a commission. Harlem's high-ranking men in the business were called bankers or controllers. Exactly how they fit in with the mobsters, or those who owned the big banks and had the muscle, I'm not sure.

As savvy as my grandmother was, she didn't know, or else refused to associate the game she played daily with notorious mobsters like Jimmy the Shiv and Dutch Schultz. Mom, on the other hand, understood gambling's seamy side quite well. Jack had a close friend who was a banker. The man lived a life of luxury, drove a Continental, had smart, well-behaved children, but it was a life spent tap dancing around both honest and corrupt police officials, a gangster network, and the jail system, because he got arrested and jailed twice.

Even in churches, where ministers pounded pulpits and preached against drugs, drunkenness and the usual laundry list of evils, they winked and nodded over the numbers. Playing was so prevalent, clergymen counted on balancing church budgets with a share of parishioner's winnings, and everyone assumed some lesser men of the cloth went so far as to place bets of their own.

Things are different now in New York with West Indian, Hispanic, black, white and foreign racketeers all vying for what's left of a dwindling gambling pie that's been diluted by legal betting, stricter enforcement and fewer racetracks. I no longer feel the pulse of the community, because I just pass through. But until recently, I knew old men who were young when I was a child, who placed their bets with new young men, as though fifty years hadn't gone by.

The game's popularity was a carryover from hard times in Harlem when hitting the number (Buddy said the payoff was 600 to 1), or living hand-to-mouth, were the only options for breaking a cycle of poverty. It endures because folks remain poor and still dream of finding a pot of gold, but practical reasons such as employment opportunities also factored in gambling's perpetuity. Respectable women with school-age children fed their kids by collecting numbers part time, when the kids were in school. Decent men who'd never do anything "criminal" made an exception when it came to this profession because it wasn't "hurting" anything.

The hierarchy of employees in the rackets started with runners who worked the streets. Trusted office people kept track of paperwork, miscellaneous helpers did whatever— watched for cops or bad guys, but controllers and bankers seemed to be the only ones who consistently got rich.

As with many bettors, my grandmother scoffed at doing business in gaming parlors (presumably like that place on St. Nicholas Avenue), but enjoyed betting with Bertie, who like Gram, only wanted to make an "honest" dollar. Bertie was a red-haired lady runner, swollen by pregnancy, and soon-to-be mother of three, who came by daily to pick up Gram's ten cents worth of bets. My grandmother's favorite pick was 369, our house number and despite long odds, she occasionally won something. She'd place a full dime on 369, or maybe five cents on the house number and the other nickel on a combination, or she picked ten different numbers for a penny each. She kept accurate records, using carbon paper to make a copy of her betting slip.

Unscrupulous bankers and underlings may have cheated people out of winnings and I don't know how that was addressed, since there wasn't a formal grievance process, but some of Harlem's yearly murders may have accounted for that process.

In the old neighborhood, I never heard of disputed numbers or deals gone bad. Once the number was out on the street, it didn't change and if you won, you got paid because keeping one's word was an important component of this business. Some folks claim numbers playing is entrepreneurialism at its best, but it's also endemic gambling of the first order for many people who can ill afford it.

Some runners, like Bertie, catered to housewives, shut-ins and penny players like my grandmother. Jack didn't mess with pennies, nickels, or carbon paper. For most of the years I knew him, he played one daily number, 302, and he placed it with the neighborhood's top dog, Mr. Big Banker, the friend I mentioned above. Mr. Big B was a family man and smart investor who, in the late 1960s, retired from the business to a home in Bergen County, New Jersey. His kids went to a private college and I assume, unlike me, they didn't need to take out loans.

Although Jack was a gambler, he was a hard-working, sober and steady man like my uncles, but he lacked their foresight. After bills were paid, his investment in the future was a gamble instead of a savings plan. Sometimes he won big, as happened shortly before he and my mother were married.

Mom was leery of his gambling, but Jack adored her, he was good to me and his bonanza meant they could put a down payment on a house. That might be why they finally set a date, since he'd been her steady beau for several years. But the only significant purchase I remember was a large RCA console, with a state-of-the-art, twelve-inch black and white screen and two phonographs.

Sugar Hill numbers men were often revered, classy looking conservative types with beautiful wives and adorable kids. They drove toned-down Cadillacs, or tasteful Lincolns and would never be confused with lowlife hustlers who skimmed the fringes of decent society in flashy suits and custom made, overdone automobiles. My mother told me, at one time in the 1940s, Harlem's secret numbers bank—where tens of thousands were kept—was in a building on the 2400 block of Seventh Avenue. When I asked Buddy if he knew about the bank, he thought it had been in The Graham Court, further south in the 1900 block of Seventh.

"I may have the address wrong," Mom said, "but more to the point, what I'm telling you about the past, can't go beyond this room."

Hmm. "Mom, we're talking about the 1940s. You're telling me about illegal gambling activity. People involved in this were breaking the law, right? Why is it a secret?"

"Because the bank was also home to W and H. Those two men weren't criminals, so their involvement has to be kept quiet. Some things are only the business of Harlem and not supposed to end up in a book."

"I wouldn't mention their names, anyway" I said, thinking of many reasons why it wouldn't be a good idea, especially if the information was wrong.

My mother's reaction was typical of how the public circled wagons around favored operatives in the numbers racket, whether smalltimers like Bertie or big bosses, like W and H. Some, but not all, of the favoritism was understandable because wealthy gamblers often shared winnings with needy women and children. It didn't occur to me at that moment, but later I wondered if someone Mom knew was a recipient of Mr. H or W's largess, because later that evening, I heard just how devastating the 1930s had been to people I loved.

"And as far as our family is concerned," Mom got to the heart of what really bothered her, "I don't understand why you want to write about us. There's nothing interesting to say.

We were ordinary." She turned her head, but I still saw tears forming in the corners of her eyes.

"Ordinary people are interesting, Mom. I'm proud of our family." I wanted to reassure her, but I felt emotions welling up, too.

"No one in this family has anything to be ashamed of," I added, "and you know Gram would agree with me." Tossing my feisty grandmother into the equation seemed to reassure us both, because Mom smiled, knowing I was right.

"When I was growing up, outsiders thought all of Harlem was a jungle, a ghetto," I said. "If you weren't Langston Hughes or Duke Ellington, you were nothing in the eyes of many. I'm sorry, but I beg to differ. The point is, there was another side—the one about ordinary people like us. Our family history belongs to me, too, Mom."

There were ordinary folks associated with numbers, and then there were people like Madame Stephanie St. Clair, a legendary numbers banker who died in 1969. She retired from the rackets and moved out of 409 Edgecombe around the time I was born. I never saw her but Mr. Thomas, a neighbor, described her as very tall with stately bearing, and as prone to violence as any man in the game. She operated with the help of a gang called the Forty Thieves, who watched her back. Her nickname was "the Queen," and like the lesser known Messrs. H and W, she was more respected than reviled, although unlike the former men, she was also feared. The 1997 gangster movie, *Hoodlum*, is about Harlem's turf wars between the St. Clair faction and white mobsters who tried to force her out of business.

Harold Thomas, who in 1994 still lived in her former building, remembered her when she was a tenant in 409. As a high school kid in the 1930s, he knew most of 409's tenants because his sister, Thelma, managed the building and got him an after-school job relieving the building's elevator and switchboard operators.

"A lot of things were going on with Madame St. Clair," he said, enjoying the recollection. "She had this place hopping. That's when she and Dutch Schultz were feuding over the numbers. One night I was relieving Sonny on the South [elevator] car; a black limousine drove up. Four guys got out. You know how you are when you're young, wondering what's happening. Someone whispered, 'Hey, they're going up to Madame St. Clair's apartment.'

"I was waiting for them and didn't even look at them. You didn't dare look at them. He had his gangsters and she had hers, but he had more. They said 10 or 8. I think it was 10 [the floor they wanted]. They stayed. I went back downstairs. Pretty soon the elevator bell rang. I went back up. I closed the door and took them down and they marched off. That's the way it seemed to me. It was like a military operation."

My grandmother was not a learned woman, but she consistently read two books: her Bible and her dream book. Newsstands in Harlem sold *The Dream Book*, a slim blue or green softcover volume of wordlists and phrases with corresponding numbers. Dream books were thought to help players hit the number by offering a "genuine, reliable system" for selecting winners based on dreams.

When I was a kid, these little pamphlets cost a dime, but today if purchased from the publisher, they sell for $2.00 to $5.00, plus postage and handling. Local newsstands and religious stores charge similar prices. Some years ago, on a whim, I picked one up at Las Americas Botanical Gardens (Subsidiary to the House of Talisman, Inc.), on 145th Street. Dream books written in popular list formats are cheaper than the deluxe model, *Success Dream Book*. The deluxe model assigns a dream a number, gives full interpretations of many types of dreams, and has a complete horoscope of the twelve planets (sic) with their lucky numbers.

The books are alphabetized in lists of columns and easy to use. If, for instance, you dreamed of baking apples, or had a nightmare about long-dead Cousin Alfred and his wife Sabina, the next morning you might gamble on Apple #194, Alfred #842 or Sabina #560. However, if you dreamed about picnics in the park and want to place money on the number for picnic, you have to improvise because picnic isn't listed in the dream book.

The "P" section does provide numbers for "pegler," "pinch back suit" and "piss-a-bed." Such words are not used in today's English language and, if they ever were in use, can't be found in unabridged dictionaries, but the public still buys this material and has been doing so for most of the century because people do win money by picking numbers from the book.

When I was learning to read, I sat at my grandmother's feet using her extra dream books like flash cards, practicing vocabulary while attempting to help her look for winners. Instead of dreams, my picks were based on words I could decipher and pronounce.

"Let's do Bs today," I might suggest, running my finger down the list until it landed on a familiar word. "Here's a good one. B-a-n-k, bank, or B-a-l-l-r-o-o-m, ballroom. I can read that long, eight letter word, and Mommy and Jack went dancing at the Savoy Ballroom. Bet on that one."

Grammy was usually too preoccupied with her own dream book or adding up her number slip for a two cent, five cent, or dime bet on 369 to pay attention to me. The better you read, the more you realize dream books are filled with archaic words and obsolete phrases (trolloping, shaking a dead's hand), and sloppy spellings (tencils, apera—possibly pencils and opera, but I found them listed in "T" and "A" sections).

The H. P. Dream Book, written by Prof. Uriah Konje, says that he's looking to help people around the world who are oppressed and/or black. His message is uplifting: he tells readers that he understands everyone cannot be highly intellectual, but they must strive to do their best, so they can be happy. Additionally, he urges the colored people to work for political equality, so they might attain social equality, as well as happiness.[1]

Buying and selling dream books is entrenched in Harlem's culture. Many buyers, like my grandmother, had several types and either believed or wanted to believe Prof. Uriah Konje when he wrote that, after years of trying, he had produced a dream book that was one-hundred-percent efficient. Besides efficiency, his book, he feels, will create love and happiness for users.[2]

After my First Communion.

8. About Good Ol' Boys, Bible Thumpers, Charlatans and Nuns

Before Mom signed me up to join St. Catherine's of Genoa, my idea of religion was saying grace before dinner and reciting "Now I Lay Me Down to Sleep" at bedtime. Then I squeezed in as many "God Bless Gram, Aunt Cee, Daddy," and so-ons, as my mother who supervised this nightly ritual, would tolerate.

We were not a family that embraced formal religion. Therefore, I was shocked to learn as an adult that my grandmother, who led me to believe she was Baptist, had also been baptized Catholic at Harlem's St. Charles Borromeo Church. I never gave much thought to Gram's church leanings, but like the rest of her, they strayed left of the usual. Take her Catholicism. In the twenty-some years I observed my grandmother's habits, I don't recall her attending Mass or entering a Catholic church, except for my First Communion, having skipped my baptism in protest. She didn't go to Baptist services either, but she read the King James Bible, sang spirituals and said her rosary—the beads she once snatched from around my neck when she caught me using them to play dress-up.

My best recollection of how she viewed the Catholic faith was her taking pot shots at nuns. "Nuns around here," she said, "are mean as snakes, because they got stranded among a bunch of niggers in Harlem and it served them right because, to be so mean, they musta been evil from the git go."

She had plenty to offer about religion in general, and particularly on hypocrites and those she called "millionaire con-men ministers," who wore $500 suits and maintained mansions in three or four cities because, according to her, they

113

were running two steps ahead of the law. Among the group she most criticized were Father Divine, Daddy Grace and, in later years, Reverend Ike; three high-powered religious leaders with close ties to Harlem.

Father Divine, arguably the most famous of all Negro prophets, preached an austere message of personal satisfaction and spiritual redemption being achieved through sacrifice, positive thinking and self-sufficiency. Many admirers said he didn't just talk the talk, but set the example by supplying guidance and resources for followers who struggled with salvation and poverty. His Divine Kingdom was generous, using commercial interests to help the needy, including profits from a bakery on Eighth Avenue that sold sweet potato pies Mom swore were the best she ever tasted. Father Divine found jobs, helped feed and house thousands of desperate people during his peak years, which coincided with high unemployment during and after the Depression.

Believers supported Divine's claim to be god the messiah, but when I was in grade school, his Peace Mission Movement was showing cracks at its foundation. By then, his church was juggling tax problems, accusations of sexual impropriety and crooked finances that critics, like my grandmother, had lobbed at him for years.

When Father Divine's troubles mounted, I remember Bishop "Sweet Daddy" Grace was right there to pick up the slack. Whereas Divine emphasized restraint and put a premium on chastity and abstinence from alcohol, Sweet Daddy's large loyal following loved his joyous, good-time ministry and his uplifting "screaming" services that rocked his House of Prayer for All People.

Both men had charismatic qualities that women in particular fed on. Daddy Grace operated on a different plane from most prophets; his long painted fingernails, flowing capes and straightened shoulder-length hair were show stoppers. Looking back at his flamboyance, I can't help thinking that James Brown, the Godfather of Soul, took more than a few pointers from Sweet Daddy. If Daddy Grace, with his multiple names, intended to align himself with Father Divine, the ploy worked with me because I had trouble differentiating the two. "What's the difference between a Bishop Daddy and a Father Divine?" I once asked my grandmother.

"No difference," she said, "those are just titles they gave themselves. The one's a self-appointed bishop and the other one sure isn't divine. But give them credit," she added. "Those money ministers are smart. They hoop and holler all day on Sunday, and those church women just start praying and sweating and swaying," she said, falling into one of her frequent impersonations of a preacher-like cadence. "The women carrying on something awful—then they turn around and give him all their hard earned pay."

She was brushing my hair dry and stopped to cross both arms over her bosom. She did that more often now that her arms got tired. But she was also distracted. I sighed. Hair drying already took too long and now, with her haranguing ministers, I'd be getting brushed forever.

"They may be full of the Holy Spirit" she continued, "but those women are also full of that so-called minister, and he knows that when he passes the collection plate around. Lord have mercy on my soul, but the world is full of fools. I know He is looking down on us saying, 'My work has just begun because these poor, ignorant black folks just won't learn.'"

"What's that high-priced phony doing on our street?" she sneered one day, sticking her head out the window, straining to follow some evangelist taking a slow Sunday roll past our house in a two-car, white Cadillac convertible motorcade. The lead car had a driver in front; a man and woman sat in back. A male driver in the second Cadillac was driving three women passengers. Everyone wore white.

"Tsk, tsk. Just look at that," she groused, pulling her head back inside. "These churchgoing sisters need their heads examined, giving him their hard earned cash. They scrub floors, look like hell all week, then plop on their wigs and Sunday-go-to-meeting clothes so they can sit in church grinning in some fool's face. Those white cars and fancy get-ups don't even look churchly. They look like some stage act traveling down the road."

Like many folks with low opinions of holy messengers, Gram was still drawn to radio evangelism. The airwaves were full of tearful testimonials, dramatic Jesus sightings and preachers eager to rescue us from sin. Religious radio was a serious spiritual tool for listeners in the 1950s, although plenty of Doubting Thomas's tuned in as well. But these shows had a way of killing the magic because Radio Reverend-What's-His-Name, always needed cash so the souls could be saved and prayers answered.

"You know what he's going to do with that $200 dollars when it starts rolling in, don't you?" Gram asked as a way of reminding me that this just the latest scam. "That's pocket change for some of these snakes. And that's where it'll go, too, right in his pocket. Poor folks sing the blues all night, then turn around and send the likes of him their last two dollars. Lord, make me judge for a day," she mimicked the radio preacher's voice. "Just one day is all I need. You know what I'd send. I'd send his lying ass to prison."

The intensity of media evangelism grew with the onset of miracle TV, a new mode of religion that allowed the public to watch people being cured of stomach cancer, arthritis of the spine and demons in the mind. Sometimes blind men were made to see for the first time. Healers came in all hues and both sexes, but in the early, razzle-dazzle days of miracle TV, only good ol' white boys, with honky tonk appeal and Bible-thumping voices hosted these shows. Gram said healers were the lowest of the low, because they preyed on people who were both poor and desperate. She claimed that some sinners were really sick and needed help, but others were pretenders, like actors in a play.

"Now, that poor fella has all the signs of being a rummy," she pointed at an emaciated little man on the TV screen who needed a miracle to cure him of drinking.

"How can you tell he's a rummy?"

"There's plenty like him around here, but he's a sorry-looking soul. Thin as a rail and weak as a kitten. Looks like he just came off a bender."

She thought a truck driver with back problems was really hurting, but he didn't need a miracle. Her suggestion was hot compresses and mustard plaster. "That's about all you can do for that lower back pain," she tells me as we watch the show. "If he used that and took four Anacin, instead of just two, like it says on the medicine bottle, it would go a long way towards fixing what ails him."

At the beginning of these programs, Brother Healer, usually in a rumpled suit because he sweated a lot, first welcomed, then castigated sinners before assuring us salvation was indeed possible if we discarded evil ways. To get to the good parts that I liked, a skillful preacher played the audience, raising his voice level as he praised the Lord and worked himself into a state of exaltation.

"Speak to me, Jesus. Walk with me, Lord." The man on the screen closes his eyes and starts trembling, then asks, "Do I hear the Spirit calling?"

"Yes, Lord," the audience answers. "Send me one of the afflicted," he tells the Father. While he's ruminating and waiting to communicate with Jesus, the camera pans the room and picks up an image that lets us know today's show will be very dramatic, because the camera has settled on a woman who is struggling down the center aisle on crutches.

"Does that lady have polio?" I ask my grandmother, who doesn't say anything, but watches intently.

"Come to me, sister. Don't be afraid. We're all sinners here. Cast out the devils and you'll discover peace and happiness today. Dear Lord, who died for our sins, make me strong this morning," he prays. "Give me the power to heal this poor, suffering woman." As she nears, he steps forward and helps her get into the right position, then with his eyes closed again, he waits for the Divine Authority or the Healing Force to enter his body so he can work the miracle.

"Oh yes. I feel it coming," he says. "I feel the power. Jesus is with me now. I'm feeling his spirit." Eyes shut, sweat popping on his forehead and streaming down his face, he prays fervently. When he's full strength, he lays his hands on her head—laying on hands is part of the miracle process.

"I believe, sister. Do you believe?" he asks the lady whose head is still down because he's pressing on it, but she's able to nod, "Yes."

Waiting for the miracle, I hold my breath, knowing my grandmother is probably right about this being fake, but I'm so loving it. Television is the only place I can watch people on crutches or in wheel chairs, without having someone whisper in my ear or hunch me in the ribs to say, "Stop staring."

On the screen, Hallelujahs and Amens roll around the church. When the minister is ready, he proclaims triumphantly, "In God's name heal, renounce your sins. Seek salvation in the Lord Jesus. Take Him into your soul. Embrace Him and be saved. Heal, sister. Heal! Stand up now. Forget those crutches. Unleash your binds and open your heart to the healing power of our Lord Jesus."

The woman rises from her knees and it makes me happy. But for some reason, the cured woman is crying, instead of rejoicing. With her head still down, she wipes away tears and an usher escorts her back to her seat, as the appeal comes on, requesting donations to continue this good work. Grams turns off the television and I ask again, if the woman was really cured of polio.

"No," she said, massaging her own achy knees.

"Why not? How do you know?"

Something hopeful in my voice makes her turn towards me. "Jean, I wouldn't know where to begin making you understand how low some people can stoop. Polio was, and is a terrible thing. If the doctors could send patients to church to get healed, they would. The man is a fraud. He gives false hope to viewers who want to believe him and they send him money." She thought for a minute. "Come here," she said, waving me over to sit on the arm of her chair. "Let me tell you something. If he or any of them performed miracles, I'd be in line too, seeing what he could do about my arthritis."

The evangelist who most interested me was Reverend Ike because I'd been inside his church, the former Loews 175th Street Theater when it was a movie theater. Jack and I went because he wanted to show me what he thought was one of the most beautiful buildings in the city. Officially, the theater's name was Loews United Palace. It took up an entire city block and was designed like a castle, although the marquee prevented passersby from seeing the full view of the front facade. Inside, soaring gold ceilings and gilded walls were elaborately carved in ornate designs. It's hard to describe this theater's dazzling decor, but a few good descriptions are out there. David W. Dunlap, a *New York Times* writer does it justice, calling it "Byzantine-Romanesque-Indo-Hindu-Moorish-Persian-Eclectic-Rococo-Deco."[1] The Loew's Theater is one of those spare-no-expense structures, like some of the hotels in Las Vegas. Words don't adequately explain it. You need to see it for yourself.

It was after I'd been inside the Loews to see a movie with Jack, that I discovered it had a new tenant. I was on the bus, passing the building on the way to a doctor's appointment with Gram. In front and along the side of the theater, there was a long line of black women waiting to get inside. The theater was huge, with seating for thousands, so it was odd to see such a long line, much less one full of women decked out in elaborate straw hats and floral Sunday dresses, but it wasn't Sunday. The marquee showed the current attraction as "Reverend Ike's Power Hour."

"Oh Gram, look," I pointed out. "When did the theater become a church?"

Without giving it much thought, she said, "I don't know, but it suits Ike just fine. He's a showman."

Further south in Harlem, the streets were lined with black churches of many sizes and persuasions, as well as religious stores such as Sister So-and-So's Spiritualist Shop. Believers were drawn like moths to flame by spiritual aids and inspiring new preachers. Often, the more flamboyant the minister was, the better. Uptown, around the 175th Street Loews, the area was more sedate and still populated by devout Irish and Italian Catholics, and Jews who walked to synagogue on the Sabbath. Reverend Ike was the new kid in the neighborhood, but within a short time, people were buzzing about this brash young man with a grandiose list of self-imposed honorifics. Ike considered himself Chancellor of the United Church of School, and was a Doctor of Mind Ministry, whose specialty was teaching thinkonomics. I occasionally ran across his radio show, *The Power Hour*, while searching for a rock and roll station and grew more curious about him, now that I knew he was just a mile away.

I asked Mom if she wanted to see him in church. She didn't. I knew Gram wouldn't, and Jack just laughed, then said something like, "Why would I waste time watching that nigger perform when I can go down to the Apollo or Radio City Music Hall for real entertainment?"

Part of Ike's shtick was capitalizing on his smooth good looks and opulent lifestyle. By declaring up front that he worshipped at the Altar of Wealth and Prosperity, he disarmed critics who lobbed the usual labels of panderer, con artist, crook, etc., at him. When he specified his need for a donation to maintain his Rolls Royces, buy new silk suits or jewelry, the cash rolled in.

Ike's ministry started sometime in the late 1950s. In the summer of 2009, I drove through Washington Heights to see two landmarks, the 175th Street Loews and the Audubon Ballroom, where Malcolm X was assassinated. The buildings are a few blocks from each other and on the outside, both looked well preserved. The theater is now occasionally hired out for concerts or special events, and even though he had recently died, Reverend Ike's name was still listed on the marquee.

Our family custom of limiting churchgoing to weddings, funerals and TV shows was about to change with me. "You're going to become a Catholic," my mother announced one evening. "Tomorrow is Wednesday and I've arranged for your released-time from school so you can walk over to St. Catherine's to begin your first day of religious instruction."

"Oh, goody. Will I get to wear one of those wedding dresses and veils?"

"They're communion dresses, and yes, you will if you're a good girl and learn your lessons. But you'll have to work hard and remember that nuns are much stricter than your regular teachers."

"Olivia, what are you doing fooling around with those nuns?" Gram asked, sounding disgusted. "Why don't you just have the child baptized and leave it at that? Don't you remember what happened the last time you had dealings with the sisters? You almost bled to death up there at that hospital they run. They call themselves nurses. Humpf, they probably know as much about nursing as I do. And do you think they'd admit to being wrong? Nooo; walking around with that holier-than-thou attitude, like their mess doesn't stink."

"Mother, the nuns didn't do anything to harm me. It's not their fault they couldn't find a doctor. I was bleeding heavily and it scared you. We'll know not to go back if there's another emergency." As if to settle the point, Mom said, "Anyway, Jean will be with teaching, not nursing, nuns."

"No difference. Have they been Upstate to teaching college like that smart Mrs. Coshburn or those cute young teachers Jean does so well with? I bet these nuns make it up as they go along. I'm telling you, Olivia, those women aren't interested in teaching children from Harlem. Look how the black sisters keep to themselves down there in their convent. And

121

the church has the nerve to call the black nuns handmaids. Now what does that tell you? They arrived in Harlem around the same time I did and they still aren't welcomed in white parishes. If the white sisters can't tolerate their own brethren, what can they offer our children?"

"It's only one hour a week," Mom said, "plus Mass every Sunday. It'll be good for her to embrace a faith."

I'd never heard of, or seen, black nuns but I loved when Mom stood her ground, which she usually did about school business. Invariably when they disagreed over me, I wanted my mother to win because it meant something radical was coming down the pipeline that Gram couldn't understand or control. The rest of the family sometimes also viewed Mom's new plans with skepticism or hostility, and sometimes her bright ideas didn't work so well, like the time I was supposed to spend one week Upstate, in Saugerties. Mom described it as attending a camp on a lake. After one hour at the place, I was scared and homesick, so I called her to say I hated it and wanted to leave.

"Oh, for heaven's sake. You just got there and haven't given it a chance. Everything will be better tomorrow after you've made friends with all the children."

In defense of what makes me sound like a spoiled brat, this was not a camp. The place belonged to a family who had a two-story country house, a swing set and swimming hole. My mother indignantly swore it wasn't, because she said money was exchanged, but the deal had all the markings of the New York Fresh Air Fund for underprivileged children. Although there's a flaw in that theory because, if there was one thing my family did not want to be, it was underprivileged. The Fresh Air Fund is a wonderful ongoing program and still sends city kids to the country to stay with a family for a week. If my deal wasn't part of that, then it was a family who had their own gig going, and charged a fee to take in kids for a week.

Sandra, Mom's girlfriend, made the arrangements and I rode up with her and her son Craig, who was only two years younger. But Craig wasn't the best company to be spending a week with, because he didn't talk much and he drooled. My father was supposed to pick us both up the following week.

I had always admired Sandra's enthusiasm. When she and Mom were together, they laughed easily and looked pretty driving around in Sandra's '52 Chevy. But unlike Mom, who watched her pennies and should have seen pitfalls in this camp plan, Sandra thought everything was "simply gorgeous," "too fabulous for words" or her favorite, "so sharp."

When she took Craig and me to Zach's Bay at Jones Beach, she promised a fabulous safe beach without thundering waves. That was somewhat true, although she and Mom were constantly scaring us away from the water because of a potentially dangerous undertow. When I met "simply gorgeous Bernie," Sandra's latest boyfriend, he was bald and looked old. Her girlfriend's new apartment was not fabulous. It had skinny modern furniture that was supposed to be hip, but was on a drug dealing block, in the back of a gloomy building with dim light.

I wasn't sure I wanted to attend camp and was nervous about being away from home for the first time with strangers. Summers so far had been just fine, and sure enough, Sandra told Mom, "Olivia, this camp is so sharp." How could snakes and bugs be sharp? And as far as I was concerned, the "fabulous lake" was the first strike against the place. Lakes had dark, inky-colored water that you couldn't see through. Their docks extended past shallow parts, and someone who could swim was always urging non-swimmers like me to jump in.

That summer, there was a severe drought all over New York state. Throughout the countryside, relentless sun, blistering heat and dry wind killed grass and left trees brown-tipped and bedraggled. Despite being afraid of lakes, the long hot ride up the Thruway had sharpened my expectations for a cool dip. On the final leg, we lurched up a steep gravel road that ended in the front yard of the L family's house.

"Here we are, you two." Sandra turned her cute freckled-nose and sunbeam smile on two silent and wide-eyed kids in the back seat, as the Mr. and Mrs. approached us. "Come on Craig, Jean, outta the car." Sandra excitedly stepped toward the house, waving generously at what might have been a vegetable garden that looked like something the locusts had harvested.

"Isn't this fabulous, and how very nice to meet you," she gushed, sticking her hand out to greet two strange people who were now in charge of me for a week. The grownups chatted a few minutes, but Sandra had a date back in the city with Bernie. It seemed like we only stood there a few minutes before she left Craig and me in the driveway, leaning against a maroon woody station wagon, watching her drive away in a cloud of I'm-outta-here dust.

The other campers turned out to be the owner's three children. There was no lake and the swimming hole had dried up, but yes, I could have a drink of water. I remember that drink of water, because I didn't finish the whole cup. The mommy of the family was a kind, but serious-sounding lady who, despite blazing heat, wore a blouse with lots of fabric and a gypsy-style skirt that came to her ankles.

"Spill the remains of your water on poor Mother Earth," she said when I started to hand back a half-full glass. I understood what she meant, but people in the city didn't speak so mournfully about our water shortage. After I poured the two or three ounces of liquid on the ground, it left a tiny dark blotch in the dust at my feet. The hopelessness of it all caused me to ask if I could use her phone.

So, when Gram couldn't think of anything else to say against nuns, or against Mom's latest idea, I knew the discussion about religious instruction would result in moving ahead with the plan. I couldn't wait to buy one of those little girl wedding dresses that you had to be Catholic to wear. Despite Gram's aversion to the idea of Catholic schooling, even part-time, she was okay with priests. They didn't live high on the hog, or whip congregates into a frenzy of shouting and fainting that clouded their judgment at collection time.

I knew what Gram meant about shouting and fainting. I once went with Sadie, our upstairs neighbor, to a Sunday baptism at Convent Avenue Baptist, one of Harlem's highly regarded churches. I saw ladies talking, clapping and shouting; one even collapsing in the aisle. A few others, who were getting baptized, ended up in a swimming pool under the altar wearing their nightgowns. But when the minister preached, he never once asked for money like on radio and TV. I liked the feel-good way they worshiped at Convent Avenue, but warnings about phony ministers and misguided worshipers made me shy and I didn't clap like I was tempted to. I left church feeling a bit like I'd been at a celebration, rather than had a religious experience.

At my new church, I got baptized in a solemn lickety-split ten-minute ceremony, so I could catch up with the parochial school girls who'd already started preparing for First Communion. To be a child of God, I had to pick a saint's name and I chose Cecelia, after Aunt Cee, who truthfully wasn't all that saintly. My Godmother Dedi was there, also a stand-in Godfather recruited from the parish register, since we didn't know any Catholic men. Gram stayed home.

A few days later, I met the nuns who would mold me into a Catholic. For nearly a year, they crammed catechism lessons into a dwindling number of public school girls, taught us when to respond at Mass, how to walk piously and kneel with ramrod-straight backs. I learned "Hands together girls, elbows in, fingers pointed to God, head bowed, eyes lowered and remember, don't chew the Host." Despite long skirts and cumbersome veils, if nuns detected poor posture or someone leaning into the pew during kneeling time, they flew down those aisles in a nanosecond.

We worked hard that year, memorizing prayers, covering questions like what it meant to be in a state of grace, to why it was a sin to eat meat on Friday. Sometimes we crayoned pictures of "Jesus Among the Children" or "Jesus with the Animals." We also got to draw our own picture of something like "Jesus Comes to my First Communion," then write a short three-sentence story to explain that he came because he loves us.

My favorite time was First Communion practice, downstairs in church at three o'clock when St. Catherine's was quiet and empty, except for the few of us. The only light in the sanctuary came from candles flickering on the altar, and from a late afternoon sun streaming through stained glass panels, making it feel like God was in there with us.

I had a growing collection of religious objects helping me be a good Catholic: the white leather-bound missal, smaller than a deck of cards; a gold cross Daddy bought me; my own pretty pink rosary that I now knew wasn't jewelry. After my baptism, Father gave me a brown scapular that I was supposed to wear around my neck, and holy water in a bottle shaped like a pyramid.

During Holy Week we got to light our own candles, then the nuns walked us through Stations of the Cross, explaining how each depicted Jesus suffering before being crucified. But as Easter approached, what Mom said about nuns being strict became more apparent. All year, they leaned more towards being mean, rather than strict, never smiling or praising, but now they were even quicker to criticize.

The nuns had remained suspicious and disapproving of public school kids and our anonymous families who didn't come to church or belong to the parish and weren't even Catholic. About ten girls started the program and four of us remained. A girl named Roberta was dismissed for poor attendance and three others didn't understand what was going on because they couldn't read well enough. I could read, but I sometimes didn't understand what was going on either. One girl got kicked out the first day for cursing our teacher who followed her to the classroom, yelling that she wasn't supposed to go in the bathroom without permission.

Back at P.S. 46, my teachers smiled or gave me gold stars and said, "Nice job dear," or showed me how to clean my pencil eraser, so it wouldn't keep smudging. Sister pointed out my wrong answers and ordered me to stop committing a sacrilege when she saw me flicking holy water off my fingers.

The boys must have come on a different day, because they weren't around, but the in-school girls' communion class was down the hall, and I envied them in their white blouses and blue plaid symmetry that looked properly Catholic. Not being in uniform was another strike against us. Released-time kids would never win the hearts of these stern women, because we didn't match and no matter how often I wore my gray plaid skirt, it was still the wrong color on the wrong kid.

Although no one wore uniforms on Sundays, our differences were further emphasized when I walked into nine o'clock children's Mass with Connie Yzergary, the other Catholic girl on my block. Because Connie was a full-time Catholic who attended St. Catherine's, she got to sit up front, on the right, in the children's pews. Released-time kids were allowed to sit anywhere but front right. In a mostly empty church, I settled for the middle, or over on the left side with old people—the majority of parishioners besides kids who got out of bed for early Mass.

I'd asked my mom to wake up early and come with me, but she wouldn't. She didn't get up for eleven or twelve o'clock Mass, either. Since learning that skipping church on purpose was a mortal sin, I worried about her soul. Gram didn't go either, but I didn't want her anywhere near children's Mass, because the first thing she'd do would be to ask why I wasn't sitting with the other girls. If she asked, I'd have to tell her and might start crying. Instead of smoothing things over like Mom would, Gram would make me go sit up front anyway, or cause a scene and get me kicked out of First Communion.

About thirty girls showed up at children's Mass and, besides Connie and me, there was one other Negro girl. She had pierced ears with gold studs in them, and long curly hair that was tame enough to wear unbraided. I wished she could tell me where her mom bought her hat, a cute beret with a little tassel on top. One thing I didn't like about being Catholic was that females had to cover their heads in church. I always wanted to bobby-pin a folded handkerchief to my hair, the way some grownups did, but if a kid pulled that stunt, it probably wouldn't go over too well. Besides, my grandmother wouldn't let me leave the house without white gloves and some dumb hat, because she said it was a shame to let them just rot in the closet.

After a year of religious instruction, it occurred to me that there might be some truth to nuns not liking colored people. Our teacher's name was Sister Margaret, but one girl called her Margaret Meanie, although not to her face. The tough, back-talking student who got kicked out the first day had just called her a bitch. Sister did not like public kids and all of us were black girls, but the color theory wasn't airtight, because of Connie and that other girl who sat up front. Also, it was the church, not P.S. 46, that asked to start the released-time program, so that Negro kids could attend St. Catherine's. The program got off the ground because Monsignor, and not one of the sisters, came to the meeting at P.S. 46. If a nun had presented the released-time proposal, parents might not have signed their kids up. Concerning the program, Mom said, "I'm glad to see St. Catherine's reach out to the black community." Then she added, "But they had little choice, since it's one of the last Irish parishes in Harlem and the Irish are bailing out of here in droves."

The important thing for me was to become a "real" Catholic who took communion. I did everything I was told and plugged away at the catechism, until we got to the part about heaven, hell, purgatory and limbo. I didn't understand why children who weren't baptized Catholics ended up alone and miserable in a place called limbo. It sounded like hell, but a hell filled with innocent kids whose only sin was not being baptized, like I had been, back in the fall. Sister said grown-ups went to limbo too, if they didn't receive Baptism, but she never clarified why children were punished for something that wasn't their fault.

I joined the church in third grade, a few weeks after I first visited the Indian Museum and for some reason, my thoughts on limbo didn't focus on my non-Catholic friends back on Edgecombe, but on the little Indian girl I'd seen inside a diorama at the museum. I'd been fascinated by her painted red lips, loved her little beaded dress and cute moccasins that I imagined her grandmother might have sewn for her. I didn't know her religion and she wasn't a real girl, but I understood she was meant to represent girls whom God had created out of flesh and blood. I thought Baptism counted too much if that Indian girl had to go to limbo. At my christening, Father held a brief ceremony, mumbled a few Latin words, poured water on my head and said, "I baptize you in the name of the Father, the Son and the Holy Ghost." Then he rushed off to Medical Center to administer Extreme Unction to a dying parishioner.

I couldn't tell Sister that limbo sounded dumb, but I drew a picture with all the parts; heaven, hell, purgatory and limbo, then used my best cursive to write a story that included the line, "Limbo is unfair."

I handed it in. She looked it over, then frostily informed me that I was ill prepared for this section of catechism and told me go home right this minute, get my mother, and bring her back to school. It was a Saturday, shortly before Communion day. To get everything accomplished, a few Saturday sessions had been added because Wednesdays were now used solely for walking through the church ceremony so Catholic and public girls could practice together.

God was on my side that morning because Aunt Annette had taken Gram down to her house so they could do each other's hair. Mom was half dressed, her hair already fixed and piled on top of her head; one of the styles I liked because it made her look sophisticated. But she was still in her bathrobe, enjoying a second cup of coffee, waiting to take me shopping for white shoes, the last thing I needed for Communion day.

"Sister says I'm ill-prepared and if you don't hurry up to school, she won't let me come back to class!" I blurted, out of breath, barely in the kitchen. "She'll do it too, Mommy. I know she will, because she put all those other girls out."

"Settle down and tell me what happened." Drawing in more smoke and acting like this wasn't an emergency, she said, "You look like you ran all the way home."

"I did run home. If we don't get back, she might leave. We were almost done when she sent me to get you."

"Don't worry. If we miss her, I'll ring the rectory bell; someone will find her. Now, what exactly went wrong this morning?"

"I don't know. She didn't like my story about limbo. She got mad and said I didn't understand the lesson, then she told me to come get you."

"Well, did you understand it?"

"I don't think so, because the way it works isn't fair. Too many good people go to a bad place."

"All right, we'd better see what's going on." Taking her sweet time, she sauntered to her room to finish dressing.

"Stop running," she twice told me when I tried to pull her along at a faster pace.

I guess Sister assumed I'd obey her directive because her pasty face in its starched white wimple stared at us from the exact spot, behind her desk, where I'd left her. Without preamble or introducing herself to my mother, she started in with, "This-is-the-most-special-day-in-a-girl's-life" tag line that I'd heard so many times. Even though I could think of other most special days—like the one at Coney Island when I drove a bumper car for the first time by myself, then won a stuffed animal because I got a high score in skee ball—I knew what Sister meant about First Communion being special.

"If Theresa isn't ready for this big occasion," she continued, "the group will have no trouble continuing without her." Sister made it clear that she had spent the better part of the year emphasizing the importance of Baptism and Holy Eucharist and, if I had other notions, that was unfortunate.

My mother listened attentively, interjecting polite "Yes, Sister" and "No, Sister," just the way nuns liked it. Mom hadn't had time to put on makeup, other than lipstick. Her clear, fresh-scrubbed face was beautiful when she smiled and spoke up. "Jean, at home we call her Jean, is a very good little Catholic. She talks constantly about church and First Communion and never misses Mass."

Mom said I always had my head in one book or another, which must be where I got such "notions." Mom was trying hard, sitting there with her classy hairdo, not acting like she wanted a cigararette, which she probably did, or like she resented being grilled by a woman in medieval garb who looked as foreign as a Martian.

I stopped biting my lip when Sister relaxed her stiff-backed position and came out to sit on the edge of her desk. Two very different women stared at each other's faces, perhaps trying to see beyond this moment and into the other's world. I don't know what the nun thought, but her suspicion and hostility was gone when she turned to ask, "Theresa, are you ready to show obedience in the next two weeks before receiving the precious gifts of our Lord?"

"Yes, Sister."

"Very well then. I'll see you after school on Wednesday."

Limbo, the reason for our being there never came up, but Sister wasn't mad at me anymore, and we were permitted to leave. Outside, Mom said, "Jean, don't contradict the nuns if you want to be confirmed. That woman is married to God and takes her job very seriously. Do you understand what I'm telling you?"

Just glad to be out of there, I remember bobbing my head up and down like a yo-yo and giving an emphatic "Yes," although I had no idea what she was talking about. Besides limbo, I thought I was doing a much better job of understanding all the rules, but now there was this new wrinkle, like how come nuns were allowed to marry God?

"No teacher has ever had a problem with you before," Mom said, holding onto my hand as we passed Trinity Cemetery and crossed 155th Street. "She's warned you and you better do what she says."

It isn't fair, I thought to myself, still unable to make an adult see my point of view. That day is perhaps the first time I truly turned to God, communing with him without just going through the motions. I held a conversation in my head, a pattern I've maintained. I didn't need to "hear" an answer to know the nuns were wrong. I knew God was on my side and welcomed all the dead children to heaven.

A short time later, I walked down the aisle in a white organdy First Communion dress, a shoulder-length veil encircling me in a little ring of glory. For my party, Gram prepared ham, greens and potato salad and the family gave me more gold crosses, silver Virgin Mary medals and money. Until college, I attended church faithfully, but I proved to be right about limbo. Like other church practices, such as meatless Fridays and full morning fasting before communion, limbo was eliminated from the Catholic rule books.

Bradhurst Avenue and Colonial Park in 1930s. Apartments at top of hill are on Edgecombe Avenue. (Photo courtesy of NY Public Library)

South view of Sugar Hill. Edgecombe Avenue and Colonial Park (now Jackie Robinson Park). Building in foreground is 409. (Jim Cummins)

Grandmom Baker   *Grandpop Baker*

Daddy

Audubon Terrace. (Jim Cummins)

*Totem Pole that stood
in front of Indian Museum.
(NY Public Library)*

Bailey "Castle." (Jim Cummins)

Edgecombe Avenue looking north from 150th Street. (Jim Cummins)

Grandpa Hodges　　　　　*Gram as a young woman*

Gram in 1950s

Owlettes social club. Dedi, my Godmother is on left. Mom and Aunt Cee are 5th and 6th from the left.

Uncle Smitty and
Aunt Annette

With my New Lincoln classmates
at 1957 March on Washington.

Annette, Mom and Cee   *Jack in 1950s*

Uncle Harry, Aunt Cee, Mom and unknown man about 1943.

155th Street viaduct and a No. 2 bus. Tall building sits on the former site of Polo Grounds Stadium. New Yankee Stadium and McCombs Dam Bridge in background. (Jim Cummins)

Morris-Jumel Mansion. (Jim Cummins)

Jumel Terrace. (Jim Cummins)

President Eisenhower's train with the train personnel. Uncle Smitty is in back row left.

Mrs. Katz's class. Front row: Reggie is on the right. Third row: Rose Casey, who gave the goodbye party, is on the left. Michele in center with pigtails. I'm second from right. Back row: Ronald, who ran afoul of Mr. Lerner, is behind Michele. Colden is wearing the sport coat.

With Jackie, Houston and Gregory, our neighbor. Ralph is standing behind us.

Me with Dedi and Mary Jo on Halloween.

With Jimmy (Jim), Reggie and Michele.

Garden at the Cloisters. (Jim Cummins)

Apollo Theater. (Jim Cummins)

Hamilton Grange in 2001,
when it was squeezed between
an apartment house and
St. Luke's Episcopal Church.
(Jim Cummins)

The Grange, sitting
in the middle of
Convent Avenue,
waiting to be moved.
(Jim Cummins)

In its new location with its porches restored. (Jim Cummins)

On left, 302 Convent Avenue, where we moved when I was 12. (Jim Cummins)

Townhouses on Convent Avenue. (Houston Jackson)

With Mom at the Polo Grounds.

Daddy dancing
at the Cotton Club.

With Houston on Edgecombe Avenue.

Hooper Fountain. (Jim Cummins)   *Directional signage. (Jim Cummins)*

South view of Sugar Hill, Edgecombe Avenue and Colonial Park (now Jackie Robinson Park). (Jim Cummins)

St. Catherine's, rectory and school. (Jim Cummins)

Hotel Theresa.
(Jim Cummins)

Edgecombe Avenue view of Harlem River; now blocked by tall buildings. (Jim Cummins)

Staten Island Ferry. (Jim Cummins)

9. The Corner

Sugar Hill's most luxurious apartment building, located near the corner of Edgecombe Avenue and 155th Street, was the Colonial Park. Its more common name was 409 and it rose above Harlem like a red brick phoenix, ascending from the lower world. Some of Harlem's most impoverished neighborhoods were lined up in the Valley beneath our street. Thirteen stories tall, the Colonial Park could be seen from miles away as a symbol of the sweet life on the Hill. I keep circling back to this building, because that is where I aspired to live someday. Since half of Harlem had similar aspirations, trying to get inside, or even peek in, didn't work with 409's vigilant gatekeepers who made a sport of shooing kids away.

Blacks became part of the building's celebrated history in the 1930s with the arrival of luminaries such as W.E.B. DuBois, as well as the previously mentioned, but more controversial Madame Stephanie St. Clair. Their names appear on original 409 billing records that Mr. Thomas kindly showed me when I spoke with him. Before blacks moved in, Babe Ruth also rented an apartment in the 1920s, when Yankee Stadium was under construction and the Bronx team shared Polo Grounds stadium with the New York Giants.[1]

When I grew up in 409's shadow, its tenant profile hadn't changed much. A few numbers bankers or wealthy gamblers lived alongside the likes of Thurgood Marshall and Roy Wilkins, who was then president of the NAACP.

One chilly Saturday afternoon, I got inside 409 for the first time. It happened because a stunning high yellow green-eyed blond friend of Mom's married a not-very-attractive gambler with a temper, who Gram said looked like he'd been beaten with an ugly stick. Blonde beauty and new Hubby, who'd recently hit the number, moved into an apartment on an upper floor, and though the marriage only lasted about a year, the wife invited Mom to see their place and she brought me along.

Gawking at the mirrors in the tiled lobby while we waited for the doorman to call upstairs, I hung on tight to Mom's hand. The doorman hadn't had a problem letting her through the front door, but he was one of the men who chased me away when I tried peeking in. Given the okay to continue, we floated over a plush Oriental rug that was longer and wider than any I'd ever seen.

"Mom, it has chandeliers and elevators," I whispered at the elevator bank. "Why couldn't we live here? I wouldn't have to wait for you to carry my bike downstairs if we lived here."

"Jack and I looked into getting an apartment in this building." Just from her tone, irritated, I knew not to get my hopes too high about moving in. Mom stared impatiently at the still closed elevator door, then rubbed her fingers together on her right hand, as if she was brushing off crumbs.

"Too expensive" she said, "and moving in here is not as simple as filling out an application. In this building, the way it works, it's who you know, and what can you do for them."

I didn't realize she was describing a grease-the-palm system that she and Jack would eventually use to "buy" their way into the apartment they later found on Convent. It also helped that the mother of the family vacating that apartment worked for our dentist.

"Jack knows everybody," I reminded her.

By then, perhaps because of not getting into 409, she was really irritated at being made to wait. "Apparently not the right everybody. I can't even get the damn elevator to come."

Thurgood Marshall was still living there the day I visited and he remained the building's most prominent tenant. With his booming laugh and back-slapping personality, he'd become a neighborhood fixture whom I saw regularly and I hoped he might exit the elevator when it came. A few days before, on my way to the store, he was out strolling with his wife, Cecelia, who appeared dwarfed next to her husband's lumbering height and bulk. The sun was shining and the wind whipping in off the river and his camel hair coat was unbuttoned and flaring out behind him and I thought, it must have taken a mountain of camels to make that coat. Marshall's long, straight black hair, lion-sized head, Apache tan complexion and prominent profile reminded me of Geronimo, or one of the fierce Indian chiefs in history books. This was during the South's lynching, bombing, school segregation era and Marshall's job was to torment bigots and step on their precedents. His photograph appeared regularly in newspapers because racial violence was about to blow the South apart, and he had just won a case that helped ignite the dynamite.

For our visit to 409, I wore my red Sunday coat. Mom had on a navy suit. Her hair was down, curled and pinned softly to the side of her face. The jacket to her suit was a long three quarter-length style, full all around like a swing coat and I would remember it forever. She wore that outfit the day she came home from the hospital with a surprise wrapped in a blue blanket that turned out to be my new baby brother. When the elevator finally came, we rode upstairs with a stone-faced operator, the perfect Charybdis for the Scylla-monster guarding the front door.

Blondie's new husband ushered us in with a sweeping-arm welcome, as cool and choreographed as the living room that looked like it should be on the cover of a glossy decorator magazine; the kind that oozes Beverly Hills or Park Avenue privilege. The walls and furniture were white; everything was white: alabaster figurines, porcelain lamps on glass tables, cotton candy carpeting, white silk drapes. They had glass ash trays, table legs of chrome and mirrored walls that disoriented me. I'd never seen anything like it.

135

After Blondie finished pointing out special effects to Mom, like a mirrored ball that was a cigarette lighter, I was still trying to figure out which wall had the view. "Are those windows?" I asked, nodding at one wall covered by draperies. "Can you see the park behind those?"

"We keep the drapes closed," she said, not answering the question, "but let's go in the bedroom." She never opened the drapes.

The bedspread was a spectacle in pleated white satin, like on the bed of a princess, which was kind of what Blondie had become now that she was sleeping in 409, instead of her old bedroom in 375, where she grew up. A detail on her dressing table that I remember well—because I admired them on perfume counters in department stores and knew they cost a mint—were two 48-ounce bottles of Chanel Number 5 and another French perfume that had Blondie lived to be a hundred, she would not have run out of perfume.

Hubby remained quiet, staying out of the way, but smiling like a home run hitter, obviously pleased by the ooh, aah, wow effect the apartment had on us. But the visit also felt staged, as though Mom and I were supporting characters in the play, *The Apartment*, starring Blonde Beauty and Mr. New Rich Husband, with sets created by the best designer money could buy.

This was a Saturday afternoon and Hubby had on a silk bathrobe that Mom later called his dressing gown. Blondie's outfit was a flowing, expensive-looking floor-length print, with kimono sleeves that kept getting stuck on the arm of her chair. Her high heels were backless slippers with fluffy white pom poms—those shoes that only rich or loose women used to wear, and I wasn't sure which kind she was trying to be.

Visiting that apartment exceeded my expectations, even though I didn't see a place for a checkerboard or think Blondie's large, lively family would enjoy spending Christmas in such perfection. Blondie didn't like it either, because she moved back down the street.

When I next saw her, I was a teenager; she had remarried and asked me to baby-sit her two kids. I walked into her new apartment, expecting elegance, but her living room was ordinary, with throw pillows scattered around, toys on the floor and a vacuum waiting to be put away.

Years passed before I stepped inside 409 again but, as a child, I continued playing that corner the way kids today play video games. It was part of my day's entertainment to run up there and buy two eggs, one kidney for the cat's dinner or a packet of headache powder for my mother. That was on the first pass. By the second or third trip, I'd gone back for Mom's Chesterfields, spent my allowance on a vanilla malt at the soda fountain, visited Bud the tailor, or Mary Jo and I walked up to buy a sour pickle, then tried sneaking in back of the candy store to read *True Confessions*.

Frenchie was the corner shoemaker, a man my affable stepfather called "An evil conked-haired son of a bitch who likes white women, and what they see in him, I don't know." Jack didn't think much of any man sporting wavy processed hair that blossomed into a pompadoured grease ball. Evil was the description for a scowling, mean-tempered person and that's how Frenchie was. Unfortunately for kids, we were drawn to his door because he not only repaired shoes, he sold records and sheet music for a few cents a song.

The store's other attraction was Willie Mays. In 1951 the New York Giants called him up from the minors and he rented a front room at 80 St. Nicholas Place, in Mrs. Goosby's first floor apartment. Within weeks, he became the new sweetheart of black baseball fans and millions of white ones, too.

Willie was brown-skinned and slim, with turned-in toes that accentuated his Alabama country boy, awh-schucks way of standing around blushing and grinning with hands in his back dungarees' pockets. He was twenty years old, with a high-pitched voice, making him sound twelve and he acted like a kid, playing stickball with neighborhood boys, but also with a bunch of men who, until Willie showed up, hadn't held a stickball bat since before World War II.

After he'd been around a few months and the excitement died down, adults gave Willie some privacy, but kids bugged him endlessly, knocking on his window, chanting "Willie come out and play," waking him up after he'd been out late the night before. A place he found some peace was in Frenchie's because boys were afraid to follow him in there.

One time, Willie and I were the only customers in the shoe shop. Actually, neither one of us was there to buy anything, since he was just killing time before reporting to the ballpark. I slipped in because I spotted him through the window. I don't think he'd made much money yet, because he was wearing his dungarees and the same yellow plaid shirt and scuffed shoes I'd seen him in before. I scrambled up, making myself comfortable in the empty leather shoe-shining chair next to him and before I said a word, he let out a low whistle and asked where I got the big scab above my nose.

I told him about Albert Hawkins hitting me with a tin can packed with ashes and that afterwards, Mommy walked me over to his house to show Mr. Hawkins my cut and two black eyes. Mr. Hawkins pulled off his belt and was about to give Albert a whipping, but Albert broke away and ran outside in his bare feet and underwear, then we all trooped back downstairs looking for him. Mom got worried and asked, "Has he run away from home before? Do you think he'll come right back?"

Mr. Hawkins didn't answer; he just got madder than he already was. I think Mom was sorry we went to his house, and I was kind of glad we couldn't find Albert, because I knew his whipping would hurt more than my nose did.

Willie wanted to know if Albert was one of the boys who hitched rides down the viaduct on the back fender of number two buses. I never saw Albert do that, but I told him that Mr. Hawkins took away Albert's bike, because he was racing on the sidewalk and hit Angela so hard he broke her leg. He wasn't supposed to race his bike, throw any more ashes, or get into trouble.

"Is Angela the girl in that heavy leg cast whose mother rolls her by here in a wheel chair?"

"Yep, that's Angela. She'll be in that thing all summer. Her leg is taking forever to heal."

Before my time ran out, I told him what I heard Billy say about wanting Willie to come down by our houses more often. I didn't repeat the part about Billy saying that St. Nick kids, where Willie lived, played stickball like chicken shit, because they didn't have to worry about hitting balls in the park. Willie kept smiling, although he seemed more interested in what Albert did than what Billy said, but then I had to leave. Two men drifted in and Frenchie shut off his loud grinding machine, turned around, spotted me and said, "Girl, didn't I tell you to stay outta here and stop being a pest?"

Frenchie's shoeshine chairs didn't remain empty long, because men sat in them to gossip about baseball, the numbers and women. I wondered if they would start talking about Shirley, the new fly white barmaid who worked four doors down, at Bowman's. I shouldn't have had to leave. At home, I'd already overheard a thing or two about this Shirley, who had been working at the bar a couple of months. She was the one Jack called a wild little thing. I could tell by the way he added the "Hmm, hmm, hmm" part, then shook his head and laughed, that he wouldn't be telling all of Shirley's story. Unless you're blind and maybe still under age five, if you grow up in Harlem, you hear men laughing and women whispering about girls like Shirley, so it wasn't hard to figure out what wild things were.

If someone had taught me how, I would have spent more time studying the bones of my neighborhood. Often I bewildered adults who, unlike me, saw no value in the small everyday dramas surrounding us, like counting the cars on the viaduct and checking to see if flags were flying at the Polo

Grounds. When I told Gram I was going to walk up towards 389 to see what the painter was doing to the park fence, she asked, "Why on earth do you want to go half way up the block to watch the wrought iron fence being painted? If you feel like painting, go get your watercolors, but paint at the kitchen table so you don't make a mess."

"But, Gram, the fence is supposed to be black," I pointed out, "and he's turning it ugly orange. How come he's doing that?"

"The painter knows what he's about. You don't need to poke your nose in his business." She forgot about the fence, but the next week, I reported that everything turned out all right because he covered over the orange with shiny black paint.

I harbored a smugness about loving my neighborhood, but I kept it secret because I feared the family might call my zeal, "One of Jean's little fits of pique." If National League flags were hoisted and flying over the roof of the Polo Grounds, it meant later that day, we would enjoy the excitement of a home baseball game. Within a few hours of the flags going up, I'd hear car horns blaring when cars got stuck in traffic, and I'd walk up to the viaduct and watch throngs of baseball fans arriving from all parts of the city. They always hurried-up to park their Fords and Chevys on Edgecombe and St. Nicholas, then tumbled out in a rush to reach the Polo Grounds before the first pitch. After the game, sunburned men, or fathers with sons wearing short pants and clutching oversized baseball gloves, strolled back leisurely, glad for the breeze blowing off the river. They showed no urgency to return to hot, dark apartments on the Lower East Side, in Hell's Kitchen or in faraway parts of the other boroughs. That's where most people lived then, since the suburbs were still being built.

Once, Mom, Gram and I took an hour-long ride on the Coney Island subway to one of those faraway places in Brooklyn. But instead of the amusement park, we got off at a different outdoor station, on a street populated with sad-looking rundown wooden houses with tarpapered outhouses in the backyards. The trip must have been important since my grandmother went along, which I couldn't understand because the lady we visited was some kind of holy bishop and Gram didn't cotton to fancy-titled theologians, especially any with questionable credentials. By then, I was a good Catholic, and a lady bishop sounded about as legit as the time Gram tried passing herself off as a police woman, which I'll explain later.

Our Brooklyn visit was a somber one, inside a dark house, with hardly anyone talking and Mom sitting across the room, high-signing me not to take another lemon drop from the candy dish. Although our hostess was dressed and walking around, I got the feeling she was sick, dealing with an unspeakable crisis or maybe getting ready to move back to Norfolk. What I remember best was how glad I was to get on the D train and head back to the city.

All my life I've been marking the history of Edgecombe Avenue. I was born there, and if it's true that tendencies get in your blood, then 369 is part of the fluid that fuels me. Doctors made house calls then and my mother didn't want to deliver me in old Harlem or Sydenham Hospital, where bloody sheets and bandages were left in plain view and the hallways and the waiting rooms smelled of ether. So, Dr. Owens with assistance from his nurse, delivered me in the small front room that would remain mine until we moved.

Refurbished Apollo Theater lobby; two photo collages can be glimpsed on right wall. (Colin Mulligan)

10. Showtime at the Apollo

Change gripped our neighborhood on a September Saturday when the Food Family Supermarket opened. Located on St. Nicholas Avenue, the new market was in the opposite direction and further away than our corner stores. For the gala opening, Mom and I walked up to see what all the hoopla was about and were treated to mini loaves of Wonder Bread and Dixie cups of Kool-Aid. Despite the giveaways, we had no plans to stop patronizing Harry, the Italian grocer on the corner where we bought dry goods. His store, with its rolling ladders and oak counter worn smooth in its sweet spot from years of doing business, was a neighborhood institution. But ready or not, change was coming and for some reason, this seemingly innocuous store opening is the marker of when outside forces most disrupted the familiar rhythms of my life.

The new market was strategically located next to the busy 145th Street subway station where hungry commuters disembarked each evening into the arms of convenience. If timing and location weren't enough to lure customers from merchants like Harry, for days on end, Food Family greeters stood in front, handing out more food samples and a new gimmick—coupons.

After work, my mother began stopping in for small items: cigarettes, milk, band aids. Both Jack and Mom cooked more as Gram slowed down and Mom appreciated the convenience of frozen foods offered at the supermarket. One day, at Jackie's house, her mother served me a glass of milk mixed with Bosco, a sugary chocolate syrup, sweeter than the malt-flavored, vitamin-rich Ovaltine that Mom bought at Harry's that I didn't drink. And just like that, my preference for Bosco turned my family into regulars at Food Family. But before too long, niggling problems we assumed to be new-store adjustments became a standard way of doing business in that market.

Their orange juice and milk tasted sour; the ground beef smelled bad. When I tried returning a container of juice, a cashier said the manager wasn't in and I had to talk to him. Meanwhile, Harry couldn't compete with the 2,000-square-foot supermarket and sold out to a Puerto Rican guy who had his own set of woes. He sold plantains, guavas, sugar cane and other foods that the store's former customers didn't eat. The new guy stocked milk, but shoppers had to wade through a maze of male friends who enjoyed playing Spanish music and hanging out in front of the store that had been stripped of its beautiful wooden fixtures.

I stopped going to the old corner and watched my life spiral in ten different directions. Something bad was happening to my grandmother. Increasingly more cantankerous than clever, she frustrated us by refusing to use her cane, resulting in frequent falls. She burned food and butchered her hair because she wouldn't wait for Aunt Annette to cut it right.

Things were already messed up that winter with Mom strangely preoccupied and Gram losing her grip. Then, one afternoon when my friend Jackie and I were playing Chinese checkers in the living room, she leaned across the board and whispered, so my grandmother couldn't hear us from the kitchen, "Your mother's going to have a baby, just like mine did."

"'She is not." I hotly defended Mom's one-child status.

It was true that Jackie had a new baby sister, although she hadn't yet made a public appearance. I also accepted that Jackie usually won when we played Sorry or Chinese checkers. She was older, smarter and better at out-strategizing me, but I didn't like her making up stories about my mother.

"She's not going to have a baby and anyway," I asked, "how would you know what my mother is going to do?"

"I'm older. I know about babies," she said. I thought she was just showing off, because she did know more about babies, now that she had one in her family. But the fact was, Mommy and Jack had been hinting about a surprise. I wasn't interested in their secret. I assumed it was about moving to a new place.

What I knew about babies was that boys could make one if you let their "thing" get too close to you. My grandmother was full of disinformation and misinformation, but she revealed enough for me to know that both Jack and my mother were responsible if any babies showed up around here. There were no babies in the family and none in my immediate circle of friends. Except for the four Goodwin boys and Mary Jo's two brothers, who were beyond the baby stage, most of my friends, like me, were single children.

I didn't give any thought to where younger siblings came from; they were just there. Having a baby was so hush-hush, pregnant women didn't even use the word pregnant. If they said anything at all, it was that they were "expecting." Expectants hid their bodies in tent dresses and ugly shoes, then disappeared in the hospital for a week, sending home reassurances, but no explanations. That's how it happened at my house.

The Chinese checker game took place the night before my mother came home from the hospital. Jackie wasn't supposed to invite friends over until her little sister settled into a better sleeping routine, but I popped over there anyway.

"Jean," I said, appealing to her mother (there were three people named Jean living on our floor), "Jackie told me Mommy is going to have a baby, but I don't believe her. She said I could ask you."

I remember Jean looking down kindly, probably feeling sorry for me. It only took her a few seconds to decide I'd been kept in ignorance long enough.

"Olivia had a baby boy. You have a brother," she confirmed. "They'll be home tomorrow."

Back in our apartment, I looked into the kitchen where Gram was plucking feathers off a fresh chicken before singeing the feet to burn off any remaining feathers. I watched for a few minutes, waiting for the kitchen to start smelling like burned hair when Gram held the bird's feet over the gas flame. Standing in the doorway like I'd done a thousand times, I didn't understand what this news meant for me, but I felt my world shift.

At some point, maybe even within minutes, Gram verified what I already knew, but I recall the smell of hair burning, and the sound of chicken sizzling in hot grease better than I remember the conversation about my new brother that must have taken place in the kitchen. At that moment, my God-like, omnipresent grandmother had somehow betrayed me.

The following afternoon, Mommy, Jack and baby Houston arrived home, and by the daffy way my stepfather tiptoed through the door with a fat bundle in his arms, I knew my life would never be the same. In a round of homecoming hugs, my mother pulled me into her arms, Grammy fussed and fluttered and Jack, who yesterday had been one of my best friends, ignored me, only coming out of his reverie to say, "Don't touch the baby."

Like millions of other pre-teens fumbling through adolescence, I sought refuge in music. My girlfriends and I were intrigued with a new kid, Frankie Lymon, who lived near us on upper Edgecombe. He was a singer-drummer in a group called The Teenagers. They had recently been discovered at Apollo Amateur Night and already their song, *Why Do Fools Fall In Love,* was climbing the charts.

The Apollo is still located in the heart of Harlem on 125th Street between Seventh and Eighth Avenues across from what was once Blumstein's, a large department store that had a foot X-ray machine in the children's shoe department. Whether shopping, grabbing a quick lunch with Mom at Thomford's or dining at Frank's Steak Restaurant with Daddy, like everyone, my eye was drawn to the APOLLO marquee to see who was playing.

In a short time, Frankie Lymon and other rock and rollers would roar through Apollo land, but this was still the heyday of big bands, or jazz divas like Ella Fitzgerald, and the deep-voiced baritone, Joe Turner. Jack regularly took me to Apollo shows, or occasionally Mom and I caught African or Caribbean dance groups. Mom and I also followed the folk singer Odetta, and South African legend, Miriam Makeba who sang *Pata Pata*, the "Click Song" that sounded like she was making clicking noises in her throat, but they were words in Xhosa, Makeba's South African language. Listening to her voice slide up and down its lilting register in that strange language sounded faraway and primordial; it could give me goose bumps. It was easy to understand why she was known throughout the world as Mama Africa.

Whether cultural or not, all shows opened with Apollo mainstays, the bawdy comedians "Pigmeat" Markham, Redd Foxx or "Moms" Mabley. Comics made their living by performing shuffling, "Yas sah, boss" darky routines while dressed in raggedy clothing, oversized shoes, hobo hats or Aunt Jemina head rags. My mother was among those who didn't like the comics. The world was changing and black buffoonery increasingly stirred controversy among intellectuals, politicians and everyday people who debated if these performances were parody, theater art, or just a disgrace to our race.

One of the hottest Apollo shows ever, *The Jewel Box Revue*, created a different controversy. They were a troupe of female impersonators who billed themselves as "25 Men and a Girl." In publicity photos, it was impossible to pick out the girl, even for people who'd seen the show. *The Revue* was hugely successful, in part because protesters drew so much attention to it. Jack went to see the show, but he didn't take me and I can't remember if it was because the theater wouldn't let kids in, or Mom wouldn't let me go.

I tend to doubt the latter reason because a few times over the years, Jack and I walked down to watch the spectacle outside Rockland Palace at 155th and Bradhurst, the avenue just beneath Edgecombe. Every year on Thanksgiving Eve, at the Rockland Palace Ballroom, the gay community held what was universally known as the Faggot's Ball. This was New York's biggest, most flamboyant party for homosexual men and transvestites who wanted to dress in drag and enjoy themselves in each other's company.

On the given Wednesday night in November, Bradhurst Avenue hummed with drag queens, *Amsterdam News* reporters, cat-callers, sullen cops and scores of curious onlookers like us. Observers stood in the chilly night air, straining to see grown men preen and vamp, while exiting taxis and limos, most of them wearing big hair, inch-long eyelashes, sequined-glitz and lots of mink. Some people yelled encouragements. "Honey, just don't worry about it. I wish my girl looked as fine as you." A few others carried signs saying, "You are a disgrace before the eyes of God" and "Freak, Freak!" It was not what the Pilgrims had in mind for a celebration, but until Rockland Palace closed, the Faggot's Ball remained a popular Thanksgiving tradition.

Until the really rocking groups stormed the Apollo in the late 1950s, I caught some of the last great performers before they stopped playing in uptown venues. Sammy Davis, Jr. was then part of the Will Mastin Trio. I heard Nina Simone sing *Wild is the Wind*, listened to Eartha Kitt's breathy *Santa Baby* song and I witnessed a twenty-minute Lionel Hampton tour de force, with him beating the mess out of a xylophone that everyone kept calling the vibes.

The Apollo never disappointed me, although the big bands weren't my favorites. I preferred when those twenty piece groups turned down the volume and played back-up for honey-voiced singers like Dinah Washington who caressed each word of *What A Difference A Day Makes*. I got to hear

Ella sing scat and watched Pearl Bailey do a sassy tap routine. Pearl called herself a singer, but I thought she was more like a classy comedian who sang and danced. I enjoyed adult music because, back then, there was little alternative. Once I outgrew *Old MacDonald* and *Oh Suzanna*, the next best thing was Sarah Vaughn, Patti Page or Dinah, at least until rock and roll was born.

Wednesday nights were legendary at the Apollo. Over the years, dozens of stars from Ella Fitzgerald to the Jackson Brothers got their big breaks at Amateur Night. But every Wednesday didn't produce a James Brown, Gladys Knight or other sensation, and audiences were merciless if they didn't like the act. Jack worked Wednesdays, but he could not have tolerated raucous crowds of rude kids and uncouth adults yelling and belittling performers. A man of impeccable taste, he dressed up to walk a block to work, then changed into old shoes and slacks that no one could see behind the bar. Though not as elaborate as some of New York's movie palaces, the Apollo was a well-appointed building with plush red seating and crystal chandeliers. Taking in a show was considered a privileged afternoon or evening of theater. It was an occasion to dress up, and before I left with Jack, Gram always styled my hair in Shirley Temple curls.

During one of our most serious moments, Jack admonished me for not applauding after a musical number. We were sitting in the fourth or fifth row and a band was playing bebop jazz, the kind of music I didn't care for. "Jean," he said, bending over so I could hear him above the audience's applause, "even if you don't like the show, clap politely to let the artists know you appreciated their efforts. It doesn't cost you anything, but your applause might be the only paycheck an entertainer receives."

If Apollo walls could talk, they would ramble on forever about music history lurking in the dressing rooms, stage and back alley of that great building. In a way, the walls did speak

149

to us, because the lobby was lined with a hit parade of posters, murals, blowups and group photos of stars who made the Apollo famous. When I first started attending, my favorite game was matching a name to one of the famous faces. Some were obvious: Billie Holiday, Jackie Wilson, Lena Horne, Count Basie, a young Ray Charles, but plenty of photos, especially of older entertainers who had completed their careers by the 1930s and 40s, remained a mystery to me.

Jack was born in South Carolina, but had already spent about twenty-five years bartending, waiting tables and mentally filing away tidbits about people he met in Harlem, including some in the lobby pictures. He knew a singer's ex-husband went to jail for shooting her boyfriend. The girl was terrified the ex might kill her when he got out of prison. He told me that before Ruby Dee married Ossie Davis, her first husband was a midget.

One day he and I were looking over the photos, when Jack cleared his throat and pointed. "Mr. Big Spender was in the bar the other night. He's a cheap, penny-pinching bastard who orders rotgut whiskey and stints on tips." Entertainers were night people, he explained. They "let their hair down" in the wee hours of the morning when the shows end, the crowd is liquored-up and the weary bartender learns what Mr. or Miss Big Shot is really made of.

"When you've worked as many clubs and bars as I have, you see and hear things, but you learn to keep your mouth shut. A lot of people know what I'm telling you," he said, "but they don't go around talking about it and you shouldn't either. There's a girl who sings backup for a male singer. You'd know him, if I told you his name. Everyone believes this girl would be a star in her own right, if she could stay off the stuff. I saw her in the bar one night, making a beeline for the ladies room, leaving her boyfriend in the booth with his head in his hands. I know she was shooting that stuff right there in the bar. I should have tossed her out when she came back from the bathroom, but tell me, how in hell are you supposed to throw a classy lady like that out in the street?"

I knew that "stuff" meant heroin, and sometimes just saying heroin made people ache inside, so stuff was a substitute word. But what surprised me about that story was that Jack thought you could still be a classy lady and use stuff. Another time in the lobby, he surprised me by saying, "That guy and I grew up in the same town." We were taking our usual stroll through the picture gallery before the matinee began and I didn't recognize the man he pointed to. "I remember when that guy didn't have two nickels to rub together," he continued. "I was a kid and he was just a poor barefoot nigger picking cotton in the fields of South Carolina and man, look at him now."

We always found our seats in time to hear the band strike up their theme song, *I Think You're Wonderful*. A ripple of anticipation tickled the audience before the red curtain rolled up and the emcee announced, "Ladies and gentlemen, it's showtime at the Apollo."

Typically, singers or big bands were the main feature, but the variety was limitless: gospel choirs, talented kids, animal acts, small combos, twenty-member dance troupes from the Congo and solo performers like Peg Leg Bates, who tapped danced with a wooden prosthesis.

I never told my mother how much I liked the comedians. I didn't always catch their dirty jokes, but Jack tipped me off by laughing his embarrassed laugh and saying something like, "Good God Almighty. It's a good thing Olivia doesn't know you heard that one. You didn't understand it, did you?" It wouldn't have mattered if I missed every joke, because I spent so many wonderful hours in that theater, I used to laugh and hug my sides with happiness from just being there.

The first time I saw Frankie Lymon wasn't at the Apollo, but in front of my house on a muggy August evening. Mary Jo, Dedi, a few boys and I were playing a half-hearted game of True-Dare-Consequences and waiting for Mr. Wimberly's ice cream cart. Frankie still lived about eight blocks north of us, near Stitt Junior High and he was storming the music scene. Disc jockeys and record producers debated whether to credit his hit, *Why Do Fools Fall in Love* with the birth of black rock and roll. Experts could debate all they wanted; I knew the score on Frankie Lymon. He was a dreamy doo-wop boy and I hoped more than anything to see him at the Apollo. Then one night, he came swaggering down our street.

Some things you hold tight to, like him walking up to me and saying the unforgettable words, "Hey gal." If my friends hadn't also been caught up in this moment of stardom, they might have heard pitter-pattering in my chest and noticed me trying and failing to say the word, "Hi," back to him. When my head cleared, I did a quick calculation of what it would cost me to follow this boy to the ends of the earth, or even down to 150th Street where he was already headed. Too much, I decided, so I just watched him and his three-buddy entourage feint, tilt and diddy bop on down the block.

"That cat thinks he's bad," Phillip finally said after they moved off.

"He sure is fine, though," Dedi noted.

Mary Jo, quick to shoot you down, said, "So what. All that curly hair doesn't give him the right to come on our street acting like he owns the place. He's too stuck up. He's not the only cute boy in the world who can sing."

"Okay, name another one," I challenged, trying to picture anyone else who could make that toe-curling, doo-wop sound. No one spoke. We all knew words to hit songs and names of our favorite groups like the Satins, Shirelles or Drifters. But we didn't always know what our boy and girl idols looked like because the only black singer to appear on television was Nat King Cole. Frankie's face was well known, because he was famous enough to make the covers of *Jet* and *Ebony* magazines.

Plenty of other local kids also had talent, including Arthur Barber, a classmate from grade school who was trying to break into music. I ran into him again when we were fifteen because he was lead singer with three other guys who rehearsed in the basement of my new apartment building. On a few Saturday mornings, I watched them do perfect pivots and high-steps, imitating Temptations' moves and singing Temps' songs or Four Tops hits like, *I'll be There*. They were ordinary kids in high-water pants and checkered shirts with dance moves and harmony as polished as the pros.

When they stopped rehearsing in the laundry room, I lost track of Arthur and never heard if they cut a record. By then, lots of teen groups were signing record contracts. The success of black rock and roll, which evolved into rhythm and blues (most kids and DJs didn't begin calling the black sound rhythm and blues until white rock and rollers like Elvis gained popularity), made it harder for kids like Arthur to join the club. Also, we were in the 1960s by then, and the Motown juggernaut was changing the industry, turning eyes towards Detroit.

Frankie Lymon found fame, but he may have already been messing with drugs when we saw him on Edgecombe. Plenty of good-news stories circulated about him, but rumors were also rampant and eventually he died from a heroin overdose. Like so many others, Frankie died in Harlem. It was as though the reality show *Death By Needle* had decided to film in our neighborhood.

Most of the music I listened to in the '50s aired on the *1280 Rocket Show* and was played by a DJ named Jocko Henderson. Jocko was the ultimate boss DJ with a snappy rhythmic lead-in: "Hi, I'm back on the scene with the record machine saying "Oo-pop-a-doo and how do you do." Thousands of kids trying to be cool like Jocko picked up his jive patter. Teenagers weren't the only ones digging Jocko's soulful sound. After he heard him, and until he died, Jack frequently copied another Jocko tag line, "Great gugga mugga."

153

From the back shelf of our television console, I unearthed Mom's converter plug that allowed me to play 45 records on her turntable and began frequenting Frenchie's shoe shop to buy 45s and sheet music. Initiating a trip to the Apollo on my own or with Jack was impossible now, because he took care of my brother during the day, and going by myself was no longer an option. On my last solo visit, I was accosted by what adults subsequently described as a masher—a word I'd never heard before and rarely since—to categorize the barrel-chested pervert who snuck up behind me in the darkened theater and pressed his hard penis in my back.

I've long since forgotten who I was there to see, but it was a standing room only crowd. I arrived too late to find a seat, but Jack had tipped Jimmy the usher enough times that, without asking him, he escorted me into a prime spot directly behind the orchestra section where I was just tall enough to see over the wall. My assailant must have been a regular, too; he seized the few moments before the curtain rose to slip in behind me, when the theater was at it darkest and seconds before the band launched its loudest uptempo opening notes of I Think You're Wonderful.

When the music started, he pinned me against the wall. There were at least thirty people around us and hundreds in the building, but he gambled that a kid wouldn't scream. Even if I had managed to swallow the fear choking off a scream, I doubt anyone would have heard me over the noise. The man was tall and he positioned his hands against the wall, not around me. I wiggled beneath him, dropped to the floor and bolted for Mom's office. Bursting into tears at her desk, I sobbed "A man...," and like a crazy woman, she grabbed my hand and tore down 125th Street in three-inch heels. In a hail of words, she relayed my still untold story to the manager who also grasped the gist of what happened, without yet asking me one question.

Cocooned in my mother's fury and the manager's calm, my tears dried up but they wouldn't let me go home. I gave a description, which wasn't bad because when it happened my eyes had adjusted somewhat to the darkness. The assailant was broad-chested, his opened coat fell below his waist, but didn't reach his knees. Before I ran far, I glanced back to see if he was following and glimpsed a dark wool watch cap, the kind sailors wore.

Mom and the manager made me stay there until the show broke, so the three of us could wait in the lobby like avenging angels, hoping I'd spot him in the crowd. The police weren't notified, even though mashing occurred frequently. I got over being frightened, but developed what New Yorkers call street sense, a hardwired awareness of my surroundings, often instilled by just such an incident as the masher. What was harder to recover from was disappointment at not being able to go back to the Apollo because, within months, rock and rollers began lighting the place on fire.

Eventually I did return, although it took five years, until 1962, but it was a doozy of a welcome-back; James Brown and the Flames were there. I was in high school and went with my cousin Charles who was an engineering student at Drexel in Philadelphia. I'd met him the year before at my father's burial in Philadelphia, and my first thought was where had the family been hiding this exotic creature who played varsity college soccer, was smart and drop-dead gorgeous, with sandy-colored curly hair and hazel eyes.

He'd ridden up to New York on his BMW motorcycle, although at my mother's behest, he parked the bike and we took a bus to 125th Street. I doubt the evening cost five bucks, but the Godfather of Soul gave a big ticket performance, best described as somewhere beyond the far side of wonderful.

Picture a lithe, muscular brown man wearing a pageboy hairstyle many women would be proud of. His shoes were pointy-toe black patents, the suit tight white and he had the brute strength of three acrobats with the pipes of a Bible-thumping chorus. After an hour, when he was lathered-up in a stone-cold sweat, one of his handlers came out, draped him in a full-length velvet cape, and escorted him off the stage. I can't remember the dozens of songs Brown sang, but *Have Mercy Baby* would have been a perfect finale, because throats were burning, hearts thumping and hands hurting from all the shouting, whistling and clapping going on in that audience.

By the 1970s, drugs and crime had tightened their grip on Harlem. The toxic climate poisoned that little piece of heaven known at the Apollo, causing it to close. Big entertainers like Marvin Gaye and Aretha began skipping Harlem, opting instead for downtown clubs and concert halls. Fortunately, a group of concerned citizens, politicians and investors rescued the theater, remodeled it and in 1985 the Apollo reopened.

11. A Sporty Kind of Guy

Someone said, "Stompin' at the Savoy...." For as long as I could remember, adults had been talking about dancing or stompin' at the Savoy. One of the last great Harlem ballrooms with big band entertainment and dancing, the Savoy had recently closed. But the closing wasn't what they were talking about. It was 1961, about an hour after my father's funeral. His closest friends and a few family members from Philadelphia were at Lula and Jack Jones' house; and the next day, most people in this room would be on the train that took Daddy's body to Philadelphia for burial.

I'd been told at school that my father was dead and I should go to his apartment. I'd seen my share of dead bodies, but no one explained why I needed to see this fastidious man lying uncovered on the floor in his underwear, one arm and leg drawn up, jaws clenched in a death grip. Mr. Peters arrived moments later and found me standing dry-eyed and shocked to see my dead father in an undershirt and white boxer shorts with a little green paisley design. In his funeral director's voice, which I hadn't heard before, Mr. Peters broke our silence.

"Jeanie, your father died from a stroke. The police and coroner have already been here."

At the word "police," I looked up. "Why were the police here?"

"It's just routine. But, now I think it's best if you leave so I can remove the body."

Neither of us spoke to May, Daddy's girlfriend, sitting numbly at the kitchen table. Mr. Peters' funeral home, Griffin-Peters, was around the corner in an unlikely spot on Seventh Avenue between the famous nightclub, Smalls' Paradise and the Hot Cha, a little bar that, in the 1930s, was a leading jazz

157

club. I only knew its present state—a small, dumpy-looking place with an oversized wooden bar and a smell of beer and sweat. But Harlem had changed a lot in thirty years. It wasn't even the same place I remembered from two years ago.

At my father's funeral, hundreds of people paid their last respects. Most lined the sidewalk standing four deep, craning their necks, unable to get inside Griffin-Peters' small chapel. Daddy was no celebrity, but exiting the family limousine in my girlfriend's borrowed black coat and walking toward the familiar funeral parlor, I felt as though I was at the Oscars and the limousine was dropping me curbside, at the red carpet. There was no red carpet, just a narrow path with neighbors and the curious standing on either side pointing, whispering and trying to figure out who was who; someone even called out, "There's his daughter."

The way my grandmother once explained dying: "Except for the length of a funeral procession, you wouldn't know if a barrister or bum is inside that coffin. They're all God's children on their burial day. Colored people," she claimed, "can cry broke all they want, but when the hat is passed for a burial, they fall all over themselves dropping ten dollar bills in." Harlem held morticians in high regard. Doctors and lawyers tipped the scale of elite black professionals, but good preachers and undertakers ran neck and neck for third. The feeling was, if you had to, you could make it through life without a doctor, lawyer or minister, but no one met their maker without first stopping at the mortuary. The three funeral homes I knew best were within five blocks of each other on Seventh Avenue, and there was enough business for the proprietors to be friends as well as competitors.

Dying in style remains a high priority in black communities. Some deceased, by circumstances or choice, don't have bank accounts or tangible assets, but it is not unusual to find a paid-up life insurance policy among their personal effects. The policy is not large enough to educate surviving children or support a spouse or companion, but the face value covers embalming, dressing, two limousines, walnut coffin, and grave opening and closing. These people may live carelessly and make no amends to their Creator, but they want to meet Him in the first-class section of heaven. Everyday that drama is played out in Harlem and, at his death, Daddy had the starring role.

Sitting on a tufted hassock in the Jones' house after the funeral, I listened as Mrs. Jones and Doc Carter, a podiatrist, continued discussing the Savoy, Cab Calloway and Lena Horne.

"Lena is older than Chink, I tell you. If you don't believe me, you can call Cab and ask him. If I'd known this would come up, I would have asked one of those girls at the funeral. A bunch of them from the old days were over there in the chapel."

"No she isn't," Doc insisted. "That gal started in show business when she was just a kid. I know they were all kids then, but she was so young she traveled with her mother. Chink was a kid too, if you know what I mean. But he was living on his own and was several years older. She was a seasoned veteran at a very young age. That's why people think she's older than she is.

"Anyway," he continued, "Cab wouldn't know the ages of those kids who worked for him. They were always coming and going and taking off to work for different gigs. I know what I'm talking about because most of the dancers lived over there at 187 W. 135th where I had my office. Those kids didn't bother us. They slept all day, worked evenings. When they got off, I was long gone from the office while they partied all night on the second floor."

"Well, you could be right," Mrs. Jones conceded, "but one thing I'm sure of, Chink's irresistible good looks and that smile lit up every stage he danced on."

—◇— —◇— —◇—

I spent the most time with my father when I was a little girl and he was lighthearted, handsome and rich. He had a smart way of dressing, like he just stepped off a fashion runway. Casual and elegant, his straight hair was slicked down and combed back, a few strands falling over his eye. He preferred sporty clothes, sweaters and spectator shoes while his contemporaries tended towards suits and broad-brimmed hats during the formal fifties; and he favored the color brown. Once he was wearing beige summer slacks with a cream and tan-colored sweater over a butterfly collared shirt. That day, women on Seventh Avenue came over to talk to me, but I knew they were really eyeing my father.

I'm sure my dad thought he was cool. He was one of those guys who asked in his smokers' voice, "May I get that for you?" then flourished his lighter or struck a match with aplomb, his hand cradling the flame from wind. When he placed a cigarette in the corner of his mouth while mixing a drink, making a phone call or counting money, the smoke trailed past his trim little mustache, giving him a sexy, squinty-eyed look like Bogey in the movie *Casablanca*. Daddy was always ruffling through a roll of fives, tens and twenties to find a five for a waitress or ten for the cabby who drove us downtown.

One memory that sticks with me was on a Sunday morning, when Daddy and two other men were counting large sums of cash in a booth at a bar he'd never taken me to before. One of the men had two children with him. My father was so jolly and busy, he forgot to notice those two boys seduce me into breaking all of his rules, including slipping into the men's bathroom.

"What's that?" I asked the bigger boy, pointing to a strange contraption that stunk like pee, but looked like a water fountain that should have been placed higher on the wall.

"It's a urinal."

"How's it work?" His little brother volunteered, "I'll show you," then demonstrated the nifty way boys and men stand up to use a bathroom. I also sneaked a glimpse of his penis; it was bigger than my brother's.

The only photo I have of my father and me together was taken that morning when his counting concluded. We're standing outside the bar, somewhere around 127th Street and Lexington Avenue. He's laughing and hugging me to his side and I think he'd just bought the bar.

I have fleeting memories of being a rich girl. For a short time, Daddy and Jack were both "cash rich," acquiring thousands by hitting the number. Daddy hit for $50 and Jack, somewhere in the same range. I don't recall a sea change in anyone's life, except that the big console television appeared and Mom got a new fox collar coat. Both men kept gambling and their arguments with Mom over money grew worse. Daddy indulged in extravagance, including a new car. Jack's greatest luxury was the big bet, or an elegant dinner in a downtown restaurant, and he took Mom to Mardi Gras for their honeymoon. For the train ride to New Orleans, she wore a clutch-style travel hat covered in tiny red, teal blue, green and yellow feathers. It was the prettiest thing I ever saw.

A train ride with my father helped me grasp the concept of privilege. We were the only people in a club car on the Broadway Limited in New York's Penn Station, waiting for our 6 p.m. departure to take us to see my grandparents in Philadelphia. To find the club car, we walked through coach cars filled with bustling travelers settling in for the short two hour trip to Pennsylvania, or the all-night ride to Chicago. For ordinary people, the excitement of saying goodbye to loved ones in Penn Station was akin to a splashy bon voyage taking place a few blocks south, along the Hudson River piers. Down in the train tunnel, anxious-to-be-off locomotives huffed and puffed like race horses anticipating open country, luggage carts rolled by, families mingled and schedule-conscious conductors yelled, "All aboard!"

But that day with Daddy, it was just him and me facing each other across a table, waiting to put in a food order.

"Would you like a Coca-Cola with your club sandwich?"

"Yes, thank you," I replied, my hands politely folded under the table.

"Do you have your toothbrush in your overnight case?"

"Yes."

"What else did your mother pack?"

"Pajamas and clothes for tomorrow and a funny book."

"Did I buy those for you?"

"No, Mommy and I got the jumper at Alexander's and Leamon Jr. bought the book and a ball and paddle when he came back from Japan."

"A soldier boy, then. Is he a friend of your mother's?"

"No, he's her cousin."

"Do you remember your cousin George? You'll see him when we get to Philly."

"No."

"No what?"

"No, I don't remember George."

After a few minutes, Daddy put on a pair of reading glasses I hadn't seen before, then pulled the racing pages of the *New York Daily News* from his back pocket.

I was quiet and well-behaved with my dad, careful to use Sunday manners. Though involved in my life, he was as much stranger as parent to me. I lumped him in the category of "special person," along with Monsignor at church and Mr. Meiselman, our school principal—men of authority who never saw the real me. My dad and I sparred at the parent-child game, feinting and jabbing without truly making contact. I was the perfectly dressed, mannerly weekend daughter. He, the stern, solicitous, overly attentive parent. It was hard to maintain perfection in his presence. He looked for it and was quick to find fault. He said, "Chew your food slowly, use your napkin, sit up closer to the table." I heard Mom say the same things, yet they sounded different. He loved me, but I think his comfort level was in the display of fatherhood over the business of being a daddy.

We hadn't left the station and I already felt stymied in my splendid quarters, missing the diversion of other passengers. Outside the window, a black family boarded the train next to ours. Daddy put down his paper a minute and together we watched about twenty family members hugging and kissing the relatives who were about to travel. They carried greasy shoe boxes of food and wore mismatched bright colored clothing like rural Negroes just up from the South, and I assumed they were returning to North Carolina, Georgia or wherever that train was headed into the night.

Children ask questions and I was no different, but knew better than to ask why we were in a special railroad car. I suspected it was from his numbers winnings. I once asked him why two little girls he took me to see were so poor. He'd left me at their dark tenement in a rough neighborhood, while he and a man I assumed was their father, disappeared for a few hours. The girls and women in the household complimented my father, but instead of getting dressed or having their hair combed, the little girls stayed in grimy undershirts and holey underpants. They patted my Shirley Temple curls and ran their hands along the beautiful clothes I always wore when out with Daddy. Poverty permeated their house, pressing on my chest, hogging the air, making me feel hot.

Gram had always told me, "Wear clean underwear. It says more about your character than a pocketful of money or a fancy home. You might have an accident, land in the hospital and the doctor will see your underwear, so you want it to be clean." This house had two smudgy little figures in dirty underclothes the doctor would not want to see. The family's attention was not unkind, but under its gaze, I was ashamed and frightened. Unable to change my dress, I tried making things even by withdrawing into crinolines and lace, standing stiffly for several hours and refusing their offers of seating and solicitation.

My prim way of dressing had put me at a disadvantage before. The fact was, not many Harlem families clothed girls in sailor dresses and smocked pinafores like the rich children Mary Poppins nannied on Cherry Tree Lane. When I complained to Mom that my Sunday dresses were itchy and formal and didn't look like everyone else's, she made me wear them anyway. Such complaints only fanned my grandmother's sense of one-upmanship. If anyone in her family could out-do the next guy, she was all for it.

I suppose my question about the girls being poor was a rebuke to my father for leaving me in a house full of strangers. He hadn't appreciated what a good job I did warding off panic and a feeling of abandonment, and he answered me with a slap across the face.

"Don't ever let me hear you make fun of people less fortunate than you are."

I'd never been struck before, only threatened by Mom with a switching on my legs and banishment to a Mississippi boarding school by Gram. There was enough trouble between my parents, so I didn't tell Mom, and certainly not Gram, who might have gone nuts or decided it was okay for Aunt Annette to have a gun, then done something terrible, like tell her to use it on Daddy.

I never asked my father another question, though I'd been meaning to ask if he was black or white. This point had not been clarified and no one mentioned it. I knew he looked white, just like my Godmother Dedi. But when it came to Dedi, the family sometimes talked of little else beyond why anyone would marry crazy black Charlie, much less a smart proper white girl from a good Boston Catholic family, like Dedi.

Meeting my Philadelphia grandparents, and Daddy's four sisters, didn't help with the color conundrum. My aunts resembled Daddy, but their mother looked whiter than any white person I ever met. That trip was the last time I saw my grandparents and they left vivid imprints of memory. Grandpop, a thin, wrinkled, brown khaki-colored man, was suffering from what looked like Parkinson disease. His speech was garbled, he trembled and lived in the grip of palsy, spending the day mopping his mouth with a towel to stem drool.

When I entered their house, Grandmom came from the kitchen, and even before she skipped my hug and kiss, I knew

I wasn't going to be grandmother's little princess in this castle. Wiping her hands with a dish towel, she threw it over her shoulder and commented to my dad, "She's grown." People said that all the time, but it wasn't normally a conversation stopper as on that evening. In her no-nonsense housedress and apron, greasy hair slipping out of its bun, this stout, triple-chin Philadelphia grandmother was all about business. She spoke sparingly, just issuing orders that left no doubt I'd pay a price if they weren't obeyed, like when she ordered me to take a second bath. She did not seem happy to see me. She did not seem happy at all.

Before leaving for that trip to Philly, Mom explained I'd be staying with my grandparents, Aunt Teresa, and my cute little cousin Georgie who was almost my exact age, born around the fourth of July, just a few months after me. The Theresa part of my name is from that aunt. As an adult, I concluded my naming must have been a fluke, a goodwill gesture on Mom's part, or a way to ingratiate herself into Daddy's family because the two women did not like each other. I'm lucky I'm not a Beulah.

After Daddy dropped me off and did a fast hello-goodbye to his parents, Georgie came in the living room to stare at me. We eyed each other in silence before Grandmom said, "Outside, both of you. I need to tend to Pop." I followed Georgie past my grandfather who was staring at a small black and white television set playing squiggly lines of static. If it hadn't been for a small act of kindness he later offered, his toothless tremor would have frightened me away from a chance to love him. Georgie and I tramped through the kitchen, where the remains of dinner were still on the table, then outside to a small fenced backyard, thick with neatly trimmed grass. Its only structure, a clothesline, sagged under the weight of trousers, dungarees and men's shirts. By contrast, the yard next door was a rectangle of dry, packed, sun-bleached dirt, and as bald as a cat's eye marble.

"What happened to their grass?"

"The kids pulled it out."

"How?"

"With spoons and their hands."

I thought about that for a minute, picturing a sandbox in the playground, then asked, "Their mother let them?"

"Yeah."

"Why?"

"Grandmom said they don't take care of anything and they're pulling their house down, brick by brick."

I didn't know if he was telling the truth about the house, but those kids sure knew how to pluck a yard clean. It started drizzling, and things between Georgie and me went downhill when we got inside. He didn't like cousins invading his space, or maybe he had another reason for gathering toy soldiers in a pile and pushing them behind his back so I couldn't play with them.

"How old are you?" he wanted to know.

"I'm five and so are you."

"But I'm older."

"You're not older. My Mom said you're a summer baby. You came after me."

"So what, I'm still older."

"No you're not. Don't you know your months? January, February, March...." I ticked off the months so he would know May came before July.

"I can tell time," he said.

"So can I."

Grandmom stopped our tiff by sending me up for the first bath while she went outside to bring in the clothes that were being rained on. Upstairs, I nervously soaped up and rinsed off fast, because the door wouldn't lock and I didn't trust Georgie not to barge in. When I came downstairs, Grandmom was back in the living room and immediately said, "I told you to take a bath." Feeling homesick in my rabbit pajamas, daylight fading outside the window, and facing my grandmother's inexplicable repeat command reminded me of what I'd been trying to forget. I was going to have to spend the night in this house.

"I just took a bath," I mumbled, hoping she didn't think I was sassing, because people in this family hit.

Though imprisoned in his plastic-covered easy chair, Grandpop had heard my water running upstairs. In a voice weak as a new born kitten's, he struggled to explain his wife's mistake. But with a kitchen full of waiting dishes, a fresh pile of clothes to iron, a husband who looked like he needed help getting to bed, and her New York glamour boy having breezed into town to dump another kid in her lap, this lady wasn't buying anything from anybody, so off I went to take another bath.

There may be more now, but New York used to have two Easter parades worth taking note of: the one downtown on Fifth Avenue and the uptown Seventh Avenue walkabout that began when a sea of pastel suits, fur coats, stoles and fancy hats, some as wide as a parasol, hit the streets after church let out. During his flush years, Daddy and I paraded along Seventh Avenue with me wearing exquisite clothes, like my taffeta dress with a matching duster, and once I remember something with an overlay of Swiss dots. We shopped in Saks or Best's where the sales help treated Daddy as if they were his personal shoppers. The service was free, but Daddy always tipped them well, not that they didn't earn it. His way of shopping was to sit back lounging in a padded brocade easy chair, smoking Lucky Strikes, while a woman presented selections for his approval. After gathering a half dozen ensembles, I trotted off with her and she helped me button, zip and model.

I enjoyed being with my father on these good-mood shopping days. We hit the stores in early December, then again around Easter time. The only catch to shopping was that I didn't like Easter coats. Despite Daddy's extravagance, he didn't buy me play clothes, so the previous year's Easter coat turned into this Spring's everyday coat. On warm spring days, I was the ninny looking ridiculous jumping rope or riding a bike in a knee-length formal blue faille coat, when other kids had on sweaters or light jackets. That, along with Grammy's usual worries about weather, meant my outfits sometimes went from ridiculous to absurd.

Once, an unseasonable early spring warm spell blew through Manhattan. When the temperature soared, it fooled everyone but my grandmother into believing June was busting out in April. After school, I found her in the usual front room spot, by the wide open window, sitting on her red kitchen chair where she shucked corn or peeled vegetables while keeping an eye on the neighborhood.

"Whew. Hi, Gram. It's really hot," I said, while carrying my heavy winter loden coat that had a hood. That morning the temperature had been in the high 40s, but now a few boys were already outside taking advantage of the beautiful day by starting the season's first stickball game.

"Can I go out like this?" I asked about the skirt and blouse I had on. Staring out the window, I hoped to spot at least one kid in shirtsleeves who wasn't male, since boys took their coats off all the time. An open window in our apartment was not an indication of outdoor temperature. We had steam radiators filled with boiling hot water. On the coldest days, the radiators hissed like tea kettles and if Mom laid a pair of wet corduroys on top, they dried in an hour. Even in winter, we often didn't close our windows unless rain blew in or wind sucked the curtains out.

"No, you can't go out like that," she said sarcastically.

"The thermometer in the drug store showed it was 75."

"I don't care what the thermometer reads, it's still April. March and April are pneumonia months. If you want to go out, put on your spring coat, and you can wear a lighter hat." She pointed to the hat waiting for me on her dresser.

"Graaaam, it's ugly and it doesn't even keep me warm."

"It protects the crown of your head," she explained, as if I was a newborn with an open soft spot.

The hat, one of Daddy's few shopping mistakes, was a dyed red straw Easter bonnet topped with cherries that I'd had to wear a few weeks earlier on Easter Sunday. This time the hat was just too heavy with the weight of grandmotherly love, and I stayed inside.

When Daddy brought me home from Saks loaded with boxes of clothing, my parents sometimes argued; at least Mom did. He mostly listened. "How many dresses does one child need, for God's sake? Why don't you stop this spending and put that money in savings bonds or a savings account, so she'll have something when she outgrows these things in a few months?"

One heated exchange occurred after an unplanned afternoon of shopping. He brought me home, then paused, hovering in the doorway, while Mom and I waited for him to come in.

"Aren't you coming in?" I asked.

"No, baby. I need to get going."

Earlier, we had popped into a dress shop in the step-down basement level of a building on 135th Street, near the police station. I figured we were just visiting, since we bought clothes in department stores and it was neither Easter nor Christmastime. At first my attention strayed to the owner's son, a little boy half my age with an uncanny resemblance to me. I knew better than to ask about this look-alike, so I focused on a dress Daddy and the owner selected; an itchy long sleeve charcoal gray wool jersey, with a jewel neckline and body-hugging cling. After trying it on, I liked it except for the itchiness, but I knew it was too dark, too fitted and more of a scooped neckline than a jeweled neck. I also knew the dress stood as much chance of getting past my mother's scrutiny as Hitler had of getting into heaven.

Still standing near the door, I took the dress from the box, so both my parents could see it, since Daddy wouldn't come in. Mom's first words were: "I know one of your new women was behind this."

And yes, the lady in the store apparently was one of Daddy's women, and from the looks of her five-year-old kid, not a new one.

"Chink, you are a fool when it comes to money."

"Olivia, she liked the dress. Didn't you baby?" he directed at me.

Since nodding yes or no would make one of them mad at the other, I left the question hanging. Mom ignored me anyway to finish telling him, "It's criminal that you won't save for your child's future. You say you want her to go to college. College costs money. What about her wedding someday? Weddings cost money. Why can't you see this? Set something up so that I can't touch it, if that's your worry. She's eleven years old and you're just throwing money in the toilet. Your child does not wear women's clothes," she yelled at Daddy's back walking down the stairs, "and she will not start now."

If there ever was an official "Mr. Seventh Avenue" title, it could have gone to my father. He left Philadelphia in the 1930s, rented a room on the corner of 135th Street and Seventh Avenue and died a block away in 1961. He was garrulous and outgoing, handsome and debonair, and everybody knew him. He and his buddies set neighborhood tempo, ran the businesses, kibitzed over drinks, and bet money. Women laughed at his jokes, subtly brushed against him, liked serving him food and pouring his whiskey.

He and I spent many Saturdays and Sundays on this turf, eating at Frazier's, visiting funeral homes, and bar hopping before they opened to the public. Our first stop was his bar, the Hot Cha, where urban legend has it Billie Holiday was first discovered. Other venues also claim that honor, including the Apollo, so it might depend on what "discovered" means. On those bar mornings, Daddy tallied receipts, took inventory and said, "Just a little longer, baby," then made his bezillionth phone call. I passed the time spinning on a bar stool and playing some of my jukebox favorites like Ruth Brown's *He Treats Your Daughter Mean*, because Jack had taken me to the Apollo to hear her sing it live.

Without understanding the allure of alcohol, I wondered what made adults keep returning to these smelly, smoke-filled saloons whose only attractions I counted were the jukeboxes and maraschino cherries I picked off from behind the bar. When Daddy finally finished calling and counting, we walked next door to Smalls.

Smalls Paradise was still a fashionable night club with a spacious dance floor that featured talented musicians and hot jazz or blues singers like Joe Turner, Helen Humes and B.B. King. But at 11 o'clock on a Sunday morning, without laughter and music, Smalls had the same beaten down look as its used-to-be-famous neighbor next door.

Inside Smalls' big boxy space, I repeated the same pattern with a new Coca-Cola and a fresh fistful of nickels for the jukebox. Part of Daddy's parenting style consisted of showing me off in my fine clothes. I performed the adorable daughter routine and liked his friends who were all more lenient than he was, especially the manager of Smalls' who turned on the stage mike for me.

"Jeanie, sing us a song," he said. "Let me see what you got. If you're good, maybe I'll give you a job. I heard you playing Ruth Brown in there. Do you know her song, *Teardrops Falling from my Eyes?*"

"Yes. No, not really," I said, starting to get nervous.

"Well, what do you know? Pick anything your little heart desires."

"Go Tell it on the Mountain."

"Wonderful, wonderful. Let's hear it."

Having called my bluff, I knew I had to follow through. In an off-key, but still sweet little girl voice, I sang one verse. When I finished, Daddy beamed, they applauded and his friend said, "Well, I'll be damned. That was beautiful, baby, just beautiful. Man, why didn't you tell me your kid could sing? If we hired kids, I'd give her a job."

That was a good bar-hopping morning but the better stops were at Griffin-Peters, Rodney Dade or Claude Sterrett's funeral homes. A common saying around Harlem was "Cry at weddings and laugh at funerals" and as far as I could tell, that's the way things were done. Mom and Jack's wedding was a simple affair with about ten guests. She wore a short pastel blue dress, got a little teary and Jack sweated a lot. Grammy didn't look too happy, but she wasn't the crying type.

Mourners didn't stay sad long after a funeral and nobody waited to be invited. Folks poured in from near and far, then stuck around for two days or a week, sleeping on couches, grieving over food and whiskey, engaging in joyous talk and praising the Lord for ending their loved one's troubles and taking them to a better place.

Mr. Sterrett's daughter, Claudette, taught me not to be afraid of dead people. She was my age and if she was spending the day with her father, we played inside, while our daddies talked on the sidewalk. Claudette was better at amusing herself in her father's place of business than I was. But to be honest, possibilities for play are endless in a funeral parlor. It's cleaner than a bar, the floor is dry and there are no rules against rearranging folding chairs, or building doll houses out of paper fans or the boxes they're stored in. Two little girls quietly going about the business of childhood was not the worst thing to happen in the presence of the dearly departed, or apparently that was Mr. Sterrett's view because we played right there in the room with dead people.

Claudette grew up in funeral parlors and knew not to point, gawk or talk about the deceased. I followed her lead. My friend Bunky hadn't died yet, so what I observed at Mr. Sterrett's fit neatly into life's natural cycle: an elder lying in repose before visitation later that afternoon. Not being afraid and not being fascinated by death are two different things, so I won't pretend I didn't take peeks. I understood why the dead person wore makeup and that someone applied it, just like Mom painted my face with lipstick and rouge for Halloween. The puzzle in the funeral process was clothes. How did a dead person, who couldn't raise his arms or legs, get into the fancy clothes? Piecing it together, I concluded Mr. Sterrett dressed bodies the same way he would cover a dining table. He cut the fancy evening gowns, jackets or pants up the middle in the back and just kind of laid the clothes on top of the body.

My father's given name was Roy Baker, but everyone called him Chink. I never thought to ask why, he didn't explain, and neither did anyone else. Chink is a slur for Asian people who generally have small eyelids. Slurs were carelessly and indifferently tossed around then. Daddy's eyelids were tiny slits that tapered into epicanthic folds like Asians have, so I assume the nickname sprung from his eyelids. I have the same eyes, but people call me Jean, Theresa or Terry.

Daddy's parents, James Baker and Minnie, nee McConaghy, met around 1910 on Philadelphia's Mainline, while working for the Stetson family, the people who made a fortune manufacturing men's hats. My grandmother, from Londonderry in Northern Ireland, was nursemaid to an invalid in the Stetson household. James, a light brown man with a receding hairline, had a hint of a mustache, wore wire rim glasses and worked as the family's chauffeur. The young couple and their nine children settled in North Philadelphia, the colored section of town. Everyone in that family, except Grandpop, could pass for white, but they lived like black people, except one son, Willard. The military classified him as white. After the war, he kept passing until he disappeared in California.

Subtleties of race elude children, and it took me a long time to figure out what was going on with these white-on-the-outside, black-on-the-inside, panda people. As an adult, when I reconnected with my aunts, I understood my confusion. Their bone structure, white skin, filmy-fine straight hair, and in once instance, blue eyes, said more than any scholarly treatise about America's convoluted interpretation of who or what color we are.

In September 1995, I reunited with my Philadelphia family, and that weekend spent reacquainting with relatives turned out to be a few months before Aunt Teresa died. She appeared to be in good health as we sat together on her front sidewalk, watching a neighborhood drill team high-step and twirl batons in the Labor Day parade. I hadn't seen Teresa in forty years. She looked sixty, not seventy-eight, and was still attractive. When I started asking questions, it made her uneasy. My cousin Charles had just informed me that the family recently learned that Daddy had another daughter about my age, named Melba Guy, with whom I would have a wonderful meeting in the year 2000. Of course, learning about a sister was not shocking news. What surprised me was that it was a sister, not a brother, who I'm sure is out there, too.

Although she was reticent about discussing some family history, Aunt Teresa did tell me that Grandpop, when he left his job with Stetson's, worked as a bartender at the Cosmopolitan Bar and Grill in North Philly. Grandmom worked nearby at the Pearl Theater on Ridge Avenue, a Philadelphia venue for live black entertainment. Grandmom was the Pearl's wardrobe mistress and her oldest son, my Uncle Jimmy, was the theater's electrician.

"Sometimes mother took the youngest kids to work with her," Teresa told me. "They were expected to play close by so she could keep an eye on them, but the boys would give her the slip. Ella and I were the oldest girls and we were back home preparing dinner and doing housework—things needed to keep a large family running. Mother didn't have to look far for Chink. He loved that old theater and he liked to dance."

A friend and contemporary of Daddy's was Charles "Honi" Coles who, like my father, ended up in show business. Unlike Daddy, he continued dancing, eventually winning a 1983 Tony for his part in the Broadway production, *My One and Only*. I wanted to meet him. If he was anywhere near as

chatty and well informed as Doc Carter, who had since died,
I figured I might learn more about my father's Philadelphia
youth and dancing career. Honi Coles died while I was trying
to arrange a meeting, but what I read in one of his published
interviews was revealing:

> In my neighborhood in Philadelphia, the only form of
> entertainment was dancing. Everyone I knew could
> dance. We used to dance on street corners at night,
> and then we'd start going to the various neighborhood
> houses and amateur contests. First I won a few prizes
> then George and Danny Miller and I formed an act
> we called the Miller Brothers. We rehearsed every day
> and night...
>
> In my day, I don't know anyone who went to school
> to learn show business or dancing. You learned it by
> osmosis, as you were exposed to it. The Miller Broth-
> ers and I used to walk out on the boulevard and into
> various places to dance. We'd dance on street corners
> for whatever coins people would throw us; that was
> our pay for the night. We'd dance in amateur contests,
> which we sometimes didn't win; then we had nothing
> but some applause for our efforts. But dancing was all
> we knew. I guess it was all we wanted to know... When
> I was with the Miller Brothers, we were a sensational
> act, but we were really a bunch of dumb kids. Hell! We
> didn't even know enough to get ourselves an agent, and
> brother, things were tough in those days.
>
> It was before Equity, the union, came in and we had
> no protection at all... For one show in particular, I
> recall, we had to rehearse every day. They gave us ten
> cents a day for carfare—period! We had to scuffle for
> food; that's all there was to it. And making a living as
> a dancer was tough... But you kept going because you
> loved your work. It was pure devotion, I guess; and

anyway, there was no other place to go. You wanted to be the best-looking act around—the best-dressed guy in the crowd—and anyway, I had no other trade. I was a dancer and that was that.[1]

When my parents met in the 1940s, Daddy was twenty-eight years old and already a retired Cotton Club "boy," the title given male chorus line dancers; females were called chlorines, because all the women were very light-skinned. Daddy's new job was bartending at Dick Wheaton's on 137th and Seventh Avenue. Mom was a pretty seventeen-year-old "A" student at Evander Childs High School and part-time waitress. World War II was raging, the Cotton Club's glory days had ended; many dancers were now housewives raising children, or men heading off to war. Daddy didn't go to war. He was a 4F, bad heart reject. That, plus whiskey, cigarettes and hard living would mark him for an early grave.

The year before he died, he seemed older than a man in his 40s. He was listless, easily distracted and his coloring was poor. His neat, slicked-down hair, now streaked with gray, often needed cutting and his suits hung on a skeletal frame. The color brown now made him look sallow, instead of snazzy. We shared a defining moment one night while dining at Frazier's. He used to sweep across the restaurant's slightly tilted, white oak floor like he owned the place, flirting with waitresses, saying hello to diners he might know, then making a beeline for the kitchen to see Mrs. Frazier, the owner and a longtime friend.

This night, he allowed a hostess to quietly seat us and it was Mrs. Frazier who later sought us out. The first thing she did when she came to our table was solve an excruciating problem for me. She said good evening, and then asked, "Chink, do you have a handkerchief?" He did, and quickly pulled it out of his pocket, and wiped his nose.

Sitting stiffly across from him, I had pondered what to do about the booger resting on the end of his nose. At age eleven, boogers take on an enormous presence and I watched in despair as this one stuck to my father's face, refusing to fall off. I'd tried placing my eyes everywhere but on that dried speck of mucus. Mrs. Frazier was a fast-talking, multi-tasking woman with guests to greet and a kitchen staff to manage, but she exuded warmth and welcome to all the diners. She was not a girlfriend kind of friend, but the kind who asked me, "How's Olivia? Tell her hello for me. I've gotta get back in the kitchen, but later, I want to hear about that new baby brother of yours."

My father and I didn't visit as often as we once had, and he was no longer the self-assured daddy who flashed large bills or went on day-long shopping trips. I didn't understand the changes in Daddy but the big puzzle, besides his lack of energy, was the current girlfriend—the one who lived with him. Everything about her felt wrong. I'd met a number of Daddy's girlfriends. They would come and go, or sometimes reappear, but none ever lived with him. Most were predictably similar: smart, soft-spoken, pretty brown-skinned women on the order of my mother.

One Sunday, Mom sent me to Daddy's house to get cash for school clothes since he no longer had the interest, energy or much money to take me shopping. Mom made me bring my brother Houston along. Lately, he'd become my personal escort, because she seriously thought his presence kept boys away. Boys had started talking to me on the street, on the bus and sometimes boys in cars would call out in stupid honey coated voices, "Hey baby, want a ride?" As if I'd fall for that. When I had my little brother with me, I had to watch out for boys and Houston, too.

May, the new girlfriend, had been at Daddy's about a year. As usual, she hung back, unsure what to say or do, choosing to do neither and acting like she never had company and except for me, that may have been the case. My visits were always brief, so I figured this would be too, and it was, because my brother kept staring at her hair tied in a kerchief and finally asked, "Are you Chink's maid?"

177

Houston immediately felt the room shift. He got scared, grabbed my skirt, while Daddy just looked at the floor. I was eleven, maybe twelve, without skills to smooth things over and my father was tongue-tied. Poor May, who just wanted to be invisible, looked like she'd been shot in the heart, and in a way she had been. After an awkward silence, I mumbled goodbye and dragged Houston with me.

I clearly knew the score on my father's girlfriends, so much so that I didn't always tell my mother about the good times I had in their company. After a day of riding in the car, stopping for ice cream and being fussed over, it felt a little disloyal to Mom. When Daddy and I were out with women, they spent the time loving him up and buttering me up, and none had been like May.

That day in his apartment, instead of dabbing on a little rouge, or changing into a skirt or dress like other women in Harlem did on Sunday, May looked like many black women's worst nightmare: the stereotypical, inarticulate Aunt Jemima figure hovering awkwardly in a house dress, head rag on, and a man's cast-off backless slippers that were two sizes too large. The only thing missing was a toothy, servile smile.

Women in our family were lipstick-laden creatures who wouldn't be caught dead with a rag tied on their heads, even if company wasn't coming. Each time I hear the old song about putting on your red dress, wig hat and high-heel sneakers, I grin. It's like a tune Gram sang to me, as I'm sure she once did with Mom and my aunts: "First thing you do each morning," she preached "is get out of your gown, throw on a dress, put some red lipstick on, and get your newspapers off the floor, because you don't know who might be dropping in." I must admit, the newspaper part always stumped me, but overall, I heard what she said.

My mother absolutely got the message. When we moved away from Gram, Mom became chief duster and cleaner-upper of her own apartment, except when I had to do it, which was often. Both of us dreaded dusting, because of New York's ever present soot; it permeated the window sills and table tops, even if the windows weren't up, which they were because of the excessive steam heat. When Mom dusted, to side-step the kerchief-head taboo and keep her hair clean, she covered her hair with a pair of panties.

Shortly before Houston's embarrassing question to May, I'd accompanied my grandmother to a doctor's appointment, something I did frequently. As our cab dropped us off, Lucy, a pretty, always well-groomed neighbor girl who lived on the fifth floor, jumped from her boyfriend's car in front of the cab, and did a three-second sprint for the front door of 369. Her blanket, tote bag, rolled towel and trashed windblown hair poking from beneath a crooked head scarf, clearly indicated she'd just gotten off the Cross Bronx or Long Island Express-way, coming from one of the beaches. Sea air and salt water have never been kind to any woman's hair, especially the kinky, nappy kind like Lucy's. In that situation, you'd think Gram would cut her some slack instead of piling on with "Lord a mercy, I'm surprised that girl let herself be seen on the street with that rag stuck on her head."

Do-rag-Negritude is back. If you're a girl and you wrap your head in a rag, you're looking "ghetto fabulous." When a guy does it, he just looks "ghetto," but that's the point. Traditions die hard: witness my mother with her panties.

When Houston and I got back from Daddy's house, Mom couldn't hide a tiny smirk when I told her what he said. Sensing her amusement, I warmed to my story, embellishing it with big sisterly scorn. "It was really terrible, Mommy. See, I told you I shouldn't have to take him any place. He's always touch-ing something, and now he's saying all the wrong things."

My brother was too young to understand what all the fuss was about, but he was smart enough to keep his mouth shut when Mom asked if he knew he shouldn't say things like that. But with the flood gates open on this girlfriend topic, I plowed ahead with what bugged me. "Why did he pick her?" I blurted out "and why does she dress like that, and act like she can't talk?" Mom bristled at my tone, stopped pretending that stirring gravy was juicier than what we were talking about, and removed the cast iron frying pan from the burner, so it wouldn't scorch, then threw me a look.

"May is your father's girlfriend," she said in a new voice and sharp tone. "She is a plain, decent woman and besides you, she may be the best thing in his life. That's all that's important and you must show her respect. What you think of her doesn't matter. Do I make myself clear?"

12. An American Original

Nearly a half century after death, my grandmother remains larger than life and is still growing. A vain, outrageous and proud woman, she was loved, loathed and respected. Born Lena Lugenia Brown on December 29, 1890 in Norfolk, Virginia, she preferred the year 1897 and adopted it as her date of birth. In our family, ages and other omissions are often kept private, but I'm confident she'll forgive me for revealing secrets because a life such as hers should not stay locked in the closet.

The family tells me I met six of her eleven siblings, but pictures are how I remember most of them. In one old daguerreotype, Grammy and her sisters Martha, Bertha and Alethia hide their youth and slenderness beneath severe gazes, choker-neck blouses and long skirts. That picture is a great piece of history because the grandmother I knew was never young, slim, buttoned-up or without mirth. In another photo, two great uncles, Herbert and Raymond, still in their teens, are mugging with confident grins and slicked-back hair. Their handsome faces and muscular bodies don't look the least bit Victorian.

My clan's mixed heritage charms me. Take Aunt Alethia, the one I first called A-Leaf-ia, whose name sounded like nature. She borrowed heavily from her granddaddy's genes; got his square-jawed coppery Indian color and thick black braids. As an old woman, she clearly resembled a tribal elder, a short squat presbyter with high cheekbones and a gray, contoured bob. Our family never owned up to its redskin heritage. Like most of their documents, it got lost on a trail of official indifference and shoddy record keeping.

181

Martha and Bertha reflected another line of descent. Both were solemn, pudgy-nosed women; their dusty brown skin mirrored the dark DNA passed down by my great grandfather Lazarus, son of slaves. The complexions change again with my great Uncle Leamon and my grandmother. Their soft blended, sand-colored faces were "high yalla," the shade just making it onto the "pass-for-white" color chart for light-skinned blacks who used to do a lot of passing. In body and soul, my grandmother was a black woman but later, I'll get to the day she went white.

In 1921, Gram married my grandfather, William Hodges, whose occupation was chauffeur. They also ran a boarding house, but my grandmother's passion was hair. Years before, as a young woman, she stumbled into styling hair while working as a maid for a woman named Miss Earlene and, from what I pieced together from Mom and Aunt Cee, it was the only white household she worked in until moving to New York.

The way she discovered her talent for styling hair started with a dog bite and the time Miss Earlene told Gram, "Jeanie, you can cook, but your cleaning ain't worth spit," which was definitely a compliment since she considered herself a cook, not a maid.

A neighbor's dog bit Miss Earlene's foot because she kicked it away from nipping at one of her horses. The foot didn't heal right. One afternoon while looking out the kitchen window, Gram watched Miss Earlene in the front yard, working the water pump, struggling to rinse soap from her hair without slipping in mud. An offer of help resulted in Gram finishing her hair, then progressing to wash and curl it on a regular basis.

My grandmother rarely talked to me about things that happened in her past, but a number of times she said, "Jean, you can learn a lot from white people." Being so stubborn and disdainful of authority, I never paid much attention because I didn't think she ever learned anything from anybody. But I didn't know about Miss Earlene's hair then.

That happenstance occurred in the late 1920s when Negro beauty culture was hitting its stride because of pioneering women such as Annie Malone who manufactured healthy hair products and created a network of schools to teach stylists. Madame C. J. Walker created additional products and started a national door-to-door business, similar to Fuller Brushes, to sell her goods. Within a few years of these developments, Miss Hattie Yeargins, an older woman trained in the Annie Malone Poro Beauty system, took my grandmother under wing and taught her how to straighten and curl Negro hair, then put her to work in her beauty shop. She worked for Miss Yeargins until about 1930.

In Norfolk, the stock market crash hit Negro businesses as hard as—if not harder than—white enterprises, including the Crispus Attucks Theater where black entertainers, such as my father's former boss Cab Calloway, came to perform. Its closing effectively shut down my grandparents' boarding house business because minstrel shows and black vaudevillians stopped touring. When Grandpa lost his job and Gram's beauty customers tapered off, she along with her two youngest daughters, left Virginia and joined the Negro diaspora heading to New York. Aunt Annette and Uncle Smitty were already living in Manhattan. Typically my grandmother departed in style, with her photo and a write-up in the *Norfolk Journal and Guide*:

> Mrs. Lena R. (sic) Hodges, above of Norfolk, who left last week to accept an appointment as teacher in Beauty Culture School in New York. Mrs. Hodges is one of the oldest users of the Poro System in Norfolk and has been associated with Mrs. Jessie B. Yeargins and Miss Fannie L. Spratley....[1]

Grandpa came to New York briefly, but chauffeuring jobs were scarce, plus Negro drivers and domestics had to vie for employment with New York's large European immigrant groups. Unlike Gram, the big city did not agree with him. He missed his dogs and the outdoors and, as a result, went back to Virginia.

My mother shared this information over a several-day period, during one of my visits home. At one point, while talking about her childhood in the 1930s, she said matter-of-factly, "When we first moved to New York, Mother still had old Mr. Jackson living with her."

"Who was Mr. Jackson?"

"Mr. Jackson was the ex-slave Mother brought with us from Norfolk."

"A slave?" I asked incredulously. "Slaves were still alive? Why was he with Gram?" With my grandmother, anything was possible, so I did a quick calculation, trying to come up with an approximate age because, to me, the more likely scenario was that Mr. Jackson had been some kind of sugar daddy. Since I sure as shucks couldn't broach that topic, I asked, "Was he her servant, or something like that?"

"Of course he wasn't her servant," she bristled, as if I was being ridiculous and sullying my grandmother's reputation, which is sort of how I felt when Mom explained. "He was her boarder. He lived at Mother and Daddy's boarding house and Mother took care of him. He didn't have any family, other than us. She couldn't very well leave him down South, with Daddy looking after him, so he came to New York with her. There were plenty of ex-slaves walking around the city in the 1930s and '40s."

As Harlem's economy grew worse and beauty college students dropped away, my grandmother couldn't find additional work in a shop. She began doing hair at home, an income stream for many black women with beautician skills and others who pretended to have them. Before chemical straighteners became the norm or natural hairdos evolved, black women straightened their hair with hot metal combs and curling irons heated on the open flames of gas stoves. With no way of regulating heat, unskilled stylists often cauterized sections of hair to the metal. Scalp and face burns were as common as ruined hair, so women tried to scrape up a few coins to pay a skilled home-based beautician like my grandmother.

Gram's other survival business was a simplified version of the "rent party." During the depression, large rent parties included food and/or entertainment. The tenant cooked a meal that neighbors, friends, even strangers paid for, and a musician or two provided the music, allowing them to earn some cash.

My grandmother gave "chitlin parties." For anyone who isn't familiar with this food, chitlins, officially named chitterlings, are pig intestines. I don't know what my grandmother charged per plate, but she sold take-out orders of chitterlings, collard greens and potato salad from the front door of her apartment. The concept had not disappeared when I was a child and I remember parties in our building or next door in 371, including a few evenings when Mom came back from someone's apartment with several stacked paper plates filled with the age-old menu: chitterling, potato salad and greens, that then became our dinner.

A ten-pound container of chitterlings was littered with fat, dirt, hair, bone chips and other foreign matter, so it took hours of cleaning to make them edible. After discarding waste, then boiling off fat, there wasn't much meat left, so multiple containers were required to produce enough for a gang showing up at the door. Chitterlings are traditionally a cold weather food, because that's when it's safe to butcher hogs and dress the meat. Even after refrigeration became the norm, particular cooks like my grandmother would only fix them in winter.

A funny thing about this food is that there is no medium ground, people either love or hate them. The dish once evoked great emotion, recalling days of scrimping and scratching to stay alive. A symbol of black culinary necessity, they remain a staple in many homes, especially for special occasion meals. Chitterlings began as an unsavory leftover byproduct that blacks had to eat because it was the only meat they got. Now they have evolved into a delicacy, and gained designer-food status, as foodies and chefs discover their fabulous taste.

One locale not usually associated with soul food is Limoges, France, where they celebrate *La Frairie des Petite Ventres*, The Brotherhood of Small Bellies, a village food festival devoted to cooking "innards," including pig fat, pig snout stuffed with pig tongue as well as veal and pig intestines:[2] in other words, chitterlings and all the kinds of food that used to be cooked in our kitchen.

For the curious, or those who might be inclined to cook chitterlings the American way, to the best of my memory, here's my grandmother's recipe:

Classic Chitterlings

- Purchase 10 pounds of frozen chitterlings.
- Defrost in refrigerator overnight.
- Separate fat from meat and rinse.
- Rinse repeatedly until they're as clean and fat-free as possible.
- In a large pot, add enough water to cover and briefly boil.
- Cool and skim off the fat.
- Add enough additional water to cover and boil again, then also add the following:

  1 large whole onion cut in half

  1 green pepper, halved

  3 stalks of celery

  1 bay leaf

  Salt to taste

  1 cup of vinegar *(It helps control cooking odor, which is a downside to making chitterlings, but the odor dissipates and the taste makes up for it).* Some cooks throw in a piece of fresh ginger or a whole peeled potato *(to help with odor).*

- Simmer 3 or 4 hours.
- Cut into two-inch pieces and, if desired, season with hot sauce and vinegar.

Despite her entrepreneurial spirit, Gram lived under a dark cloud during the 1930s. The depression was slow to release its grip on the nation and her first years in New York were not financially successful. With the gas already turned off in their apartment on 142nd Street and Bradhurst, Gram received notice that her electricity was being shut off, too.

Ten years ago, my mother told me what happened that day. "When the gas got turned off, it eliminated Mother's source of doing hair, cooking chitterlings as a side business, or even making normal meals for Cecelia and me. To prepare simple foods like scrambled eggs, Mother devised a crude hot plate from a flattened tin can suspended over two light bulbs."

"Couldn't she have paid the gas bill first?"

When she answered, Mom was starting to cry. "It wasn't an either-or situation. Your grandmother was trying to hold on to the rent money and couldn't pay the gas or electric bill. The gas company just lost patience sooner."

"You know she was not a downhearted person or one to give in to defeat, but we were poor and she was tired of living from crisis to crisis. The day electric service was to be disconnected, Cecelia and I woke up to find Mother sitting in the dark by the window. She was in her navy blue dress with the white shawl collar. But we knew something was wrong because she had on her hat and gloves and it was 7:30 in the morning.

"We were frightened because she sat there all morning and afternoon, softly singing spirituals. To this day, when I hear a spiritual, it makes me think of that time in our life.

"Around three o'clock, after sitting all day in some private hell, it seemed like she got a signal, because she grabbed her pocketbook, jumped up, told Cecelia and me she would be right back and charged down three flights of stairs.

"She'd been waiting for the electric company truck to roll up, so she could 'accidentally' run into the serviceman and stop him before he went down to the basement meter.

"When Mother got down to the front vestibule, Cecelia and I were standing at our door listening and we heard Mother say, 'I have been sent from the Home Relief to inform you that Mrs. Hodges has paid her electric bill and service to this apartment is not to be interrupted.'"

"Did it work, Mom?" I asked in a tiny voice. "Did the lights stay on?"

"I don't remember," she said, crying harder. "Our gas and electricity was turned off a number of times back then, and we moved a lot. It's your grandmother I'm talking about here. She always had a hope and a prayer, or some wild scheme, like impersonating a white social worker."

By 1935, both the American economy and my grandmother's finances improved enough for her and Aunt Annette to open their own beauty parlor, the New York Beauty Box. The shop was a source of pride and even made money. They closed five or six years later, but each retained a small home business. By then, Gram was a respected Harlem beautician who emphasized the care component of beauty culture. She was critical of lazy operators or those with "heavy hands" who burned or damaged hair with hot combs. She started a job by using the least amount of heat possible, always testing her irons on clean white rags that she used as a temperature gage. If the curling iron scorched the rag, it was too hot. Sometimes she tested it in the palm of her hand, like she did when she spit in her hand to test the clothes iron's temperature.

"Take pride in what you do," she said about her work. "Study each customer. Hair is a woman's crowning glory and God only gives you one head of it. These good professional products eliminated lard (as a hair grease) over fifty years ago, yet some unskilled operators still think they're supposed to get in that "kitchen" (nape of the neck) and cook. Go lightly; you can always add heat, but you can't replace a ruined head of hair."

When I came into the world, my grandmother had been living on Edgecombe several years, was sixty-one, but preferred being age fifty-four and went by that. Current New Yorkers are probably more neighborly than they used to be, because in the 1950s and '60s, you could live in a small building like 369 for half a lifetime and not get to know neighbors in the next door apartment. By the time I moved at age twelve, I had been there my whole life and only knew three of the twelve families on the floors above ours. But for a number of reasons, everybody knew my grandmother. First of all, she cussed and for some quirky semantic reason, that's what she did; she cussed, but didn't curse. Day and night can't describe the difference between cussing (or cursing) then and cussing now. But, the way she goosed-up words like hussy, bastard and sonofabitch, it would make a sailor blush.

An equal opportunity offender, she had it in for dumb bastards, white bastards, no-account bastards and the group she held in highest contempt—poor ignorant black bastards. "The only thing we colored people have to do," she used to preach, "is stay black and die and if you're black, there's a good chance you're going to be poor, so you better not be ignorant to boot."

One bastardly encounter took place in the halls of 369 when she was a new tenant and it must have been memorable because people were still talking about it twenty-five years later at her funeral. In the 1940s and '50s, bill collectors, like door-to-door salesmen, came to collect fifty cents to five dollar payments for everything from life insurance premiums to encyclopedia sets. Most people didn't answer the door when they wanted to avoid a bill collector, but Gram relished confrontation. At any rate, she chased the man from her front door, embarrassing him and everyone within hearing by yelling down the stairwell, "Now I dare you to come back again and tell me what I have to do, you long lanky cracker bastard."

Neighbors at the time thought she might be jailed, dispossessed or, worse, get all the black people thrown out because of the way she treated whites who needed to work in the building. It was not uncommon for people say to in my presence, "Miss Jeanie is crazy." Sometimes, but certainly not always, it was said with affection.

Mr. Levine, the bill collector she cussed out, had a job to do, so he did return. The suite of living room furniture I grew up with is what took Gram most of my childhood to pay him for. I was an infant during their early run-in, but I remember him well. He obviously figured out how not to antagonize her and, until I was eight or nine, came to our apartment sharing small talk and photos of his wife and two little boys.

"There is no explanation, rhyme or reason for what your grandmother did after she divorced Daddy and found out he was going to marry Miss Florence, his lady friend in Norfolk. I don't know what she expected the man to do," Mom said tensely, taking another sip of beer. "She wouldn't go South to live with him.

"During the war, there were many unlikely romances, but Mother must have been out of her mind when she met John Luacau, who was here in New York on leave. I remember him showing up at the house with a bouquet of white orchids, the kind of flowers we used to wear in our hair. Doing it up big, Luke took her downtown to see Benny Goodman, but all the soldiers were wooing women with flowers and expensive dates."

Gram's last name was Luacau but I had never understood why, since the only ex-husband she ever referred to was my grandfather, William Hodges. Instinctively, I always sensed that I should not ask Gram, my mother or aunts to tell me why her name was Luacau. Now with Mom crying harder and choking on her beer, I held my breath and shook my head at her next question: "Then, after a few weeks, do you know what Mother did?" I only knew a bomb had been released and was about to drop into this room; I just didn't know how big it would be.

"She married him. But Mother was fifty-seven years old and Luke was thirty-two."

Beyond commiserating with her sisters, Mom had never discussed my grandmother's May-December marriage with a living soul. I let out my breath and after a long stretch of silence figured it was my turn to speak, since she was spent.

"Were they happy?" I whispered.

"Happiness!" she practically spit. "That is hardly the word for that match or that time in our lives. Mother didn't like bastards. We'll never understand why she married one."

Despite the skeleton that came out of the closet after all these years, I was not aggrieved by news of my grandmother behaving badly. What quickened my heart was the decades of ache still in Mom's voice.

I should have been a source of comfort after watching and listening to her surrender this painful story. But a saucy in-your-face image of Gram kept interrupting our serious moment until the only thing I could do was laugh. I laughed a deep, tension-breaking guffaw made possible by the grace of fifty years and a mother who had not done such a thing to me. This rich piece of history was one more reason to love my brash grandmother and her talent for mocking convention.

"Mom, I understand your distress and embarrassment. All your friends' mothers were proper middle-aged women with husbands their own age. But I didn't live with her impropriety and I can't censor her for it. All I can say is how like her to fly in the face of custom and do what was expedient for her. I bet she never apologized to anyone or hung her head."

"No," Mom snapped, still indignant but I hoped she wasn't mad at me. "Mercifully, the marriage didn't last long and Luke eventually drifted back to Boston. His family was probably as relieved as we were. Mother never broke stride or cared what people thought. She didn't keep a low profile, either. For the rest of her life in New York, she grandly used the name, Mrs. Lena Lugenia Hodges Luacau."

"Mom, do you still care so much about this? It's really a remarkable story. How many women marry men half their age? He certainly didn't marry her for money. She was still a handsome, vivacious woman in the 1940s. I say more power to her. Besides you and Aunt Cee, who's alive who could possibly care and if they do, it's probably because they're jealous that she pulled it off."

"Her friends in Norfolk didn't know and wouldn't approve," my mother offered by way of explanation. "A few of their children are still in touch with our family. Your grandmother may have proudly worn the Hodges-Luacau name in New York, but the few times she visited Norfolk after divorcing Daddy and marrying Luke, she coyly remained Mrs. Lena Hodges."

"Give or take a few years, her friends would all be pushing 110 now," I reminded her, "and do you really care what their children think of something that happened over fifty years ago?"

My mother cared. Clearly, she had never looked upon this family secret as some sort of coup and despite my feelings, she never would. Telling this tale took a lot out of her, so we moved to another subject and I never considered bringing it up again.

To everyone's relief, Gram never said "I do" again. The only other gentleman to appear in her life was Ralph Walker, who knocked at our door one day after being told by Uncle Smitty that Mrs. Luacau had a room for rent. Ralph was a waiter on the New York Central Railroad and an ideal boarder because he spent half his time on trains, shuttling up and down the East coast.

Unlike Luke, Ralph was only about nine years younger than Gram. He also wasn't a high-strutting soldier with a dress brown army uniform. More on the order of a colored Mr. Peepers-type, Ralph was small, baby-faced, yellow-skinned with a hangdog look, a long Jay Leno chin and a strong Bay Rum scent. Soft-spoken and meek, he had a liking for Great

Gordon's Gin. It was only after drinking Great Gordon's that we might hear a peep out of him because he said, "It (gin) makes me want to straighten up and fly right and do the hucklebuck."

Although it caused him no end of trouble, Ralph had a favorite watering hole, the Fatman Bar and Grill on 155th Street and St. Nicholas. They traveled in different circles, but this was the same bar Thurgood Marshall frequented. Two or three times while at the Fatman, Ralph got "rolled," a term for getting your pocket picked. The last time it happened, he came home, his head hanging, confused and drunk, turning his pant pockets inside out.

Gram did what she could to battle the bottle for Ralph, mostly by chiding him for making a fool of himself in front of "those hustling high class St. Nicholas Avenue hussies." His slight frame, lurching-drunken gait and goofy grin marked him as easy prey, both at the bar and on the street. He showed up one night with a black eye, split lip and all his pay stolen. Gram told him it served his fool-ass right, but if he wanted to live in apartment twenty-two he had to pay his rent. That's when she got serious about straightening him out, and in the process became his sweetie. For six or seven years, until he moved back to Altoona when his mother took sick, Ralph lived in our apartment. Gram was his protector and nemesis. She bossed him around, made him take baths, wear clean shirts and stay sober if he wanted to sit at the table and eat a home-cooked meal with us.

I've salvaged a few impressions of one other man in my grandmother's life, Grandpa Hodges. When I was born, he was her ex-husband number two, Luke was number three and the first one, Mr. Hayes, Aunt Annette's father was long dead.

When I was eleven, Mom and I spent a week in Norfolk with Grandpa Hodges. A tall, handsome outdoorsman, he immediately charmed me by the way he grabbed our bags, tucked two suitcases under each long muscled arm, easily climbed a flight of stairs and led us into his living room where a shotgun was propped against the wall. Wearing a sweater vest, long socks and tweed knickers that bloused at the hips like jodhpurs, he welcomed us with the same slightly head-tilted smile as my Daddy's smile when he melted women's hearts.

"Welcome home, baby girl," he said grabbing Mom in a bear hug before giving me a sloppy, cigar-smelling, scratchy-face kiss and calling me his little baby girl. My grandpa was a chauffeur by trade, but his passion was hunting and his mannerisms those of a Southern gentleman used to having women wait on him.

Unlike Aunt Alethia, who still lived in my great grand-parents' one story house in the Broad Creek section of Norfolk, Grandpa had a newer, two bedroom, second floor apartment that was close to the downtown area, on a quiet, shady street lined with lush hickory and walnut trees. We were Grandpa's guests, but no sooner had we said hello, than Mom started doing all the work that week. She cooked the meals and washed the floor after Grandpa clomped through the rooms in mud-spattered boots. Later, he took a bath leaving a ring in the tub that looked like his five hound dogs and the dead raccoon he killed that morning were in there bathing with him. When he nervily expected one of us to clean the tub, I didn't feel so charmed anymore. I felt more like hitchhiking back to New York five days before the train left, because that seemed preferable to cleaning a scuzzy tub for a man who was strong enough to lift four suitcases and whose bathtub had been well scrubbed when we arrived.

When I balked, "I'm not touching that tub," Mom said, "Oh just settle down." Then she added, "and go up to the front room and show your grandfather some respect." She hadn't seen her father in four years and must have felt it was important to please him. With her job and having to care for Houston and me, now that Gram wasn't up to it, Mom rarely got to visit Grandpa and he never came to New York. But shoot, he was basically a stranger to me, because I hadn't seen him in six years and barely remembered him.

I walked out of the bathroom, leaving Mom awkwardly bent over the tub, smoke trailing from the lit Chesterfield in her left hand, scrub rag in the right as she tried not to splash Ajax and water on her new orange silk blouse. In the living room, Grandpa, his feet resting on the hassock and looking happy as a hyena, was chomping on his cigar. "Baby girl," he said when I warily eased into a chair across from him, "Go get me a beer out of the Frigidaire."

If I didn't learn anything else from that trip, it became a little clearer to me why Gram was no longer married to him.

I sometimes wonder what my grandmother would have been like if she lived in the latter half of the twentieth century, instead of the first part. Maybe she'd be ordinary; just another loudmouth rebel in a crowded field of contenders. When I think of her daily toilette, my heart skips a tiny beat of affection for that glamorous old gal. Early each morning, girdled and corseted, she did her hair, dabbed on make-up, got dressed. There were no purple-flowered muumuus or dowdy green housedresses in her closet.

With an eye for design, she was always placing orange-colored gladiolus around the living room and filling vases with fresh schefflera leaves. When I was halfway through high school, Gram was in poor health but she bought a new white, pickled-wood bedroom set, because she had saved the money and, in her old age, decided the dark furniture had to go. Completing the makeover was a pair of off-white drapery panels subtly splashed with red Chinese lettering. On her death bed, she told Mom to give them to me.

Gram spent her last days wearing one of two new pink nightgowns that Mom had rushed downtown to buy on sale at Macy's. Gram was in a private hospital room, poking at mushy meat, criticizing overcooked vegetables and complaining bitterly about using a bedpan. In those days, doctors did not plug patients up with tubes and wires. When the organs shut down, you were allowed to die in dignity, but it never occurred to me that my grandmother was dying. On her last day, I left the hospital to have dinner with a guy that I still dislike because it's easy to blame him, instead of myself, for leaving my grandmother. He was cheap, wanted to go Dutch when guys didn't do that, and he wasn't worth knowing anyhow. The previous two nights, I'd eaten dinner in the hospital cafeteria with Mom. When I got up to leave for my date, Gram told me something I didn't understand. She said, "Slow down, Jean. It's too late to be rushing." She must have been telling me she was going to die.

Late that evening, I walked into the hospital room and found my mother frantically manipulating Gram's mouth. She was wrestling with the silver clips on her dentures, not thinking yet about grieving, or calling the nurse or telling me what was painfully obvious; that I missed by minutes, saying goodbye to my grandmother.

Mom looked up, saw me standing in the door and blurted out, "As God is my witness, she'd never forgive us if we buried her without teeth, but I can't figure out how to get them in her mouth."

13. Cubans and Cousins

We didn't know it then—we just took things for granted—but my grandmother was a linchpin, and the only member of the Brown family with the personality and drive to hold our extended clan together. For years, she hosted Sunday dinners, and one regular guest was ninety-two-year-old A-Nette (short for Aunt Nette). A-Nette was a fragile, sweet-natured, white-looking lady with a mass of wiry white hair hanging to the back of her knees that Gram washed and untangled for her. Our family matriarch, and the last of my great grandmother's five sisters, A-Nette was always accompanied by her daughter, Vernetta, a beautiful copper-tone replica of her mother, but with long black hair.

Vernetta worked as cashier at the Hotel Theresa's coffee shop, a glam job if ever there was one. Her duties entailed sitting on her butt all day looking good, while making change for playboys, entertainers and heads of state. I'll tell you about the head of state in a minute, but first it should be noted that for a short time, Aunt Cee took over Vernetta's job when she left. Like most of what takes place in this book, these visits were in the 1950s and early '60s when Harlem was under siege by drug lords and addicts, but also when the community developed into a national center for civil rights activity.

When World War II ended, the nation finally started responding to Negro demands for equal rights. A major policy shift occurred when President Truman desegregated the Armed Forces. Then, in 1955 the Montgomery, Alabama bus boycott resulted in a Supreme Court decision outlawing segregation on public transportation. The momentum brought forth Dr. Martin Luther King, Jr. and spawned a crop of young

Northern activists such as Stokely Carmichael, leader of the
Student Non Violent Coordinating Committee (SNCC).
Established organizations like the NAACP and Congress
of Racial Equality (CORE) were energized, leading to the
South's lunch counter sit-ins and Freedom Rides, then culmi-
nating in the 1963 March on Washington, where Dr. King
delivered his seminal, "I Have a Dream" speech.

Despite drugs and crime, Harlem's location appealed to
national civil rights leaders who needed to strategize without fear of being shot at, or lynched, and they chose Harlem.
Uptown was a hotbed of political change, but Negroes weren't
the only folks acting up; so were the Russians. Ten years earlier,
the Russians were America's staunch ally—a mighty force
that helped bring down Hitler. Now with Cold War tensions
running high, Nikita Khrushchev, Russia's UN representa-
tive, turned up the heat by demonstrating exactly what sort
of loose canons we were dealing with. In an incident heard
around the world, red-faced and angry, Khrushchev started
pounding his fist on the table. When that didn't achieve the
desired result, he took his shoe off, and used it to bang the
table during the United Nations General Assembly meeting,
previously an inner sanctum of decorum.

American officials had one wary eye on the Russians and
the other on Negroes, when Fidel Castro chose this inopportune
time to declare victory in his "Democratic Front" war against
Cuban President Batista, the "legitimate" but repressive ruler
of their country. After vanquishing Batista, Castro stunned the
US with the "C" word, meaning the United States now had a
Communist country just ninety miles off the coast of Florida.

If you were an affluent New Yorker in the 1950s and '60s,
Cuba—with its white sand beaches, year-round tropical
climate and flavor of bad boy Hemingway mystique—was the
go-to Caribbean vacation spot. But up in Harlem, beyond
an appreciation for Afro-Cuban music that was far from
universal, I think blacks were generally unaware or neutral

198

towards Cuban affairs. All that changed the day Castro showed up at the Hotel Theresa.

There are a number of explanations about how that happened. As a new head of state, he was in New York for the same UN General Session as Khrushchev, and scheduled to stay downtown at the Shelburne Hotel. One screaming head-line version of why Castro switched hotels claimed he arrived with a flock of live chickens that he intended to slaughter for food and the Shelburne refused to admit him with the birds. Another story said their staff freaked at the sight of twenty or thirty battled-toughened and visibly armed revolutionaries wearing fatigues. It's not as though downtown hotels weren't familiar with Communists, but the Russians at least hid their guns under suits.

Whatever his reasons, Castro's appearance on 125th Street shook up Harlem, its ailing economy and ended all community apathy toward Cuba. His stay also focused international atten-tion on the civil rights movement because Castro expressed solidarity with the Negros' quest to win their fight for equality. If the Cuban leader was trying to unnerve the establishment, he succeeded by first chatting amicably with Khrushchev, then holding a high profile meeting with Malcolm X. That matchup helped legitimatize Malcolm, who was then a fiery young member of Elijah Mohammad's Black Muslim sect.

My family and neighbors considered Black Muslims little more than a band of ex-convicts like Malcolm and were not happy hearing him preach about self-sufficiency without cooperation from white society. After all, most everyone said, that's what we've been doing for 200 years, and it hasn't produced the desired effect. Such radical views and calls for violence against "whitey" resulted in Malcolm being expelled from the Muslims. In time, he would moderate his extreme views and start his own Organization of Afro American Unity, which he headed until his assassination in 1963.

Vernetta was working at Hotel Theresa during Castro's stay and passed along as much gossip as she could, considering the hotel was in lockdown mode, and under siege from revolutionary guards and half of the NYPD that wasn't downtown keeping an eye on Khrushchev. Apparently the chickens were a no-show at the hotel, which was a great relief for the housekeeping staff, but for years a trail of chicken jokes remained embedded in hotel lore, like the one that said the birds died of fright on the way uptown when they heard fried chicken was the colored people's national dish. More likely, if they ever existed, the birds were left behind because Castro felt safe at the Hotel Theresa and no longer feared his food would be poisoned.

Beyond music collaborations, Harlem never bonded well with its Cuban population. Before Miami, Manhattan was a central hub for Cuban immigrants. After Castro's take-over, black and white islanders flocked into New York by the planeload, many settling around 135th Street and Broadway, in that nebulous area that's a block too far west to be Harlem, and too far south to be called Washington Heights, so it became New York's Little Havana. There were language barriers and cultural differences between Negroes and their neighbors, but a simpatico also existed, as it often does among people of color in this race-conscious world.

Part of the frostiness stemmed from skin color and that complex word, mulatto. American slave owners had pretty much stomped out the word mulatto and black people rarely used the term. In our country, even if you came out white, you were black and less than human in some eyes. In the Caribbean and in Central and South America, mulattos were accorded more recognition as a subgroup of the African, Indian and white races. But here in America, we were colored and no one cared if you were part something else, so don't be acting like you were. So, as far as Harlem's blacks were concerned, that mulatto nonsense was the rap against Cubans who often looked blacker than us, but eschewed the black race.

Putting differences aside, when it comes to Fidel, the love affair that began in 1960s Harlem has not completely ended.

People don't always understand what conditions are like in Cuba under Castro, but to many he remains the good guy. Ask some older black men or women what they know of Castro's affiliation with our community. If they know anything at all, they first mention that he stayed there. They will also tell you his long-ago war was good for Cuba because Castro took all the rich people's money and redistributed it to the poor.

No story about Harlem can be told without introducing Southern relatives like mine, who annually visited us from Virginia. These family folks were so much more colorful than the literally and figuratively colorless Philadelphia clan. The Virginians also provided a reality check. When they showed up, little New York sophisticates, who considered themselves long removed from anything backwoods or countrified, got an object lesson in what it meant to be part of a gene pool. Such reminders in my life would be my two great aunts, Alethia and Martha who, over the years, showed up for quite a few Sunday dinners at our house.

Alethia was caboose shaped—a tiny rectangle of a woman with a motormouth. One of the last times she stayed with us, I recall her being in our house about ten minutes before she changed into her housedress. Next she filled a glass with ice and placed it near a box of starch, then settled comfortably on the couch. With her short legs dangling above the floor, she started eyeballing the hint of a figure taking shape beneath and above my purple pedal pushers.

"O-liv-e-Ah," she boomed her thundering bell-tone roar at my mother, who was seated across the 11x12 foot room, "can this be your baby girl?"

Standing in the doorway, I was a head taller than I'd been when she last saw me in Norfolk. Nodding along with my mother, I spoke up, "It's me, Aunt Alethia. I'm not a baby girl anymore."

"So I seeeee." She wiggled a half dozen "e's" in my direction, exaggerating the importance of a few inches and making me feel special with her relentless cheer.

"Since I last saw you, you've grown faster than the weeds in my yard. You're looking more and more like your pretty mamma." That, I thought, was going a little far, since this was my pimply, bad-hair era. Patting the empty space next to her, she tingle-linged me over. "Jee-een-ee, come sit by your old auntie, and see what surprises I bought you." Leaning forward, she pulled presents from the suitcase at her feet, and handed me a box of salt water taffy. She was also on a new kick with her present-giving. For the past two summers, she had given me a keepsake that once belonged to my great grandmother. This year's gift was a cream-colored platter with red trim and spider veins crackling the ceramic glaze that I did not want, but still have. I also have great Grandma's pressed glass salad bowl that Mom wisely stored, then re-gifted to me fifteen years later.

I ate the taffy and listened to Aunt Alethia fill Gram in on news from Norfolk, starting with Henry, who had apparently gone and done it this time.

"Henry really showed his behind. Hattie put him out for good after the police found him wandering around downtown. Liquor and women. Always was his problem," Aunt Alethia said, opening the box of starch. "If it wasn't one, it was the other." Stopping to catch her breath, she looked at Gram. "Jeanie, didn't you used to have a thing for Henry when we were girls?"

"No," Gram denied, "and our friend Hattie should have known better than marry him. I couldn't tell her anything because I had kept a little company with Henry, but I knew that boy was trouble from the git go, because he thought he was cuter than me."

"You're right about his big head," Aunt Alethia agreed. Before moving on to news of Miss Louise's daughter's wedding, they concluded Hattie would take him back because she always did.

The news on Miss Louise's daughter (a child in the family Aunt Alethia worked for) was about her coming home to marry the Northern boy she had been keeping company with, and how her family gave the largest wedding Norfolk ever saw.

"Being an only girl," Alethia said, looking in the starch box, then jiggling her glass of ice, "you knew her daddy was going to marry her off big. Some bridesmaids and groomsmen came from as far away as Massachusetts, near that college where they met.

"Remember Fletcher, Jeanie? He's still living in those three piss-poor rooms; refuses to fix them up. And speaking of fixing houses, I saved the best news for last. You wouldn't know the old house. I replaced the water pump with an inside faucet and got a real cook stove. (When I'd last been there, she used a wood-fired cooking stove and drew water from a pump at her rustic kitchen sink). No more wood for me. The city came through a while ago offering incentives for senior citizens to modernize our homes."

Small and jolly, Aunt Alethia laughed with abandon, drank bourbon lustily and gave hip checks to prove she could still "cut a rug" and "...shimmy like a four-legged ape." When her motor ran down, she started chewing ice and daintily plopping clumps of starch into her mouth. She looked like a kid eating cracker jacks, but Aunt Alethia ate Argo laundry starch, the kind intended to stiffen clothes. The adults never mentioned her odd habit and until recently, I hadn't heard of a condition called pica. It's an abnormal desire to eat unusual substances such as chalk, ashes, dirt, clay and ice.

My other elfin great aunt, Martha, waddled into our life like a toothache you figure you can live with for a few days until the dentist returns, but after twenty-four hours, you just want that sucker gone. She was Gram's middle sister, a no-fun-at-all tightwad, sporting wooly hair mashed under a Ma Clampett-style hat she often wore inside the house. One time she showed up with a man named Bill, her new husband, who she called

Mr. Blevins. The oddest thing about him, other than being married to her, was he had no other obvious defects. I can't remember if she had teeth, but an occasional smile would have done wonders to soften her lantern jaw.

Martha was the money manager in their marriage and she allowed him to have a daily quarter so he could buy cigarettes and, as far as I could tell, that twenty-five cents per diem was all the money either of them spent while in New York. Bill always handed her any change from his cigarette purchase, and for the next few minutes she picked over pennies, as if one might be made of gold. Just before Gram was about to serve dinner one evening, her count didn't add up and she growled at him, "Go back to the store. And straighten this matter. Out."

This aunt was christened Martha Fanny Brown but, for some inexplicable down-home reason, kept her childhood nickname, Ma Fanny. Everyone called her Ma Fanny, except me. I called her Aunt Martha, steering clear of the Fanny part, because she had the biggest butt I ever saw. Until I learned how the story went, I assumed the family called her Ma Fanny because her backside looked like she carried a suitcase on it, and with her being so weird and all, she just put up with sixty years of insults.

I guess Alethia and Martha and their peculiar ways were more like country cousins than women who hailed from the big city of Norfolk. At the time, Norfolk was Virginia's second largest, with a population around 300,000 people. Being from the northern-most Southern state (Maryland doesn't count, because it still isn't sure if it's North or South), the Virginians considered themselves genteel and somewhat worldly. True, Virginia was racially segregated and it claimed Aunt Martha as a resident, but it wasn't, say, Mississippi. Almost every Negro in America thought those poor black folks in Mississippi just lived in pure hell.

Having visited Norfolk helped me understand a few things about the South, like why Aunt Martha could spend the better part of a week sitting on our couch, arms crossed over her bosom, waiting until it was time to go home. In Norfolk, time was a state treasure measured by day-long waits for the telephone party line to free up, our ride to show up or the day to cool down, before we could do anything. We visited an ancient neighbor lady up the road and had to speak in whispers while we waited in a dark parlor that smelled like moth balls until she woke up and finished having her say about my great grandfather Lazarus' mean old mule.

Trooping dispiritedly back up the road in the pitch black to Aunt Alethia's, even Gram said, "Lord, that did take awhile, didn't it? But I could never show my face in Norfolk again, if I didn't make a courtesy call on Miss Erskine. You'll enjoy tomorrow's planned visit better," she assured me, "because we are going to see Mag."

"Will she keep falling asleep, too?"

"I don't think Mag ever sleeps. She has enough energy for two women."

"Who's Mag?"

"It's Magdalena, but she goes by Mag, and it's Aunt Mag to you. She's my ex-sister-in-law. Before he died, she was married to William's brother. They lived in the country on a farm, and we'll ride out there in a car."

Norfolk's bus service was limited, but Gram wasn't going to ride in back of a bus anyway, so she paid a man named Mr. Hudgins to drive us. Hiring oneself out as a driver was commonly how blacks earned money, and their passengers got to travel short or long distances with dignity. The night before the hour-long journey, Gram reminded Aunt Alethia that they needed to get going early. That sounded good to me, because some days we didn't get going at all.

"You can set your clock by Earl (Mr. Hudgins). He's as reliable as the day is long."

"Say what you will, Alethia, but we don't need to be out after dark. If we meet any peckerwoods on those roads tomorrow, we want it to be in daylight."

205

This time, because they wanted to get back before dark, we headed off after breakfast, which was about lunch time back home. We didn't run into any peckerwoods, or much of anything else besides a lot of hot, dry wind blowing through the car. Sometimes the straight ahead highway and monotonous scenes of tall roadside grass was broken up by a false lake shimmering ahead of us in melting road tar. What we did eventually come upon was a chain gang. It was a punishing hot day and it took too much effort to talk, but there at the side of the road were about ten black men in gray prison uniforms scything down tall grass. A white man in a wide hat, sweat stains soaking his khaki shirt, sat on horseback watching them work, a rifle resting across his saddle. There was enough cleared brush to reveal lengths of chain attached to the men's ankles. Mr. Hudgins speeded up. Gram saw me staring at them, and in a thick voice, said, "Jean, turn your head. We don't stare at those poor fellas."

When we arrived at Aunt Mag's, I thought farm was a bit of a stretch for a vegetable garden and several acres of hardscrabble land Aunt Mag lived on without lights or running water, although she kept chickens, a cow and a pen of pigs that I watched her slop. Slop was a good description for what she did, because it entailed feeding them a late lunch of dried, scraped-from-the-pan leftover morning grits, orange peels, egg shells and other garbage. Animals down there, like Untouchables in India, led a hard, almost invisible existence. Each time I came within ten feet of a cat, dog, pig or mule, someone warned me away with, "Don't touch." That some animals survived at all was a near miracle, since their caregivers didn't dispense much care or notice missing ears, tails, patches of fur or mangled body parts. One-eyed, rheumy dogs and cats limped around, and no one took them to the vet or tut-tutted over their hurts. To earn a few meager scraps of food, animals had jobs to do, like chasing strangers away from the house or rabbits out the garden. Cats controlled mice, terrorized fruit-eating birds and as a reward, routinely got their kittens drowned. Four-legged creatures were banned from the house, routinely kicked, told to shoo, git, scat and called ugly names like mangey-flea-bitten-mongrel-bitch.

The short stay at Aunt Mag's was unfortunate because once we disembarked from the St. Charles ferryboat on our trip down to Virginia, the woman with the weathered, heart-shaped face and Annie Oakley cowgirl vibe was the best thing I saw in Virginia. After serving us a lunch of homemade biscuits and gravy, a couple of fresh-killed fried chickens, and corn and tomatoes from a jar, Mag grabbed her rifle. "For snakes," she told me, then took hold of my hand with her free one. "Jeanie," she said to my grandmother, "you don't mind if I walk a ways with Olivia's young'n, do you? I'd like to get to know her some, and she'll want to see the litter."

Gram, Aunt Alethia and Mr. Hudgins were feasting on homemade ice cream and a pie filled with red fruit and tart berries I'd never tasted before. My grandmother waved goodbye to me as though wading into a yard full of pecking chickens was something I did everyday.

"They don't do anything," Aunt Mag said when I flinched and squeezed her calloused hand harder. "They're just birds. Cat got your tongue?" she asked.

I shook my head no, but couldn't speak in the presence of something so formidable as this aunt who wasn't an aunt, but an ex in-law twice removed—a lady named Mag. "That's okay, honey. You don't remember me but I've knowed you since before you were born. I watched over your mother, Olivia, when she was just a bit younger than you."

At the pig pen, I finally spoke. "Can I go in there and pet the little pigs?"

"No, their mama wouldn't understand. You can't touch the pigs."

Despite that one setback, I'm still in awe of that pioneer woman with gooseberry stains running down her apron. Just like Gram had said, Aunt Mag had enough energy for two women, plus, strength to push a 500-pound sow out of the way so I could see her babies, and she produced mouth-watering food in a kitchen that was about as updated as a cowboy's chuck wagon.

Aunt Martha didn't wrestle pigs out of her way, like Aunt Mag, or eat starch like Aunt Alethia—she dipped snuff. At our house, once the hugs and so-glad-to-see-yous ended, I detected an undercurrent of ill will, and things best left unsaid when Martha was in town. Respect for elders was engrained in all three generations of our house, but watching Martha squirt tobacco into an empty, 20 ounce cling peach can gave Mom dry heaves. I avoided Aunt Martha, too. A lipful of her snuff turned into a watery brown reminder of the bottle of Father John's I'd hidden in the bedpan on top of our toilet tank.

Gram, who told you off in a minute if you crossed her, was born into a culture of snuff-dipping, tobacco-chewing women and silently accommodated her sister's nasty habit. Gram was also uncharacteristically charitable about what the rest of us thought were Martha's bad manners. When Alethia visited, she pitched in to wash dishes, clear the table or help tidy up. Martha arrived empty handed and hunkered-down, as if she was stranded in a snowstorm, until it was time to go back to Norfolk.

Like Alethia, Martha had a voice, but hers was deep and mannish. She hiccuped words, bit off ends of sentences, punctuated at will, and remained as out of step with the rhythm of language, as the rhythm of life. "Can't get used to those new gas stoves. Jeanie," she chipped. "Now if you had some wood for Mr. Blevins. To chop. He'd kindly oblige. Used to chop my own. Til I married. Bill Blevins. Here. Yes siree. I did. Lend a hand. Dinner. But know how par-tic-u-li you are. In your kitchen. Best not disturb you."

One summer, Alethia and Martha were in New York at the same time and all the women decided to have a beach party. Several years before, when I didn't drown in the country club pool, I promised God I wouldn't complain anymore about going on day-long picnics. But I'd forgotten my promise, and being almost a teenager, I had new ideas about having a good time, and spending all day with Aunt Martha wasn't one of them. Still, the beach trip had potential since we would go in Aunt Annette's sharp white and baby blue Ford Fairlane that she hardly ever took out the garage.

Actually, before events proved me correct, the going to Queens part of the plan was what made me think the day would go wrong. Negroes had started patronizing Long Island's Jones Beach. With its Olympic size swimming pool, clean concession stands and concrete bathrooms that didn't resemble Rockaway's shabby, splitter-filled shacks, Jones Beach was like a resort. But we were going to Far Rockaway Queens, because the Southern aunties formed a conga line of protest, with Aunt Martha sticking her fat lip out and Aunt Alethia insisting, "We're not going all the way out to any Long Island where half those people haven't seen coloreds. We'll just stay right here with our own kind, in New York-thank-you-ma'am-City." That's how things unfolded; on a sour note.

Aunt Annette found the beach despite six women, including my mother and Aunt Cee, directing her to a place in Queens that none of them knew how to get to. On the beach, while they organized the usual mountain of food these trips entailed, I spotted a pint of bourbon in Aunt Alethia's beach bag and knew this would be one of the longest days of my life.

The fussing and instructing was endless. Aunt Annette thought Mom's ice tea could have used more sugar. Mom thought it tasted fine. Aunt Martha, her bottom lip, bulging with snuff, didn't try to hide the fact that she was spitting in a can she'd half buried in the sand, often missing her mark. In her fog horn baritone, she growled, "I feel peckish. What'd ya'll pack. To eat."

Turning her back on Martha, Mom instructed me, "Jean, go get your feet wet. Don't just sit there. Or build a sand castle," she added.

"I don't want to build a castle." Already miserable, I watched a beach full of toddlers and little kids with bright colored buckets, digging and dumping sand to make sand castles. Many of them had siblings or a friend along. I did not bring friends on these trips, nor was I asked to accompany Mary Jo or Dedi when they went on picnics. Family bonds were so sacred among black families, the practice of including outsiders was not encouraged. Not too far from our blankets, a group of young teenagers, not much older than me, were rubbing baby oil onto each other's backs while listening to a transistor radio and managing to have a good time without six adult chaperones and enough food to feed forty people.

Gram kept offering me ham, baloney and egg salad sandwiches. The fried chicken was for dinner. "Don't get sand in your hair," she reminded me, "it's too hard to wash out."

"Put your shoes on," Mom said, "before you use the bathroom; and stop asking when we're going home."

I wasn't feeling it, but this was love being passed around. These women were the body and blood of my ancestry. Unused to full days of pleasure, they deserved their fun in the sun. For my grandmother, certainly, getting her to relax or behave in a frivolous way was just short of expecting Jesus to show up and part the waters of Rockaway Bay. A picnic or beach outing were the only times she got out of her corset and stays.

All day the women just laughed, shooed flies, nibbled on limp sandwiches and warm potato salad that, for some reason, in that pre-frozen blue ice era, never killed any of us. I was impatient with the old-fashioned ways of my great aunts, embarrassed by their outdated bathing suits, felt they cooked too much food, toted too many baskets and didn't act groovy like Mom and Sandra, when I went to Jones Beach with them.

By five o'clock, fighting tears of boredom and frustration, black from sun and gritty with sand, I longed to be back home, where I pictured my friends licking creamsicles in the shade, hoola-hooping, or maybe Mary Jo was showing them how to dance the Watusi. For my trouble, the women ignored me.

"Little Jeanie," Aunt Alethia piped up late in the afternoon, "you tickle me to death, acting like old folks who just want to sit up at home."

I dared not, but I wanted to tell her to leave me alone. Instead, I took another walk down the beach, returning after a detour to the concession stand, for a snow cone I was too full to eat. Now with evening coming on fast and Aunt Alethia full of happy hour bourbon mixed with a stiff, eight-hour sun chaser, I was suddenly the funniest thing she'd seen since Moms Mabley. "You're just like a Grandma," she said, doubled over with laughter. "That's what I'm going to call you from now on, Grandma."

Everyone was amused, and at first I was, too, because it was the only halfway funny thing that day. But the name stuck like gum on a shoe, following me home, then into my teens, until it mercifully died before Aunt Annette—especially, but occasionally even Mom—ever called me the no-longer-funny Grandma, in front of my friends.

Banner seen on Edgecombe Avenue. (Jim Cummins)

14. Unfortunately, She Didn't Care What the Neighbors Thought

One of my bi-monthly chores was delivering $33.00, half a month's rent, to the landlord's office. We had a large apartment, but $66.00 was a substantial sum of money to live anywhere, especially Harlem, although Sugar Hill housing was perennially high because it started out inflated in the 1920s and '30s, when buildings first "went black." To fill units and recoup loses during the depression, developers and landlords saw little alternative to adding Negroes to the area's best housing stock. Watching desirable Sugar Hill apartments get snapped up by black folks must have been painful for many white landlords, although they assuaged some of their hurt by jacking up prices. In the early 1940s when my grandmother moved on the block, rents were steep and salaries low.

Mom, a bright young woman with excellent secretarial skills, earned $1,500 a year working at the *Amsterdam News*. Jean Beverly's husband Jimmy, a subway conductor, made $1.00 per hour, a little more than my mother. Mr. Drayton, Mary Jo's daddy, likely received a similar Transit Authority salary for manning the subway coin booth on 145th Street. These men and postal workers, such as Uncle Harry and a host of neighbors and friends, were glad to pull all-night shifts for $1.00 an hour because many of their parents had picked North Carolina tobacco and Georgia peanuts for $1.00 a day, if that. Though proud to have dignified employment and thrilled to live on Sugar Hill, it was hard for many folks to make ends meet. Families juggled and finagled, bought necessities "on time," and sometimes pawned a personal item until payday. But it was also common to do without and treasure what little you had.

Our family had several income streams, including my grandmother's personal injury settlement from the City when she fell and injured herself in the street, but another safety net was Ralph, the roomer. To accommodate him, Gram changed the front parlor into a bedroom (creating a fourth bedroom by eliminating a dining room) and shared a closet with me.

Leaseholders and boarders cohabited under arrangements of dignity and survival. There was no stigma to being a roomer, nor in having one. If anything, you were thought to have good business sense for snaring a large apartment, or four-story townhouse that outsiders helped pay for. There were exceptions, but Sugar Hill boarders tended to be honest, quiet, fiscally responsible subtenants who paid on time, and if they didn't, someone else was waiting in line to take their place.

Most boarders were single people, like Ralph, who opted for a simple lifestyle and didn't want the responsibility of a full-time apartment. Until Jack and Mom married, he was a boarder in an apartment on St. Nicholas Avenue. Mirrored walls were all the rage then, but Jack's landlord used a mirrored bar to brighten up a corner of his living room. It helped create depth and reflect artificial light in what would have otherwise been an ordinary dark, back-courtyard apartment. Subtenants lived contentedly in other people's home for years. They admired the decor, shared neighborhood gossip and a sense of community that occasionally led to them taking over an apartment, when principal tenants died or moved out.

When it came to housing, a man named Mr. D. Edward Smith was a prominent figure around Sugar Hill. Mr. Smith was our landlord, and he operated an insurance and real estate business from the second floor of his St. Nicholas Avenue townhouse, about a ten-minute walk away. Mr. Smith did not believe in friendly chit chat or small talk; he got right to the point when I walked into his office. "What can we do for you, young miss?" he always asked, as if there were two of him sitting there, or he didn't know I had been coming to his office for eight or nine years with my grandmother and she was no longer standing beside me.

A solemn and formally dressed black man, Mr. Smith was a throwback to an earlier time, when gentlemen wore cutaway morning coats and hightop lace-up shoes, which is how he dressed. During business hours, he wore a tight-fitting jacket and pinstriped pants that looked like he might have worn them to someone's wedding thirty years ago. Mr. Smith was the prototype of a successful West Indian businessman who was resented by Negroes from the South. In Harlem, West Indians were often perceived as haughty outsiders who established businesses, then set high prices or rents to enrich themselves at the expense of black customers. West Indians were also respected and grudgingly admired for their achievements, including strides in the medical field, because Negro doctors and dentists were often Jamaican, Barbadian and Trinidadian.

In comparison, over thirty million Southern blacks who moved North were leery of a country that for generations had stacked the deck against them. Many were under- or uneducated and used to being cheated, humiliated and physically harmed by officials. West Indians deplaned at Idlewild International Airport with confidence, big expectations and some degree of business sense, including a rigorous British schooling system that went far in helping them achieve their big expectations.

The divide between black Americans and islanders was wide and the relationship complex. Both banded together to protect themselves from a common enemy, the white man, but they didn't always like it. My grandmother was not a fan of West Indians. She thought they were arrogant and clannish, didn't like their cooking and said they squeezed a dollar so hard, she could hear the eagle scream. Being our landlord, Mr. Smith was her favorite target, and I will say this about him, he was deadly serious about collecting her dollars.

Sitting through his procedures felt like I was buying 369, instead of just paying a half month's rent. He used an inkwell, like the one in my desk at school, only his had ink in it. The transaction was recorded in a large blue ledger, on the page that said 369 Edgecombe. When he finally found the

215

right page, he scratched a number three, rolled a blotter over it, inspected it, dipped the nib in the well, then did it again and again until $33.00, date and name were just the way he wanted them. He repeated the same steps to fill out a receipt. I ran this errand during what should have been about twenty, not forty-five minutes to an hour slashed from my play time. I remember watching him writing, blotting and messing around and thinking he seriously needed to use some of that money and hire a secretary.

As a family, we didn't have a lot, but in Harlem the gap between haves and have-nots was fuzzy. Positive thinking was common among children on Sugar Hill because adults instilled it in us, but I knew enough about social order to realize everyone on the block wasn't as well off as I was, especially the Franklin kids. They wore dingy, too-large, hand-me-downs. Every morning on our way to school, we watched Mr. Franklin head for work in his wool tweed suit that was too long in the arms, sagged at the knees and dragged at the cuffs. Later around 5:30 p.m., trying to, but not fooling anyone, Mr. Franklin did a tight tip-toe down the middle of Edgecombe, determined to be dignified, through drunk. The oldest Franklin boy was my friend, and after seeing me give him half my popsicle, I came upstairs and Gram said, "You know, those boys all need haircuts and it would only take me a little while to cut their hair." Gram liked Mrs. Franklin and felt sorry that her husband drank up the little money he made.

The Franklins were down on their luck, but not lowdown, like the new people in the basement, whose arrival set the neighborhood's teeth on edge. "Their fast daughter, with her bosom hanging out," Gram complained, "is nothing but lowdown basement trash. And that conked-haired son is a lowdown national disgrace."

When cool weather chased everyone indoors, most complainers forgot about the Lowdowns and found something else to gripe about. But then Gladys, who lived in their building, reported to Gram that she had been in the basement laundry room and peeked in Mrs. Lowdown's open apartment door and saw her preparing potato salad for a chitlin party.

"Mrs. Luacau, I waved at her, but all I could see were the eyes on those boiled potatoes. I saw those eyes, and half-peeled skins looking at me and I just wanted to tell her to give me a knife and I'd help make the potato salad."

"It's no wonder the daughter's the way she is," Gram backtracked to the summer theme, "with a slovenly mother and dumb father who's blind to everything that goes on around him. What could the landlord have been thinking when he let them in that building? They already pay next to no rent, and she has to have a chitlin party. Would you please tell me who in their right mind would spend good money to eat that woman's food?"

It's no secret that underemployed, marginally educated and disillusioned citizens populated rundown sections of Harlem. Like all residents, the poor wanted better lives, but as soon as they moved up, down or around town, they brought criticism and unease, like the basement family.

Upper, middle and lower class Negroes didn't just square off during my childhood in the 1950s when the community was the symbol of poor black America. The duality had long been there and today's residents continue grappling with Harlem's uppity, versus its lowly image and lifestyle.

When I was young, some black people openly pointed the finger at rural Negroes just up from the South. They felt that their ignorant, unsophisticated behavior and lack of familiarity with indoor plumbing, for instance, not only damaged buildings, but fanned racism against blacks in general.

As you can imagine, Gram had strong opinions about maintaining Edgecombe's integrity, and neighbors weren't shy about using her as their mouthpiece to address problems of unmopped halls, or loud teenagers hanging out on benches or stoops. Three qualities made her an excellent enforcer: she was outrageous, fearless and she didn't know what embarrassment was.

According to our upstairs neighbor, Sadie Spratley, "When Jean got something stuck in her craw, she didn't swallow the way most people did. No, whether friend or foe, Jean chewed you up.

"I once sent your grandmother a Christmas card," Sadie recalled. "She'd been visiting in my apartment when I was addressing the cards and saw my box of really beautiful cards. To neighbors, I sent out plain inexpensive cards, plus one of my boys addressed them for me because I didn't need to write special greetings for people I saw almost every day.

"Well, Jean got my card and called me on the phone to say, 'Sadie, why would you send me a lesser card like this? I know you had nicer Christmas cards and I'm hurt that you sent me a cheap card like this one here, and you didn't even write it out yourself.'"

"I tell you, she never missed a trick. You shouldn't have even tried pulling one over on her, because she'd tell you about yourself in a minute. She caught me good the time I threw her hat away. We used to wear hats all the time, and Jean bought this hat, but decided it wasn't a good choice for her, so she gave it to me. I didn't like the hat either, so I threw it away. I thought I'd stashed it carefully in the trash, but she saw the hat on the dumbwaiter when it got down to her floor and, Jean being Jean, was not about to let it go. Man, did she let me know how she felt about throwing that hat away. But Jean was my good friend. Boy, could she make me laugh. When she was around, things never stayed dull for long."

Mom's best neighbor friend was Eloise Drayton, Mary Jo's mother. They visited while hanging clothes on the line, or passing borrowed sugar back and forth from the middle bedroom window in each apartment, the point where the buildings connected.

Eloise was a huge Jackie Robinson and Brooklyn Dodgers fan, even though I thought she should switch to the Giants after Willie Mays became our neighbor. She explained that baseball fans don't pick teams based on where players live. I didn't understand intricacies of the game, but Willie seemed a good enough reason to like baseball. I developed a little girl crush on him and became dismayed when, a few years after becoming one of us, he married a lady named Margherite. I had hoped he might wait until I grew up so he could marry me.

In warm weather, Eloise's kitchen radio stayed tuned to Dodger baseball and, in those pre-air conditioned days of summer, we heard whoops of joy echoing through the courtyard when Jackie did something wonderful at Ebbetts Field. "Hey Eloise," someone, maybe Mr. Spratley who lived above us, might call across the courtyard, "what'd your boy Jackie do this time?" In the strange language of baseball, she answered, "Jackie just threw Dusty Rhodes out at the plate," or "he pulled off a double play... stole home... hit a triple." Happy talk, signaling all was right with the world.

It was a world where, in summer, neighbors opened all their windows, sometimes doors too, to capture cross breezes blowing off the Atlantic. We didn't have our radio turned up to baseball, but our apartment stayed in the spotlight because of my grandmother's antics, although she had plenty of help from company who paraded through our house, especially crazy Charlie.

My Godmother Dedi was married to Charlie. As we evolved into their surrogate New York family, they came regularly for Gram's cornbread and oxtail stew Sunday soul food dinners and Dedi, who was Irish, dipped into a steaming hot bowl like everyone else.

Our hearty meals were cooked from scratch and laden with fresh vegetables and fat. Healthier cuisine hadn't reached Harlem kitchens, or if it had, no one was interested. For weeks at a time, Gram went on a soul food tear, cooking up animal parts like tongue, pigtail, pig feet, snoots and oxtails, which I

219

bought for her at the corner butcher. Like all these cuts, oxtail is what the name implies, the tail of an ox. But when oxtail is cut up, seasoned and cooked in a thick brown broth with onions, potatoes and carrots, oxtail looks and tastes just like beef stew meat.

I wasn't squeamish about soul food, but drew the line at snoots and pig feet. I mean, who could look at fat toes on a flesh-colored foot stuck in congealed meat juices and not lose his or her appetite? Fortunately, I acquired a liking for chitterlings and ate at least twenty-five pounds before I learned exactly what intestines were. Chitterlings are deliciously soft and chewy, a comfort food that slides down the throat as easily as a crush of cherry popsicle on a hot summer day. Chitterlings are also the best tasting mother lode of artery clogging, heart attack, soul food that God and woman ever created.

On soul food nights at our folding dining table, Dedi sat next to Charlie, anxiously batting her long eyelashes under Buster Brown bangs while trying mightily to keep Charlie in check. "Charles, remember your manners," she enunciated in her crisp New England accent. "Did you thank Mrs. Laucau for inviting us to dinner? We don't need to hear your plaid bathing suit story again, Charles. Nobody cares about your muscles. Charles, please sit down. You can show us later." Her words bounced off a cute button nose that sometimes sounded exasperated with Charles. It was wonderful though, the way she took him seriously because no one else did.

Jean Beverly, who mostly enjoyed our family at a safe distance from her apartment next door, told me Charlie was a Gullah. Gullahs, sometimes called Geechees, are descendant of slaves and live in the sea islands along the coast of South Carolina. When I was a girl, they were a curiosity around Harlem because they still spoke their own language, a patois of English and African dialects that was unintelligible to outsiders. Some people laughed when Gullahs talked. Others described their way of speaking as a Geechee language. Such teasing may explain why Charlie decided to become French, a creation that remained part of him as long as he lived. I knew Charlie for twenty-seven years and never heard him drop the fake French accent, and I never saw Charlie sober.

Drinking and smoking were endemic, and not just in the black community. Most everyone around me, except Gram and Uncle Smitty, were too busy drinking, smoking and groovin' to good time melodies of Joe Turner or Nat King Cole, to think about their health. Concerns about alcohol's dangers were rationalized by drinking "safe," name-brand whiskies. You could float through Harlem on a sea of Dewars, Jack Daniels and Johnnie Walker Red. Wine was for winos or foreigners, although Charlie, our Frenchman, preferred Scotch and nobody but Ralph, to Gram's everlasting dismay, ever touched wine except champagne on New Year's Eve. Sherry was a woman's drink that cured the vapors, cramps or some female disorder, but the same bottle of ruby red Sherry remained on our top shelf until we closed out the apartment when Gram died.

At some point Charlie decided true Frenchmen should bear gifts. Creating more than his usual commotion one evening, he arrived with an armful of long-stemmed red roses. Bowing extravagantly, kissing our hands, pursing his lips with "Psst-psst-Mademoiselle" gibberish, he gave one to Gram and the women in the apartment, including me, then knocked on Jean Beverly's door. She knew him a little, accepted the flower, but was politely skeptical and not interested in the French flourish part of his presentation. Mrs. Boseman didn't answer her door and he skipped Hazel in the back apartment because Aunt Annette, who'd had a few drinks herself, told him to "Shut up, sit your crazy drunken ass down and don't go ringing that girl's bell. If her jealous boyfriend's home, there's no telling what that man might do."

Being like family, the ladies were often protective of Charlie. Jack and my uncles put up with him, but thought

221

him a bit of a fool. A smooth-skinned handsome man, he was a shorter, darker, loopier version of Harry Belafonte with a similar thick head of hair and Belafonte-style shirts unbuttoned to mid-chest level. Instead of fretting over Charlie's endless inebriation and odd behavior, our family emphasized the positive. He reported daily to his shift at the main post office and despite naysayers who thought an interracial marriage would never last, especially his, he remained devoted to a beautiful Italian-American wife who loved him.

The way Charlie died was painful and ugly. It was painful to see him shake, waste away and end up with brain damage and true unintelligible speech. It got ugly because by then, Dedi had started down the same alcoholic road.

I guess it was fitting for a house that attracts nutty people to end up with a strange cat. To be more accurate, we eventually drove our poor cat crazy. We got Angel because of a mouse problem, plus I had been begging for a pet. I hoped for a puppy, but Mom didn't like dogs and Gram wouldn't hear of confining a dog in a city apartment, then letting it relieve itself by fouling Edgecombe Avenue.

Angel was a sweet-faced, black, white and orange calico who didn't scratch or bite and took quickly to her litter box, but she never was what you would call friendly. She sunned in windows but peevishly flicked her tail, as a keep-away signal, if someone got too close. Until my brother joined the family, the cat enjoyed a year and a half of peace and relative quiet.

Before she had to be put down, Angel had two near-death experiences that proved cats are tough as nails, or else they really do have multiple lives. Her first close encounter occurred when we had painters in the apartment and my brother kicked over a half-sealed and mostly full can of white paint that splattered everywhere, but primarily on him and the cat. In the seconds before we figured out what to do with a wailing, paint-covered toddler and a panicked animal who was slick with oil-based Stark Ceiling White, I experienced a moment of fury that this could happen to my cat.

"Oh, Lord, Jesus," my grandmother cried when she found her voice. "Catch her, Olivia, before she runs across the rugs."

"Mother, I already grabbed the cat," she said, hanging on to the scruff of Angel's neck, trying not to get clawed. "Get some towels to put on the floor and let me have one to wrap her in. Jean," Mom yelled at me, "calm your brother, take off his shoes and wipe him down with one of those towels and keep him from tracking up the house. And," she added sensibly, "find a can down there on the floor that says, Paint Remover, so I can clean her up before she licks this off."

Because she had no choice, Angel let my mother towel her off with benzene or turpentine, whichever one burns like hell, because that's the only thing we had and we all needed to use a ton of it and my hands were on fire. After getting scrubbed in a caustic chemical, Mom washed the cat in baby shampoo, then flooded her with water.

After that, the cat didn't become any friendlier and unfortunately, a few weeks later, Houston shoved her out the kitchen window. For his sake, we carefully monitored my lightening-quick brother around open windows and honestly, he never mistreated the cat before, because she hissed when he got too near. The paint was a fluke. After she tumbled out the window, I ran down to bring her up and handed her to Mom, who slowly explored the cat's body.

"She doesn't seem to be in pain and nothing feels broken, but she's agitated," Mom said, watching Angel hang her head and breathe more rapidly than normal.

"Is she going to be okay?" I asked, starting to cry, and more visibly upset than the cat; I was fed up with my brother causing toddler chaos in our house. "Mommy, I see a little smear of blood on her nose" I said. "She's getting a nose bleed." After petting her, Mom placed her on the floor and Angel walked down the hall, flicking her tail disdainfully, as she often did, so we agreed she was shaken, but basically unharmed.

We weren't like the callous Southerners whose dogs and cats had better be darn glad for any kindness or decency owners offered, but that day, no one thought about a veterinarian for Angel. Understandably, the cat's personality went from touchy to toxic. One evening, about a month later, I noticed Angel pacing. Having been aloof since we got her, I was delighted. "Look Mom," I squealed, happy to finally see the cat's playful side. "Isn't she cute, walking back and forth like she's in a hurry to go somewhere?"

About a minute later, her hair stood up and she started pacing in circles, snarling and caterwauling as though communing with Death and telling him all the unintentionally terrible things we'd done to her. When she stopped moving, she looked at my grandmother and from somewhere deep inside that eight pound body, let loose a bloodcurdling yowl that made hairs on my arms stand up, right along with the cat's.

That's when my grandmother shouted, "Olivia, grab Houston. Jean, run for the door." In her way to safety, Gram picked up a broom to fend Angel off and managed to back the snarling, hissing animal into Ralph's room. I loved my cat, but when the door slammed and the lock clicked, I knew we'd dodged a bullet.

It surprised me that both Jean Beverly and Sadie Spratley hooted with laughter when they recalled this forty-five year-old cat story. It's true that neighbors were drawn to the hallway by the cat's screams and our yelling and stampeding for the door. Maybe if I'd been outside the apartment, with them, instead of inside with that cat, I would have been tickled too, to see Gram move so fast. After all these years, I know we were lucky not to get mauled by a crazed animal, who had every reason to hurt us.

It all happened about 7:00 at night, on an evening when Ralph and Jack, who were always at work during a crisis, were at work. My mother called the ASPCA, nervously explaining that we had a cat emergency. Through the phone, the dispatcher heard the high pitch wails and asked incredulously, "That's a cat?"

"Yes," Mom answered, "that's our cat and she's gone crazy."

Within the hour, a responder arrived with a box, a long-hooked stick and padded gloves that looked like the kind used to defuse bombs, which is exactly what ticked in that back room.

"Please wait outside," he asked us, "in case the cat slips by me when I go in after her." We gratefully trooped into the outside hall with a half dozen curious neighbors crowding our floor. After mom explained what was going on, Mrs. Boseman said, "Thank God, Olivia. Until I saw the man go in there, I thought it might be a person screaming for help." Most of the other people just stood around chuckling at the commotion.

Ralph's room was just inside our entry door, where we stood listening to the cat's howls, but we also heard thumps and bumps. It wasn't until that man emerged sweating and grinning, his hat askew, with the cat in the box, that we knew who won a chilling half-hour battle.

Wringing her hands, Mom asked him, "What were the thumping noises?"

"She ran over and under the bed and behind the night-stand. What you heard was her throwing herself against the walls. When she was too exhausted to run anymore, I grabbed her, but she put up a heck of a fight."

The cat night left an indelible imprint on my family and neighbors, but a few months later, a dog epitomized how my world and the people in it were betraying me. This time, witnesses weren't adult neighbors, but a group of teenagers, including Billy Goodwin, who were sitting across the street, clustered around a boy playing "Bobalu" music on a bongo drum. This was the era of the Afro-Cuban jazz craze, which Castro's visit would intensify. The *I Love Lucy* show was also one of the hottest programs on television, and the boys were outside getting pointers on how to play the bongo like Lucy's Cuban husband, Ricky Ricardo, might play.

I was upstairs in our front room, standing on a red step-ladder, dusting the top ledge above one of the front windows.

Taking peeks at what was going on outside, I hoped the boys saw me standing on the stool in my pink shorts. Seated next to me in her favorite chair, Gram pushed her trifocals back from the tip of her nose and kept trying to thread a curtain rod through one of the sheers.

"These glasses need tightening in the worst way. I guess I ought to make an appointment at the eye clinic," she said before telling me again to wipe off all the dirt. "I don't want my clean curtains brushing up against sooty woodwork before they're even hung properly, so do it right. And for your information," she threw in, "you're not going anywhere this evening, so you might as well stop looking out there."

Swiping my finger across the ledge, I held it up for her to see. "Look, no more dust," I said, far from defeated. "If I do a good job, can I go out then?" If I couldn't change her mind, that meant I had to say upstairs with her, while she spent all evening by the window watching and criticizing everything my friends did.

The kids on our block were growing up, especially the group on the bench. Boys were sprouting peach fuzz above their top lips and girls were growing breasts. Suddenly this was the summer when boys I had known my whole life were labeled, "Trouble with a capital T."

"You can't go out, period. Doing a good job on these windows has nothing to do with it. Those fast hussies are out front," she started in on the girls. "You don't have any business associating with them. All they want is a whiff of those randy boys and then, Lord, look out."

"But Gram, Dedi's out there, too. She needs someone our age to sit with."

"If she's so lonely, when we're done with these curtains, you can invite her up here. The other day," she said, squinting over the tops of her glasses for a better look, "one of those fresh girls, I think the one in the blue skirt, started talking that gutter talk (pig Latin) when they realized I was sitting at the window and could hear them. You don't need to be in anybody's company who can't come right out and say what's on their mind in plain English."

Besides an age difference and make-believe language, I knew what Gram didn't like about "fast" girls. They had a cool way of snapping gum, wore gold anklet bracelets, pasted Dippity-Do spit curls at their temples and put metal taps on their shoes, then dragged their feet down the street, giving off that fast, bad-girl sound.

"Oh Gram, that's not fair. They were only talking in pig Latin. Everybody does it, not just fast girls. Please let me go downstairs," I pleaded. "Those big kids are nice. The boy with the drum lives around the corner and told us he's in a band. He won't bother me, I promise."

"Fairness? Promises? A band? Now that takes the cake," she scoffed in a voice that would have carried across the street, if the drum hadn't drowned her out. "I could tell you a thing or two about these dope fiends who make promises and call themselves musicians. You're too young to even pee straight, so don't try to act grown. I can smell trouble a mile away, and I don't like what's in the air this evening."

"What's so wrong with listening to the drummers, or playing Red Rover?" I tried again. "That's all we do."

"Nothing's wrong with that," she snapped, "but don't try to be cute. And who's that shifty, riney-looking, bigheaded boy sitting out there next to James Grisham?" she asked sinisterly about a kid whose only offense, besides being a male teenager, was having red hair and a face full of freckles. Like many other older black people, my grandmother was superstitious and considered Negroes with red hair bad omens, or else some kind of genetic freaks. "I don't know him" she said, "and there's no telling where he came from. He probably plays in some band, too, instead of going to school. You're staying upstairs."

Deciphering the complexities of coolness wasn't easy, but I'd been making progress until a few days ago when Johnny Williams, a cool boy who seriously played drums and was starting Music and Art High School, came up to me and said, "Give me some skin." When I went to slap him five, he moved his hand and a bench full of his buddies nearly fell on the ground from laughing so hard. Five minutes later, everyone seemed to have forgotten it, but I stayed flush with humiliation, and now days later, still felt like I needed to get outside to repair my image.

Next, I tried the go-to-the-store angle. "Gram, before it gets too late, do you need anything from the store?" Instead of answering yes or no, she said, "Who's that?" pointing at a man across the street and near the kids, who was letting his boxer squat and drop a big load on the sidewalk.

"I don't know," I said, "I never saw him before."

"Mister," she bellowed out the window at the man, "take your dog and get away from this house." A few seconds passed, and he ignored her while the boxer continued its business and all the kids looked up at our window.

My thoughts flew to Billy. He was such a confidently cool kid, and before this situation got any worse, which it did, I just hoped he wouldn't hold an embarrassing grandmother against me.

"Do you hear me? Do you know who I am?" she yelled again at the man. Instead of moving, the man turned his back and looked out over the park, the dog now sitting quietly beside his master. Long off the stool, so no one could see me, I stood on the other side of the room, holding my breath, thinking, Oh God, who is she going to be? I think this was the day I decided I was going to grow up to become a very polite person who never embarrassed people. Lately, Gram was crashing and burning into any conflict she could find or manufacture, like this one.

"I am the law," she boomed importantly at the dog walker. "I am a policewoman and if you don't move your black ass, I will come down there and arrest you!"

Oh God, I groaned. A policewoman! I'd never heard such a thing and if the NYPD really had them, no overweight, near seventy-year-old grandmother could ever pass for one.

But the policewoman ploy got the man's attention. He turned around, shook his head and started laughing before walking back up the street.

This was about the third time that month I had cringed to see her engaging in yet another outrageous confrontation. She cursed strangers, vetoed my plans or yelled downstairs when I was sitting outside on a bench to say, "Jean don't sit so close to that boy."

Everything was going wrong. Mom said she and Jack were about to close a deal on an apartment. Although Gram wasn't as much fun as she used to be, the thought of living without her was giving me stomach aches, but living with her did the same thing.

There was so much to worry about. At age twelve, I had breasts and had blossomed into a five-feet-four-inch size eleven, pimply faced sixth grader in pig tails and ankle socks. Some of my girlfriends were shedding little girl clothes. I lobbied for my first pair of stockings and flats, instead of the usual clunky Buster Browns with straps; and I really wanted a straight skirt.

"Don't be ridiculous. You're just a child and aren't going to wear women's skintight clothes," Mom repeated the same words she had used with my father a year ago.

"Mom, your skirts aren't tight; they're just straight. I don't want it tight, but my clothes are ugly and I look stupid. A girl at school has one."

"What on earth are you talking about? Just look how pretty you are," she said about my acne and legs that needed shaving; another improvement I wanted to make, but couldn't yet face asking her to buy a razor, fearing she would say, "You're too young to have a razor."

"You have nothing to be ashamed of. Don't you remember all the compliments you and all your little friends got on Easter Sunday when you looked so adorable in your dresses?"

I thought Mom was being unreasonable, but I didn't know how to counter her claims because I didn't understand puberty was making me tall, pimply and teary. In a sewing class, I made my own skirt, a big flouncy full one, instead of the straight style I wanted, because Mom wouldn't buy the straight skirt pattern. When it was finished, I thought I looked okay in five yards of Woolworth's discounted red-floral chintz. I wore it to the store and ran into James Grisham coming from the opposite direction. "Hey Jeanie," he yelled, "you look like a duck walking down the street in a pair of draperies." James wasn't mean, so I couldn't even get mad at him, and in a way I knew he was right, at least about the fabric.

A month earlier at school, we had to make collages for a math project and Jeffrey, a bashful boy in my class dressed up in his sleeveless navy blue sweater and bow tie to come over and work with me in my living room. He didn't live on our block. Boys who did wouldn't come near our apartment except, en mass, years earlier for a birthday party when I was seven. Gram didn't know Jeffrey, but I remember her acting like a normal grandmother that day, not using bad language or shouting at anyone. Jeffrey and I were working with a compass and straight edge, cutting geometric shapes from black construction paper and he wasn't a neat cutter, because his circles looked more like pears.

"Here, hold the scissors like this," I showed him, "or let me cut the circles, so we don't run out of black paper." I was reaching over to take the scissors when Gram walked in and I pulled back. She watched me for a few seconds and I thought, Oh, Oh, we're sitting too close; she's going to say something. She did. "Jean, your legs are bare. It's too chilly for bare legs. In this kind of weather, you might catch cold in your tubes and have female problems. Go put on socks."

Another challenge that year was my brother, whose terrible twos were lasting well into his third year. Jack was proud of Houston being "all boy," which meant he was allowed to run amok, touch all my stuff and act like he didn't understand the word "No." But he was smart enough to hide my blue flip flops in Ralph's closet where I couldn't find them for weeks. I thought he needed a good spanking, but no one in our house believed in corporal punishment.

One of my jobs was to take him outside after dinner to run off some energy. One evening, he was wearing his light blue sweater and I wasn't supposed to buy him a snow cone because of the mess. To keep the peace, I got him one anyway, with less cherry syrup.

"Here." I said. "Now sit still and don't spill anything on your clothes."

Momentarily fascinated with red ice crystals, he sat with me on a bench, popping small pieces of ice in his mouth without dripping. When he had enough, he bolted to the curb and dumped the snow cone in the street, then whined for mine.

"Dang," Mary Jo said, "somebody needs to do something about that boy."

"Yeah, I know, but what? You make him behave. He won't listen to me. How come Dennis and Ronnie know how to act right?"

"Girl, don't be crazy, but they weren't as bad as him."

Mary Jo and I were trying to have a conversation and Houston kept running toward the street. Frustrated, I grabbed him and smacked him across the face and sure enough, as if to nail my coffin shut, he got a bloody nose and started crying and so did I.

"Hey, Jeannie," Mary Jo said, "you can't be hitting him in the face."

"I know, I know, I'm sorry. Don't cry," I begged, picking him up to calm him down and trying to remember tricks Gram used to stop bloody noses.

"Mary Jo, my grandmother's not in the window. Quick, go get some ice from the snow cone man."

It wasn't a bad nosebleed; most of the red came from cherry juice, and ice on his forehead just made him cry harder. No one in the family found out, but the slap across his face echoed around in my head. I was angry all the time, but hurting my little brother scared me. I knew how disappointed Mom, Gram

231

and especially Jack would be. Jack didn't have much time for me anymore, but we were still pals. He told me I ironed better than anyone he knew, even better than the Chinese lady at the laundry, and he gave me a quarter for each of his shirts I ironed. That was twenty-five cents more than the zero sum I got from anyone else in the family when I ironed their stuff.

Though they were hopeful, no lease had been signed on an apartment, so Mom and Jack took one more house-hunting expedition and invited me along. I appreciated being asked, but couldn't believe what we dragged through that day. The house wasn't within Sugar Hill's borders, supposedly a requirement of the move, and we stumbled through its damp dark interior by the beam of a flashlight. In the second floor gloom, Mom's cheery chatter sounded desperate when she told Jack, a man who didn't even own a hammer, much less ever fix anything, "If we don't get the other place, you could take the walls down and remodel this into a single family building."

"Olivia," he said sensibly, "I think we can pass on this one."

Apparently not hearing Jack, nor a peep from her shellshocked daughter, Mom walked over to where I was standing by the window, trying to warm myself in the sunshine. Waving at the few rays trickling into the gutted room, she said, "Don't you think this would make a lovely teenager's bedroom?"

In August, after two years of searching, what they finally found was an apartment on Convent Avenue.

15. Siddiness and Black Society

Our move would take place in September, the autumn after I finished grade school. Mom had already started investigating private schools for me. A few other parents were doing likewise, or checking out parochial schools, but most of sixth grade was heading ten blocks up Edgecombe Avenue to Stitt Junior High. For eleven and twelve year olds, Stitt was the great unknown, a treacherous place full of mean teachers and neighborhood bullies that we'd been dodging since fifth grade.

Sixth grade was ending in a blaze of glory since Michele, my best friend, and I were the principal's monitors, an honored position loosely described as co-goody-goody gofers. When Mr. Meiselman, the principal, planned after-school meetings or needed to contact one of many teachers scattered throughout the five-story, block-long building, he waited until sixth grade recess. While a couple of hundred kids raced around the yard, Michele and I spent the hour in a private office, placing forks on the left, spoons and knives to the right, or big-timing it in the hallways.

I still attended religious instructions, but after four years, the glow of released-time had dimmed considerably and I was still trying to figure out how to make those nuns understand the privileged life I led at P.S. 46. Michele was the Alpha girl in our relationship, just as I'd been with Colleen; a protector of sorts, but also a provocateur. She called the shots, had cool ideas like suggesting we learn to play tennis, but her goody-goodyness only went so far, because she also thought up mischief, usually with some fancy, whim-wham finish.

She could also hold tight to a perceived insult or grudge. One afternoon, I was at the office conference room sink washing and slicing apples for a teacher's meeting, and her job was to take the cake out of its wrapping, slice it and open a fresh can of Maxwell House to prepare the coffee pot.

"That's stupid," she said, all pissed off at Mr. Meiselman's secretary. "She can't tell me what to do. I know how to cook better than she does. I bet her food tastes like mess."

"She still wants you to fill the pot and measure the coffee," I pointed out, "just not heat it up. She said she would do it because it gets too hot and boils over."

"So? Recess isn't over, I can turn it down."

Most pissed-off kids, who'd been told not to touch the hot plate because it had a faulty thermostat and might catch on fire, would just get even by pilfering a piece of Sara Lee pound cake. Michele said, "Look," then picked up each of six dessert plates, licked them, polished them with spittle until they shined, then placed a piece of cake squarely in the middle.

I was dazzled by such wickedness and unable to articulate how we might get caught, lose our cushy jobs or get our privileged little asses whipped. Expulsion was the least likely route because teachers didn't need it when smacking kids around worked just fine. Gram spoiled me silly, but even she would be at a loss to defend me if I got caught in this dirty deal.

Mr. Lerner, our sixth grade teacher, was firm but gentle on girls, although we had good sense not to cross him. I watched him beat-up on a nice boy named William. He made William stand in front of class with his arms spread to the side at shoulder height. His palms were up and in each hand he was supposed to hold a dictionary. Every time William dropped a dictionary, which was a lot, Mr. Lerner picked it up and hurled it at him. The rest of us kept our heads down, pretending to be busy with work. His punishment went on for several minutes, and for the life of me, I couldn't figure out what William did to make Mr. Lerner so mad.

Women teachers usually didn't hit, but they didn't mess around either. A perfectly innocent transgression, like lack of neatness, sent them over the edge. It happened to me, five years earlier, when I was in first grade and two girls on the playground wanted to style my hair, so I let them. After undoing my ribbons and pigtails, we started playing beauty parlor. When we had enough of that, everyone went back to running around the humid, sun-baked school yard, without any of us knowing how to re-braid hair. When I wore my hair down and unbraided, it was styled in Shirley Temple curls and held together with pomade, water or Dippity-Do, if not all three. "Down" was reserved for Easter, birthday parties and other special occasions since heat, humidity and active play were known to have a lethal effect on down hair. After recess I lined up with the other children. Mrs. Schneider was on yard duty. She was the door-banging teacher who wore a wig, had a whiny, high-pitched nasal voice, and taught across the hall from our classroom, where we heard her constantly saying, "Okay people" when addressing her first graders. She pulled me out of line.

"Young lady," she asked, "what is wrong with you?"

"I'm hot," I confessed.

"I mean, what's wrong with your hair?"

"I don't know."

"Well, can you fix it back the way it's supposed to be? It's come loose and you can't go back to class looking like that."

"I don't know how to braid braids and I lost my ribbons," I told her miserably, "My mommy fixes it for me."

"Well, if you can't fix it, your mommy will have to, because this will never do. Come with me."

Today, yard patrol can be hazardous duty with teachers breaking up fights and occasionally confiscating drugs or weapons, but loose braids are no longer on their list of unacceptables. This incident occurred during the uptight, tuck-it-in 1950s, before boys wore ponytails, or Afros grew two feet wide, or curly girls went wild with untamed locks.

Mrs. Schneider was faced with a situation, so she had to do something.

Instead of the principal's office, I landed in the nurse's clinic, a grim fog-colored room with a glass cabinet full of stainless steel medical implements that looked like horror movie props. Even four years later, when 1,000 kids gladly filed through for polio shots, nothing could remove the stink of fear from that clinic. On the bad hair day, there were no other patients. My only company was the accusatory teacher who left me with a head-shaking nurse who'd never seen such a case.

"Here," she said, shoving a circular white porcelain pan in my lap when I started crying. "If you need to throw up, use this. Your mother has been called."

The diagnosis was a messy-hair health crisis that required isolation from other children. By the time Mom arrived, the school day was almost over, so she stormed home, dragging me along.

"Mommy, can you please braid my hair," I asked timidly, thinking she was mad at me. Proving a point that I didn't understand at the time, she refused to re-braid my hair in front of the nurse, or in the hall or anywhere, and I had to walk all the way home wearing the cause of so much trouble, like a flying buttress on my head.

Now, five years later, Michele and I roamed these halls carrying our badge of distinction, the wooden office pass wrapped in tinfoil. We routinely delivered messages to the nurse's clinic which had not changed, but no longer scared big girls like me—at least not as much.

My favorite errand was to the custodian's office, down a hidden staircase, deep in the bowels of the building, a spot other students didn't know existed. Custodian's office was a woefully inadequate term for his subterranean suite filled with upholstered furniture, cooking odors and a wife who met us at the door and signed our note wearing pink kid curlers in her hair. Behind her, it looked like she stepped from a homey little fiefdom, which their apartment may have been, since New Yorkers learned in subsequent years that public school janitors had, over decades, moved families into school buildings and built personal dynasties through nepotism and abuse of authority.

Michele's nickname was Mickey and she lived on upper Edgecombe, close to Stitt. At lunchtime, she went home to walk her dog Bambi, and during those last months of school, before we split up to go separate ways, I sometimes joined her.

Late winter in New York can be windy and raw, or bring cloudless blue skies with moderate temperatures. I remember those last joyous months of grade school when elms, lindens and tree varieties that Mrs. Katz tried so hard to get us to appreciate, suddenly budded, then delicately leafed-out in a first blush of spring that I had never noticed before. There was a party at Rose Casey's house where our closest sixth grade friends promised to stay in touch forever. We exchanged addresses and phone numbers, some for the first time since being in classes together since kindergarten.

Strolling over to Michele's the next day, I asked "Do you know yet which school you're going to?"

"Probably shitty Stitt, but I don't know. Daddy doesn't talk about it, so I stopped asking. How about you?"

"I'm supposed to visit some new schools soon, so probably one of them."

For lunch we fried bologna circles until they puffed in the pan, made our sandwiches, then took the dog out.

"Come on, the coast is clear," she said, stepping from her lobby onto the sidewalk.

"No it's not." I nodded to my left. "Two boys across the street are walking this way."

"Oh, so what. Come on. I have to walk the dog and we don't have all day."

When the boys came parallel to us, one yelled, "Hey girl, you live in this house?"

237

"Don't answer and don't let them know where you live," I whispered to Michele, who was pulling on Bambi's chain, trying to make the dog look mean. Already five-foot-eight and built like an up-and-coming WWF wrestler, Michele mostly pretended to be afraid of tough kids because that's what nice girls were supposed to do. When Bambi started coughing from getting strangled, Michele eased up on the leash, but ignored my warning and said back to the boy, "Who wants to know?"

"We like your dog," his friend said. "Does he bite?"

"No she doesn't, but you better not mess with me, 'cause I'll kick your ass."

Before slinking back up toward Stitt, they threw a few dirty looks. I didn't say anything, but in retrospect, I figured the boys were flirting because Michele was pretty. She stayed hot for the rest of the walk, and on the way back to school, acting like she was disappointed that her dog and best friend were both wimps.

That incident ended any more posturing about her being scared of junior high kids, because she wasn't. Contradiction was Michele's best weapon. Generous to a fault, she would give me her last dime or best sweater, but not until she finished calling someone a faggot or an asshole. Beneath her turned-up nose, perfect bangs and silky braid that hung down her back like a Coolie's queue, she had the capacity to get a little bit crazy.

One day, the fury beating in Michele's breast flew out when a man came walking toward us on Broadway. He gave us an admiring look, as men had started doing, as we grew up and our figures developed inside school girl clothes. Michele stepped in his path, got in his face and hissed, "Watch your eyes, Mister."

"Why you little bitch," he said to her back, as she hustled ahead in the opposite direction, leaving me and the astonished man in her wake. Where she got her language and those bad-girl ways, I don't know. When our friends cursed, they sounded like ordinary adolescents experimenting with syllables and boundaries. Michele got her mouth around cuss words and wrung out the juice, or reamed you out, just by the way she said asshole. Even as a kid, she would expose a man's darkest secrets by calling him a faggot. Neighbors knew he was in the closet and everyone, but Michele, was willing to let him stay there.

That kind of mischief tormented Mrs. Q, her mother. Michele was an only child of two proper, bordering on stuffy, parents. She went out of her way to provoke her mom, but she adored her father, a tall, handsome, humorless man who viewed his daughter's devilish side as the sparkle other girls lacked. Her daddy was a waiter on the Penn Central. The other railroad waiter I knew well was Ralph—tiny, timid, comically under my grandmother's thumb, and totally opposite Michele's father. That comparison made it difficult to picture Mr. Q scurrying around doing the bidding for some rude diner. Light-skinned with freckles, Mr. Q wore combed-back hair, round, horn-rimmed glasses and had a keen interest in the greater world. He looked professorial, and more on the order of the United Nations dignitary, Ralph Bunche, than Joe the waiter. I suspect he also harbored some statesmanlike disappointments about a life that relegated him to a dining car with so many other potentially talented, riding-the-rails-to-nowhere black men. If I had dinner with them and he was home, we all minded our P's, Q's and everything else. He once told me, "Get your elbows off that table, young lady," and he didn't say it as though I was company, or like he was channeling Dr. Bunche and trying to be diplomatic.

Soft, busty and matronly, Mrs. Q wore dark colors and high-neck blouses with bows and was fifteen years older than my young, slim mom, whom strangers assumed was my big sister. As an older mom, Mrs. Q conveyed a wise-woman confidence that I'm not sure was legit, living in that house with those two powder kegs.

My mother once sniffed that Michele's mom had "social climbing dignity." When Mom talked like that, I thought she was being catty because she was jealous of my friendship with Mrs. Q. But Mom was a bit on target, too, because Mrs. Q dropped names or talked about her family's accomplishments, like the big house they owned down by St. Phillip's Church. Right now, I can't remember their other accomplishments, because statements she made about Mr. Q overshadow most of what came out of her mouth.

I don't know why she confided in me, unless being a good listener and keeping Michele's secrets qualified, but any friend would do the same. I was much older, maybe sixteen, the day she asked my opinion about an intimacy concern between herself and Mr. Q. Michele was not in the room and partly to cover my shock, I thought long and hard because no grown-up, or kid for that matter, ever came this close to exposing her soul like this woman just had. Such trust was humbling, but burdensome too, because our friendship might hinge on not saying the first stupid thing to pop in my mind, which was that I didn't know people as old as she was even had sex.

Fortunately, I settled on, "Mrs. Q, I don't know. I can't answer that for you, because I don't know about those things." Despite her sweetness, I don't think she had a confidant, like Mom had her friend Sandra or Aunt Cee to talk to. Mrs. Q's sisters and a sister-in-law lived close by; all lovely, intelligent ladies, but maybe one of the family accomplishments was not confiding in each other.

It bothered Mrs. Q a lot that Michele had a vile temper and used bad language. "Watch your mouth, Mickey," she said, trying but failing to sound authoritative. "I can't believe a daughter of mine talks like that. You're a young lady, so please start acting like one."

"Well, he is an asshole," Michele emphasized, "only paying me two dollars for babysitting his brats half the night."

"Stop calling the man names. You agreed to fifty cents an hour; that's good pay."

"Not when I had to make dinner and clean the place. There were dishes all over the kitchen. I scraped a week's worth of jam off the table. You should see the leftover mess she planned for their dinner. I wouldn't feed it to Bambi. I fixed mashed potatoes and they ate like they hadn't been fed in a week. And later, while he's taking forever to dig two measly dollars out of his wallet, she gets undressed, like I'm invisible or just hired help or something, and starts parading around showing off her big tits."

"Oh, Jesus, Mary and Joseph," Mrs. Q crossed herself like a Catholic. I don't know if she did that because she was High Episcopalian, or did it in desperation. I tried not to laugh.

"Just go. Go to your room, right now. I'll clear the table."

Mr. Q, was never home when these things went on, so he had no idea his daughter knew profane words, much less used them. Sometimes it was so much fun being Michele's friend, but not on nights when Mrs. Q used me as bait to point out her daughter's bad habits.

"Mickey, just stop it. Why can't you be more like T (that, of course, was butter-wouldn't-melt-in-her-mouth me)?" When she started in on comparisons, I tried to change the subject or defended Michele as best I could, like about the babysitting family. Michele and I double babysat for that family a few times and she wasn't exaggerating about the condition of their house.

"Mrs. Q, the place really is a pig sty, not just the kitchen," I said. "Toys everywhere, nothing put away, unmade beds, dirty sheets, the toilet filthy. Mrs. C leaves her fancy clothes laying all over the bedroom. There's so much stuff, there's hardly space to sit down in that house."

Michele knew I was oil to her vinegar, and she appreciated my efforts to smooth over her rough spots. Sometimes, but not always, it helped. Michele liked to walk on the wild side and let people know she was different. As a teenager, she shopped at thrift stores, redesigned patterns and made everyday clothes from elegant fabrics like silk or velvet, because she didn't want to dress like other girls. Michele made fun of what she said were silly girls in pony tails, all wearing the same copycat trends, like poodle skirts or pink sweater sets with pearls.

241

Despite living on Sugar Hill, in proximity of beautiful people, I didn't personally know many. Michele changed that, because she was my one friend with enough pedigree to hobnob with the black bourgeoisie. She didn't care about social status but smart, good-looking boys were a different matter, even though she scared them half to death. Jack and Jill, the la-di-da social club for children of black muckety-mucks, was a place to meet such boys, but plenty of stuck-up assholes too, according to Mickey.

I guess I could say Michele first "introduced me to society" simply by describing Jack and Jill boy-girl parties. Her mother held a professional position in a hospital, so I'm not sure why, but Michele didn't belong to Jack and Jill, either. The muckey-mucks might have denied her membership because Mr. Q waited tables, but Michele had entree to Jack and Jill functions through relatives in Queens.

"T," she told me, "the walls are lined with cute boys who don't just stand around giggling like Colden or acting bashful like Reggie." Colden and Reggie were two cute, well-mannered kids we palled around with at school. "Jack and Jill boys ask you to slow dance," she explained, "without stepping on your feet. But if you go to a party with me, you'll have to get a pair of stockings, like I did, because that's how you're supposed to dress."

Michele arranged for me to tag along with her to a St. Albans party given by a girl who belonged to Jack and Jill. St. Albans, Queens was one of several new suburbs opening up to blacks, because whites were moving out and heading further east to Long Island. I was spending the night of the party at Michele's house, so we got dressed in her room and Michele just shook her head in disgust when I took socks from the overnight bag. "I know," I said. "I still can't make my mother buy me a pair of stockings. Can't I go like this?" I asked about my party dress, patent leathers and the thinnest-weight nylon socks Woolworth sold; in other words, the same look I'd worn since age one.

"We don't have any choice, since we're getting picked up in ten minutes."

Looking back, I realize we weren't that good yet at being deceptive, because it never occurred to either of us that I borrow a pair of her stockings, something my mother would not have discovered. So off I went to this big deal event, dressed like a little girl.

The party was held in a paneled rathskeller. Trooping down basement stairs behind Michele, I focused on the wet bar's sparkling brass fixtures. A man I assumed was daddy of the house, had an enormous feminine-looking, soft roll of muffin fat encircling his waistline, and he kept wiping down a spotless laminate countertop, as fascinated as I was by such advanced engineering. Wet bars, I decided, were why people left the city and ended up riding the Q line, or whatever subway came out here to Queens. Michele kept hunching me in the ribs and saying, "T, come on," but I'd drawn a bead on the daddy who was saying, "Okay, kids have a good time tonight. There's soda in the refrigerator behind the bar. No beer tonight, ha, ha, ha," to six people who all, except me, ignored him. Eventually I had to find something else to focus on when the daddy headed upstairs.

We'd arrived at seven sharp, and the other early birds were two girls huddled in a far corner and a handful of boys, including Samuel, a super shy boy whose mother drove us to the party, because she had a car, worked with Mrs. Q and had offered to drive us. Neither Michele nor I had met Samuel before tonight, and now he was leaning against a wall, trying as hard as I was to act natural.

To get the party going, someone had cranked the volume up on the Hi-Fi and it was blasting the Diamond's song, *Little Darlin* into the room. I yelled at Michele, "Do you know any of these people?"

"I don't know these short little assholes." Being twelve years old, and standing five foot eight, was not a social asset in the 1950s. Michele regularly towered over boys our age, including the few already there, but she was better than me at hiding her nervousness. My stomach was in a knot, as I watched kids pour down the stairs, into a small room that was already uncomfortably warm. The best idea so far was when Michele suggested, "Hey, let's go to the bathroom."

The bathroom had the same wood-paneled walls and red tile floor as the main room. I wished it had a hair dryer. I still didn't have stockings, but I'd gotten a new mod dress, a trendy futuristic style with dolman sleeves, in a light blue shiny cotton, that showed every stain and probably looked exceedingly absurd with ankle socks and Buster Browns. The arms and body were one continuous piece of webbed material, like the wings of a flying squirrel. Peering in the mirror, dribs and drabs of armpit sweat stared back at me, from blue cotton material that looked like it was stamped with rorschach inkblots. "Oh God, I'm sweating up my dress and it's not even tight under the arms."

"They need some windows in this basement. Take it off and dry it with these," Michele said, grabbing up most of the evening's supply of guest paper towels, a fancy brand, designed with black fleur de lis.

"I'm not taking my dress off. I don't trust that lock. Besides, it'll take too long and won't do any good. What I need is a hairdryer. When's that lady picking us up, anyway?"

"When the party ends at 10:00."

"Oh God, it's only 8:15. I'm starving," I said, doubling over with hunger and nerves. We couldn't even finish dinner because she came so early, and she better not be late on this end. That prissy little bitch passing around chips and onion dip won't even come over by us."

Back in the main room, someone had dimmed the lights, encouraging a few brave souls to slow dance. The spot we'd claimed all evening was now filled with other kids. I wasn't shy anymore, didn't care, and just wanted this dog of an evening to end. I had to squeeze into a new standing spot. It was by a boy who turned around, stuck out his hand and said, "How do you do, my name is Warren. Do you want to dance?"

"Yes, thank you," I answered, momentarily setting aside my foul mood. We did a slow dance to Johnny Mathis, and Warren didn't try holding too tight or breathing in my ear. He didn't seem to mind, either, that I was an outsider in ankle socks but by then, lights were dimmer and the room so crowded that no one saw much, including my sweat stains.

Besides the two boys, Warren and Samuel, whose mother, bless her, picked us up early, I didn't speak to or befriend any girls that night. Nor, in subsequent years, was I ever a close friend with any Jack and Jill girls. Some, but not all of them, preferred socializing exclusively with other girls and boys in that group. The social snobbery in black families often started with these ten- to fourteen-year-old girls who were as clever as their mothers at protecting their entitlement against undesirables whose parents weren't married, or had bartenders or waiters as fathers.

Not all "qualified" Negroes were interested in "going society." Many well-connected black people dismissed that crowd as a bunch of social-climbing phonies. Wallace Thurman, a dark-skinned Negro novelist writing in the 1920s and '30s, during the Harlem Renaissance, penned the following commentaries years before I was born, but what he said about Negro society was still true when I came along:

> [They are] the more successful and more socially inclined professional folk—lawyers, doctors, dentists, druggists, politicians, beauty-parlor proprietors, and real-estate dealers. They are for the most part mulattos of light brown skin and have succeeded in absorbing all the social mannerisms of the white American middle class... These people have a social life of their own. They attend formal dinners and dances, resplendent in chic and expensive replicas of Fifth Avenue finery. They arrange suitable inter-coterie weddings,

preside luxuriously at announcement dinners, prenuptial showers, wedding breakfasts, and the like. They attend church socials, fraternity dances, and sorority gatherings. They frequent the downtown theaters, and occasionally, quite occasionally, drop into one of the Harlem nightclubs which certain of their lower-caste brethren frequent and white downtown excursionists make wealthy.[1]

Even a visiting foreign journalist, Nancy Cunard, a British woman and daughter of the shipping family, was taken aback by the amount of snobbery among Harlem's light-skinned groups; those she called mulattos and dark-skinned members of society who snubbed one another over money, clothes, family position, and especially the degree of melanin in one's skin. She called the snobbery around skin color "terrifying."[2]

When I was a young woman and more sure of myself, I could have written a laundry list of pushy, social climbing mothers I knew who micromanaged their children's social lives. These women worried about the skin color of their daughter's dates. They shopped cotillions so their girls would be presented in the Waldorf Astoria Hotel ballroom with the wealthiest kids from brand name families. Society dressmakers were prized commodities, reserved a year before the event, so the deb's mother could tell her bourgeois friends, "Mrs. X made Judy's cotillion dress with freshwater pearls and imported Belgian lace."

Boys were encouraged to date girls with straight-ish hair and if these young men inherited their mother's worst qualities, they wouldn't go out with anyone who wasn't "light, bright and damn-near white." The daddies just reared back and grinned with approval, many of them having married light-skinned trophy wives, creating a trickle-down effect of racial, class and color snobbery.

Mothers, fathers and children who behave this way are not bad people. This is just what some black folks do, and they don't just do it in Harlem. It's society, it's siddity and despite rage, braids, Malcolm, Obama and changing our name from Negro, to black, to Afro-American and now African American, some things never change.

In the midst of my preteen coming of age, the private school visits began. Elisabeth Irwin, Walden, Dalton and New Lincoln were four of the best that accepted minorities, including children needing tuition assistance. Education was always a priority for my mom, but I think private schooling was also a way for her to circumvent our exclusion from black society. She was not a social climber, but wanted me to have every advantage, so she trumped the black middle class by bumping me to the head of the class—the wealthy white world.

All New York private schools had rosters of famous families; infamous ones, too. Had I gone to Elisabeth Irwin, two schoolmates would have been Angela Davis, later the radical Black Panther and also Mike Meeropol, whose parents Julius and Ethel Rosenberg had recently been executed for espionage. In the funny way that paths cross, the day I visited Elisabeth Irwin, I met Mike Meeropol in the lunch line. He was the messy-haired, sharp-faced, hyperactive eighth grader ahead of me in the lunch line, wearing a ripped flannel shirt. He captured my attention because he couldn't stop fidgeting and talking about the wait, his torn shirt pocket and the flapping sole of his shoe that he kept making worse by folding back and standing on. But his subway story helped me decide not to come to his school.

"Yeah," he said in his jittery way, "it's no big deal living uptown. A lot of kids at this school live uptown. They catch up with each other at the 96th or 72nd Street station, then ride downtown together on the express train." That sounded friendly and all, but I was partial to bus rides and had particularly disliked awaking to an early morning alarm, followed by a long, stand-up subway ride down there to Greenwich Village.

I learned Mike's family history only because I ran into him seven years later when we ended up working together as counselors, in Upstate New York at Camp Thoreau, a summer camp owned by Karl and Ann Rodman, two popular teachers at New Lincoln School. Both New Lincoln and Elisabeth Irwin had populations that were more diverse than many other New York private schools. They appealed to minorities, left-leaning political families, and those in the performing arts who'd been blacklisted during the McCarthy madness.

By the time I worked at Camp Thoreau, I understood the dynamics of Cold War politics, got the significance of who Mike's parents had been, what happened to them and how it shaped him. Mike's eighth-grade hyperactivity had morphed into a sweeping, mop-headed personality bursting with edgy musical talent. He was camp music counselor, attached all summer to his twelve-string steel guitar that he used to strum about injustice, or about the ill winds blowing in Southeast Asia, or he'd urgently finger-pick his way through roots music while paying tribute to the downtrodden. His music also memorialized Andrew Goodman, who'd recently been killed.

Andrew had been our age, had gone to Walden School, and earlier that spring, he and two other civil rights activists, James Chaney and Mickey Schwerner, had been murdered in Philadelphia, Mississippi while trying to organize black voters. Andrew's younger brother, Peter, was a camper that summer, in the same age group as my little brother, Houston.

I chose to attend New Lincoln School for a number of lofty adolescent reasons. Students were welcoming when I visited, kids called teachers by their first names and it was located in Harlem, on 110th Street, allowing me to continue my last-minute-out-of-bed routine of waking up to the *Klavin and Finch* morning radio program. The school also had Cecil, a crusty elevator operator who sometimes let students drive his elevator and since I caught him in a good mood, he gave me a turn that day. The second floor was a well-stocked library, the cook had made chocolate pudding for lunch, and there was a swimming pool in the basement.

Spring weather on the morning of my visit had reverted to winter and the building's old furnace was losing its battle to throw off the chill, except in the toasty basement locker room where my hostess took me after lunch. I only knew her half a day, but she acted like a friend, instead of the girl who got stuck wasting time with some new kid.

"Oh, a real pool," I squealed when we got to the basement. "I love this place. They didn't tell me you had a swimming pool. Now I can finally learn to swim. Don't you just love it?"

"Are you kidding?" She rolled big blue eyes at me. "We hate it," she said in the manner of a privileged girl who spends summers at the lake, or in the pool at her country house and already swims like a fish.

"Watch out if you take life guarding," she warned. "To pass, everyone has to rescue Lou Fink, our gym teacher and that asshole tries to drown you during the panicky swimmer drill."

"He won't be drowning me," I assured her. "I just want to learn to swim."

"Having swim for gym is a total drag. It's warm down here but forget it, the water's always freezing," she said.

I dismissed the day's only sour note, just happy to be coming here and knowing I would soon learn to swim properly. And I was happy there, but like all the other girls, I spent the next six years using every trick in the book to stay out of that damn pool.

That fall I shed parts of my old self. We moved twelve blocks from Gram, but I ran back and forth daily, checking on her and trying to stay tight with old friends who were slipping into the past. It didn't help that, contrary to my firmest belief, Gram didn't seem broken hearted without four noisy, active people crowding her space. And as Mom promised, the reality of a bigger room with modern white furniture and my own Hi-Fi to play Johnny Mathis and Harry Belafonte albums was an adjustment, not a hardship.

Our new apartment thrilled Mom, who suddenly took a shine to cleaning and organizing. About a week after moving in, the kitchen still wasn't organized, although we'd finally finished washing and drying the cabinet shelves. The shelves rose up to the ceiling on one entire side of the kitchen, so washing them and lining them with contact paper had been a big, time-consuming job. It was about eleven at night, and instead of waiting until the next day, Mom was determined to empty the last boxes and put everything away. She was shoeless, working in stocking feet, still wearing her shirtwaist dress, while standing tippy-toe on a stool and reaching over her head to place her new, special occasion dishes on the very top shelf. I turned to grab another stack to hand her, when I heard eight freshly washed, never-before-used, gold-trimmed Noritake soup bowls crash and shatter on the linoleum.

"Ooh no, the dishes, my dishes. Why is everything such a struggle?" she sighed, reaching out imploringly, as if to catch them. Taking a deep breath, she stepped down, flopped on the floor and burst into tears.

"Mom, you're going to cut yourself! Don't sit there. It'll be okay. It could have been you that fell. Get up. They're just dishes." I pulled two from the pile that were badly chipped but potentially usable.

"You're not happy here."

"Yes I am, Mom."

She ignored me and the two bowls. "What next? Bills are piling up. I don't even have a decent pair of drawers to wear; they're all nothing but rags," she said mournfully, but she always said that when she was feeling sorry for herself. Usually, my mother wore panties—which by the way, always looked quite decent coming out of the clothes dryer—but when she was laying a guilt trip on me, or things weren't going well, her pretty nylon panties turned into pitiful raggedy drawers.

250

Sweeping up shards of white porcelain made the tears flow faster, smudging her cheeks with runny black mascara, making her look utterly woe-begone. Despite the underwear comment, a surge of guilt, sorrow and tears spilled out of me, from seeing my generally optimistic mother so exhausted and inconsolable. Sharing that late-night crying session forever closed the gulf between Edgecombe and Convent Avenue, and the new home crisis ended.

If you were moving up in Harlem, the southwest corner of Sugar Hill, where we landed, fit the bill. An otherwise desirable location was Riverside Drive, the street Michele's parents settled on when they left Edgecombe. Technically, Riverside wasn't in Harlem, even though people thought it was, now that blacks lived there. The couple from whom Mom and Jack "bought" our new apartment (money got spread around to lobby the landlord and generously tip the super to fend off other "donors"), turned around and bought a house in the suburb of Mount Vernon. For whatever reasons, they did not remain in Westchester County and after a few years, when Upper West Side buildings became more accepting of black tenants, came back to live on Manhattan's West End Avenue. Riverside Drive and West End were close to both the number four and five bus lines, locations that were definitely an "improved lifestyle in a better neighborhood."

Aesthetically, 302 Convent Avenue was certainly a step up from our former home. A stately category "A-" building with ten-foot ceilings, 302 had a polished brass-trimmed elevator, large, gracious lobby and seven-room apartments with spacious kitchens, multiple baths and maids' quarters. Our smaller five-room unit lacked the latter two amenities. Harlem's "A" buildings had all of the above, plus a part-time or full-time doorman. The neighborhood was architecturally diverse, full of well-appointed apartments, brownstones, limestone town-houses, freestanding mansions, churches, cultural institutions and schools. Four blocks south, Music and Art High School sat in the midst of City College campus. In their book, *Touring Historic Harlem*, Andrew S. Dolkart and Gretchen S. Sorin noted there had once been an old building on CCNY's south campus that was a Convent of the Sacred Heart, the institution thought to be responsible for the street's name.[3]

We were surrounded by "society" neighbors who attended society functions requiring them to hire sitters, so soon after settling in, I established a babysitting business. One of my first jobs was for the Carter family, whose son Stephen was a quiet, serious child I should have borrowed to show my brother how behaving was supposed to work. Houston had acquired the habit of shooting any boy who came over to the house to see me, with rubber bullets from his bazooka gun. Stephen is now a distinguished professor at Yale Law School and a best selling author, perhaps most notably of the novel *The Emperor of Ocean Park.*

Immediately beside us, in apartment forty-three, Mrs. Dixon, an elderly widow, lived alone in seven rooms. Behind her thick Coke-bottle eyeglasses, we suspected she was blind, senile, or else we had beside us the consummate Sugar Hill snob. Her accent was West Indian, but the few clipped words she uttered in our presence tilted towards a veddy veddy British way of saying "Oh, now who are you again?" Few women wore hats on a regular basis anymore. Mrs. Dixon wore hats and white gloves to walk to the corner for a loaf of bread. After one of her outings, we sometimes found her standing in the hall, clutching milk or bread to her bosom, fumbling with the key, trying to open her apartment door.

If Mom said, "Hello Mrs. Dixon, it's Olivia and Jean from next door. Do you need any help, or want me to open your door?" she reared back, looked down her nose, but handed over the key. Lonely, reclusive, or maybe blind, Mrs. Dixon never acknowledged us, the common people next door.

An occasional quiet, cordial visitor to apartment forty-three was Mrs. Dixon's son, Dean. Unknown to us and most Americans, Dean Dixon was the principal conductor of the

Gothenburg Symphony Orchestra in Sweden. That fact was not shared by him. We learned of his acclaim through chatter in the building. Considered a prodigy as a child and a maestro in his prime, Dean couldn't overcome American racial restrictions that stymied his career. Despite being Ivy League educated and classically trained and gifted, the only major symphonies willing to hire him were in Europe, where he lived out his life.

I first met Stanford at Snooky's Sugar Bowl Restaurant on Seventh Avenue. Most everybody working or living near Seventh Avenue knew Snooky, a five-foot-tall firebrand with crossed eyes and a Napoleon complex. Kids were tempted to make fun of his eyes, his size, or his loser-sounding name, but didn't, because he was scary. The rumor mill was full of stories about Snooky tossing kids out of his restaurant for defying him, or committing minor infractions, like touching the salt and pepper shakers before food arrived at the table.

I had eaten dinner in the Sugar Bowl with Daddy, not realizing it was an after-church, Sunday morning hangout for Jack and Jill teenagers whose families belonged to St. Phillips Episcopal on 134th Street, around the corner from the restaurant. Outsiders, like me, who didn't belong to Jack and Jill or even practice the right religion, also showed up to mingle over milk shakes and banana splits.

Michele didn't ordinarily worship at St. Phillips, but arranged to attend service with her aunts, so afterwards we could go check out boys at the Sugar Bowl. By this time, I was even more skeptical about some Catechism rules, like the one about burning in hell for worshiping in any church that wasn't Catholic. But, I also didn't want to chance it, so I caught up with Michele after my usual Mass at St. Catherine's.

I'd just turned thirteen, was finally wearing a garter belt and cinnamon-colored stockings, straight seams in the back.

I knew I looked dynamite that day in Aunt Cee's snazzy two piece, hand-me-down white lace suit that I'd had my eye on for years. Michele and I strolled into the busy restaurant, edged to the back and prayed we'd find an empty booth, because ending up at the counter with adults wasn't what we were aiming for.

As luck would have it, Frank Hudson, a boy we both knew from Edgecombe, waved us over to join him in a back booth where he sat with another kid. Frank was a long, tall beanpole and he quickly rose to greet us, then motioned to his friend. The friend was an even taller, eager, smart-looking boy with thick glasses and yards of arms and legs folded under him like a newborn colt's. When the friend got untangled, he stood up and Frank bravely fumbled through introductions.

"Jean, I'd like you to meet Stanford. Michele, this is Stanford. Stanford, this is Jean and Michele."

That got us through eight bumbling seconds before everyone sat down and listened to Stan sucking on a large chocolate milkshake, his eyes on the cup. After an uncomfortable amount of slurping time, I sensed Michele was ready to jolly us along and tell Stan to "Stop it," or ask, "What's wrong with you? Can't you talk, or are you retarded or something?" But Frank rescued us by mentioning that I'd recently moved.

"Stanford," he said, looking at his friend, "I've known Jean since we were little kids. She used to live three houses from me, but just deserted the old neighborhood and moved to 302 Convent A..." Before Frank finished uttering my new address, Stan gulped, choked and knocked what remained of his shake into my lap and spit the rest in my face.

A pile of napkins addressed the immediate catastrophe, but nothing stopped Michele from hee-hawing like a jackass, and drawing every eye in the restaurant to our table. Michele kept laughing and Stan, his voice rushing up and down multiple registers, kept eeking and squeaking a repeated apology. "Oh my God. I'm sorry, I didn't mean to do that."

Damp and mortified, I swiped napkins across my face, woodenly repeating "It's okay, it'll dry," but thinking no bigger fool existed in the universe. I wanted to leave, but remained in a sticky wet seat, too afraid to walk through a gauntlet of snooty kids with what looked like diarrhea running down my legs. Thank God Snooky wasn't there; the only thing more humiliating than walking out would have been getting kicked out.

Stan finally started speaking in sentences, words knocking each other over with nervousness. "The reason I got so carried away is because, cause that's so, so amazing," he blathered incoherently. "You see," he squeaked, the point still eluding us, "that, that, that's just great because if Frank hadn't introduced us today and if I just saw you on Convent, I couldn't have said hello properly," he cluelessly explained.

"Instead of living three houses from Frank, now you live next door to me. You're my neighbor," he finally got to the point, as if I cared where the big doofus lived.

Stan and I got through that crisis, which was memorable for two awkward kids, and the neighbor-thing did become a factor in our lives. His parents' townhouse was next to our building and until he left for college, I saw him hundreds of times while running errands. Errands were now simply chores I needed to get out of the way. The new neighborhood had more people and real estate than Edgecombe. The stores were on Amsterdam, and some as far as Broadway, two of Manhattan's busiest thoroughfares with unyielding traffic and soulless businesses that cared little about customer service.

When I chatted with Stan, or a few other neighborhood kids I later met, we mingled briefly on the sidewalk, since there was no place else to go. The weird thing about the city, and our move to a fancier street, was that most park benches within five blocks were now claimed by junkies, winos and pigeons.

Stan was a work in progress. First he got contacts, then grew into those impossible arms and legs, and his voice settled into a deeper octave, conveying intelligence and gentlemanliness. When he started driving his father's cream and black Buick Riviera, I figured the remaking of an unbroken puppy was over. Stan became my best date and lifelong friend. During his first year at Dartmouth, I was still in high school and he invited me to Hanover, New Hampshire for Winter Carnival. Later that summer, we rode around Westchester County, ate spaghetti at Stella D'oro's Restaurant in the Bronx, and once drove twenty miles out to Coney Island so we could buy two of Nathan's Famous hot dogs.

Stan has had a long distinguished career, including interim president of CCNY, up the street from where we lived. In his final position at the university, he was appointed dean of the college's medical school. But after forty years, Stan still blushes and stammers like a fourteen-year-old when I remind him how we met.

16. New Lincoln School

"Hi, my name's Stewie" were the first welcoming words that encircled me that morning when I stepped into the lobby of my new school. All around me, returning students were busy getting reacquainted after a three-month break. But there was sweet Stewie, a cute curly-haired black kid, with a sunburst smile and square-sounding name.

An hour earlier, before she put a halt to our conversation, Mom and I had gone round and round about her taking me to school. "No, and don't keep asking" she said. "It's ridiculous. Just think about it."

"But Mom, please, I'm nervous. It's not like it was at P.S. 46. I won't know one single person."

"You've been going to school by yourself since second grade, and now you want me to walk you into junior high! Think how that would look."

Her refusal was completely out of character because, in maddening ways, she stuck her nose into everything I did. Although it happened four years later, she pulled one of her most over-the-top maneuvers the time my friend Billie invited me to visit her at Howard University. Billie was a college freshman and I was a high school junior. Howard had a reputation as a wild party school, which my mother some-how knew about, although I didn't. But I was a responsible seventeen, almost eighteen-year-old who felt this weekend request should have been a no-brainer. Earlier that winter, in February, Mom had let me go up to Dartmouth's Winter Carnival with way fewer questions asked, and a minimum of drama.

When I got back from that trip to New Hampshire, I couldn't stop bubbling with excitement. "Mom, they had an ice sculpture contest. You wouldn't believe some things they carved, like a twenty-foot dragon and Mickey and Mini Mouse characters. And you should have heard the Dartmouth Glee club. Every one of those guys could be a professional singer. How do they do that?"

"Lessons, years of hard work and practice. If you had kept up with your tap lessons," she couldn't help reminding me, "you could be a very accomplished dancer by now, just like those Dartmouth singers."

"I hated tap dancing and wasn't good at it. Maybe if I'd taken singing lessons, I wouldn't sound so off-key in chorus."

"Well, we could consider singing lessons."

"No, that's okay," I quickly added. "I meant maybe I should have taken them instead of dancing. Hugh, our music teacher at school is teaching us to sing different parts for the spring concert. I stand in the back with worse singers than me. I'm an alto."

"That's wonderful" she said, presumably about being an alto, then asked, "does Hugh give private lessons?"

The weekend at Dartmouth really had been terrific. We hung out with Stan's friends, who were also smart, polite and intent on showing their dates the best of what Dartmouth had to offer. I saw no need to tell Mom the campus also had its share of beer chuggers, up-chuggers and wild fraternity boys. If I'd drawn the entire map for her, there probably wouldn't have been any discussion about visiting Howard, because I knew how her mind worked. She would have said, "I knew I shouldn't have allowed you to go galavanting off to a place without adult supervision. In another year, you'll be leaving for college. That's time enough to spend a weekend on some campus"—or words to that effect.

Despite my glowing report about New Hampshire, obtaining permission to visit Howard turned into a tennis match, with me pleading and Mom vacillating back-and-forth for days on end before finally giving the okay, but with one stipulation. "You may go" she agreed, "but I'll have to call the Dean of Women."

I thought, oh shit, she's gotta be kidding, but she was speaking in her throw-up-every-obstacle voice, the one she had adopted now that Gram wasn't doing all the dirty work for her.

"Why do you have to do that?" I asked, hoping she might just want to make sure boys couldn't visit girls' rooms, or perhaps check to see if freshmen girls were allowed to invite overnight guests. "Yesterday, I thought you said it would be a good idea to visit Howard so I could compare an all-black college to a mostly white one, like Dartmouth."

"You can do that, but I also want the Dean of Women to know you're coming, so she'll be sure you're properly chaperoned. She may be too busy to check on you personally, but surely Billie's dorm has a housemother who looks after the girls and I want her to know you're there."

My mother didn't often say flat out "no" to my requests anymore, but I couldn't get a simple "yes," either. She'd started acting as if all teenage business was linked to the devil and kept me off balance by coming up with Faustian conditions, like the call to Washington. If I wanted to go to Michele's house on Saturday afternoon—something that used to be fairly automatic—I first had to clean my closet, tidy my room or do some other make-work project that might cause me to lose interest or forget what I planned to do. If I asked to stay at a school dance until it ended at 11 p.m., I could. But, at 10:30, I had to leave my friends, find a dime and go stomping around the building looking for a phone so I could check in and let her know I wasn't dead in an alley, or alive and smooching in the back seat of someone's car.

A boy named Douglas caused a lot of this trouble. I met him that summer before my junior year of high school, when he was visiting his aunt and uncle, a "society" couple in our building, who had a weekend home in Sag Harbor, an exclusive section of Long Island, where blacks had carved out their own small, but exclusive enclave. Douglas was a very good-looking, sophisticated Southerner who'd just been accepted to Meharry Medical School. Before he left town, even Jack, who usually just concentrated on my brother, said to me, "You better watch yourself around that slick, fast talking North Carolina nigger." It was the winter after Douglas wowed every Harlem girl he met that I went down to Howard and got an eyeful of how some of those smooth Southern sweet talkers, like Douglas, interact with certain young ladies.

During the train ride to Washington, a half dozen scenarios whizzed through my mind, especially the one with Billie ordering me out of her sight, once she realized we were being shadowed by the dean. But when my taxi approached a large university complex with multiple dormitories, large classrooms and administrative buildings, I relaxed somewhat and hoped maybe the dean had brushed Mom off as a crank caller.

I suppose the fact that men weren't permitted in women's rooms could be construed as chaperoning. Except for a few conscientious girls studying in cubicles at the end of Billie's floor, the women weren't around either, because they were in men's apartments where all the action was.

With her new, home-away-from-home freedom, Billie had reinvented herself into a wild child who ran with a fast crowd. Her idea of a good time was tramping around DC looking for purple Jesus parties, where male-female twosomes called dibs on the next empty bedroom. At one stop, a dark-skinned girl came out of a bedroom and did a little self-congratulatory Geraldine-type song and dance routine, à la the comedian Flip Wilson. "The blacker the berry," she sang, snapping her fingers, whirling and drunk-jitterbugging in circles, "the sweeter the juice."

The sexual revolution hadn't hit my friends in Harlem, and if it had, nobody was telling. Before that weekend, I thought our generation's promiscuous behavior was confined to a few fast white kids at school who crossed limits and severely distressed their elders.

A handful of students at New Lincoln were well acquainted with marijuana, abortions, bulimia, analysis, weekends that stretched into a week at home alone while their folks traveled, and telling their stepfathers to "F-off." Black students at New Lincoln were mostly like me, from homes where grandma, or her clone, demanded basics like please, thank you and a good night kiss for mommy and daddy. If you got pregnant, you feared the threat of being sent to Mississippi could come true, and with a father like Michele's, count on getting your butt kicked before it landed in front of the Vicksburg, Mississippi poor house. Howard proved that clearly, another group of us was out there.

Back in seventh grade, I waited in a lobby devoid of parents. A teacher named Fred, with a mop of very blonde hair, read my name as part of the group going to a class called Core 7B. In the elevator, I stood quietly next to a still smiling Stewie and said a prayer of thanks to my mother for getting this one right.

When New Lincoln opened in 1946, education was slowly changing because of reformers like John Dewey. New progressive schools emphasized a child's individuality. Rather than writing, reciting and sitting still, the modern approach now focused on student involvement and hands-on interaction. Freedom, informality, writing, history, economics and literature were integrated into our core curriculum. But for the first few months, I kept wondering what happened to plain old English and history.

My transition to New Lincoln from the silent, workbook-oriented, authoritarian classrooms of P.S. 46 was not easy. Under the old system, I'd been a star. Here, we sat at movable desks that constantly shifted to form large or small circles. No one slammed doors, rapped knuckles or demanded silence. Classes were fast-paced, lively affairs and we were encouraged to ask questions and make comments, as though our opinions actually mattered. I loved being there, but was politically naive, out of step and mostly silent among glib conversationalists who, at age thirteen, understood that Russia's frigid weather wasn't why we were in a Cold War. Many seventh graders had moved up from the lower school and were already progressive, or blessed with affluent parents who had exposed them to a life of intellect and discovery.

Sometimes we worked independently and on those days, I bet I wasn't the only one confused. The committee studying China's natural resources clustered in the west corner of the classroom, so they wouldn't disturb the Chinese military group by the coat closet. My pod, assigned to the library to research industry, might produce little all morning except too much noise, then recriminations from a librarian who said, "Get serious or I'm sending you back upstairs," but never did.

"Work" often got put on hold to watch a film, take a field trip or welcome guests who demonstrated Chinese calligraphy, arranged flowers, told stories, or showed slides. Today, this is how much of America teaches, and kids who seemingly get nowhere are often learning fact, as well as how to think independently and work cooperatively. In the 1950s, New Lincoln was cutting edge, and it took me awhile to understand that, indeed, the school taught English and history and did it very well.

Initially, I found my center of gravity with foreign language. Spanish was Spanish; it was taught through memory and drill and, as far as I could tell, was not part of Core. We not only called the teacher Señora Loos, instead of Dorothy, but she called me Señorita, rather than Theresa.

Some days were a blur, but everything didn't come with complications. I partied at bar and bat mitzvahs, got a picture of my clay pot published in an art book, snuck cigarettes, sat in fifth-row center at theater birthday parties, and I learned what rich meant. A visit to Teddy's house got me on track about real wealth, because I'd been way off the mark on that one. Years later, when I read *Bonfire of the Vanities*, Tom Wolfe described Teddy's house:

> Why, his building was one of the great ones built just before the First World War! Back then it was still not entirely proper for a good family to live in an apartment (instead of a house). So the apartments were built like mansions, with eleven-, twelve-, thirteen-foot ceilings, vast entry galleries, staircases, servants' wings, herringbone-parquet floors, interior walls a foot thick, exterior walls as thick as a fort's and fireplaces, fireplaces, fireplaces, even though the buildings were all built with central heating. A Mansion!—except that you arrived at the front door via an elevator (opening upon your own private vestibule) instead of the street.[1]

My evening in this apartment was spent in the boondocks part of the house: the children's wing. We were shown into a large playroom with a sagging couch and a few pieces of scarred-up furniture and dim lighting. Teddy and his siblings had destroyed all the table lamps, leaving only a naked, sixty watt light bulb hanging thirteen forlorn feet above our heads.

Having a seventh grade party was sort of like inviting over twenty-five puppies who weren't house broken. Only brave, strict or naive parents allowed large amounts of hormones and braces into their beautiful homes. Teddy's parents probably permitted it because they had that big buffer zone that was already stripped of anything breakable. Despite being told to stay in the kids' area, we did some wandering and running around. The apartment had guest rooms, alcoves, store rooms, dressing rooms, two or three unnamed rooms that could've been living rooms, an office, the library and a grand staircase leading to the terrace or the penthouse, maybe both; I'm not sure. After seventh grade, Teddy left New Lincoln to attend a boarding school. I don't know what his family did or who they were, but they showed me rich.

Besides the plain rich, the rich and famous also sent their children to New Lincoln, and it was favored by parents in show business. Harry Belafonte's daughters, Adrianne and Sheri, were in the lower school, and Josh and Toby Mostel were a few grades behind me. Their father, Zero Mostel, would soon star as Tevye, the leading role in the Broadway production of *Fiddler on the Roof*. Before Brandon DeWilde withdrew to focus on his acting career, he'd already been nominated for an Oscar for his role as Joey, the little boy in the movie, *Shane*. Barbara Buloff's father, Joseph, was a famous actor on the Yiddish stage and Mr. Carnovsky, Steve's dad, performed in Shakespearean plays.[2] Herbie Sondheim, in the class ahead of me, had an older brother named Stephen who had something to do with the play, *West Side Story*. Except for Josh Mostel; a wild, zany kid, who was good at disrupting class with one-liners and Harry Belafonte, who everybody knew, I had no inkling of my schoolmates' connections to fame until I was long gone from New Lincoln.

While enrolled, much of what I did discover about the world of theater came from Susan, another new seventh grader. Susan's father, Frank Loesser, wrote the music for a Broadway play called *The Most Happy Fella*. Broadway was awash in mega hits in the late 1950s–60s, which helped explain why my seventh grade class was full of drama queens who peppered their conversations with the word, "lovely," but pronounced "lov-er-ly," the way the character Eliza Doolittle said it in the play, *My Fair Lady*.

Melodramatic girls floated through hallways and danced in the locker room, emoting song lyrics from *My Fair Lady*, but also *West Side Story*, *Most Happy Fella* or any number of other shows. On Saturdays, my classmates went to see one of the plays for a second, third or fourth time, then waited for autographs at the stage door, so they could continue filling up their Playbills.

When her father's show opened on Broadway, Susan's parents moved from their home in Hollywood to New York so, like me, she was a new girl at school. New Lincoln was welcoming, but there was still an old-school culture, with an in-crowd that neither of us belonged to and as a result, we became friends. Susan was not one of the drama queens. Having spent twelve years around California movie stars, she was beyond star-stuck and as far as I was concerned, many days at New Lincoln were mind-bending, so a few Broadway tunes and dances didn't do much for me, either.

For months at a time, *Most Happy Fella* sold out its Saturday matinees, but on several occasions, to the consternation of fussy lady ushers, Susan invited me to see the show anyway. She got us there late, waltzed regally into the darkened Imperial Theater and plopped down on the front mezzanine step, with me tripping along behind her; both of us in flagrant violation of the fire code. Once, when the lady next to me wouldn't stop tsk-tsking because no one made us move, I leaned over to whisper, "This is Susan, Frank Loesser's daughter. She's allowed to sit here." The lady nudged her friend with the news, left us alone until intermission, then tried to suck up to Susan.

Susan was a big part of my progressive experience. She and her parents invited me to Carnegie Hall, Sardi's and the Russian Tea Room, where I made the mistake of ordering my first club sandwich on an evening when everyone else was just having drinks.

My social life wasn't all one-sided. Mom thought I should give a party, too—a small one—to reciprocate for all the nice children who invited me places.

"Are you sure they'll come?" I asked, worried that I'd be stood up at my own party.

"Of course. These parents," she declared with certainty, "are liberal-minded and won't deprive their children of a pleasant evening in Harlem."

The party was also Mom's chance to feel good about the apartment and show off her modern unskirted, slim, low-back living room furniture that was all done up in custom-made plastic slip covers. Still, I sensed a couple of flaws in the plan. The first one was caviar. "Mom, what does caviar taste like? All the other mothers serve cocktail franks that we dip in a mustard and BBQ sauce."

She waved that idea away. "Caviar is just tiny pieces of fish you spread on rye bread and anyway, no one sells miniature frankfurters in Harlem."

About fifteen kids showed up and she served them caviar, horrible little fishy-tasting black peas. Where she found caviar and miniature rye bread, I never asked, but it sure wasn't in Harlem. My friends ate the bread, but didn't like caviar and disposed of it in ways that Mom deemed inappropriate.

A second problem was Susan and Michael. I guess it was inevitable that, at one of these parties, two bodies would start heavy hugging and smooching on a bed. I just wish it hadn't been my party. At other gatherings, kids were making their way towards this natural boy-girl behavior but up to now, they mostly cuddled up on the dance floor or sat holding hands on the couch.

Jack was working, my brother was asleep and for an hour, Mom did a credible job of leaving us in peace, until she spotted mashed black caviar in the fibers of her orange shag rug, then came in to wipe it up. After that, her room checks turned into a nonstop parade, up and down the hallway. Then for some doggone reason, she went into my bedroom, probably because Susan and Michael were noisily necking under the coat pile. Mom didn't like that, got loud, and said all the wrong things.

"Susan, Michael, get off that bed, right now. I mean im-me-di-ate-ly," she enunciated in a loud, steely voice that made me cringe, even though I was a good twenty-five feet down the hall from my bed, and around two corners. "Michael," she continued, "you've got your dirty shoes on some other child's coat. Take them off. No, not the shoes, your feet. Get off the bed, right this minute. Susan, put your shoes back on. Who turned this lamp off? Turn these lights back on right now, and go back in the living room. Look at this mess."

Until then, the evening had been a partial success of drinking Cokes and dancing to everyone's favorite hits like *Silhouettes* and *Little Bitty Pretty One*. After Mom spoiled the fun, kids started digging their coats from the pile and heading downstairs to find cabs, except for Jimmy. He lived in White Plains and had to get picked up. With my mother scraping more squished caviar and rye bread from her rug, and about a millisecond from boiling over again, I came up with the idea for Jimmy and me to hang out the window, watching for his father's car to pull up. It was either that, or sit in the living room, waiting for my mother to blow up. By the time Jimmy left, I decided I didn't want to have any more parties.

Just as I got into a rhythm, I also got the new teacher, Mrs. Margolis. Stout; corseted, gray-haired, she was a throwback to old public school days. Why the administration went to suburban Connecticut to find her, instead of recruiting on the West Side or looking in the West Village, where most of the hip teachers lived, I don't know. She was like a nun in street drag, just meaner, more sarcastic and masterful at public humiliation. She also held "cubby parties." Instead of lockers, we had open cubbies in the back of the classroom. If you didn't keep yours neat, you might return from art or music and find your stuff on the floor with her stomping on it.

When she was in a really foul mood, she waited until everyone was seated and watching, then marched to the back of the room to trash your belongs and your stupid inability to get it right. I was never the recipient of a party, but I incurred her worst wrath one day in the balcony of the auditorium.

She was rehearsing the cast of the spring musical and didn't permit anyone to watch. I thought I'd take a peek anyway. Big mistake. She saw me, stopped rehearsal and screamed, among other things, "Get out of that balcony and down here, you dirty little sneak." Instead, I headed to the girl's "lounge," the bathroom floor near our classroom. It was a place to retreat and offer counsel, like the time we consoled Laurie, the only girl in our class who still didn't have her period. Yeah, what a bummer, we all agreed.

Mrs. Margolis stormed in five minutes later and found me huddled in the corner, hiccupping in hysterics. I wouldn't have felt so bad if she had skewered me in front of my class, instead of all her pet, upper grade, goody-goody theater students. New Lincoln was a permissive school, but I thought I was a goner when I yelled, "I hate you, you bitch."

"Theresa, I'm shocked to hear one of the nicest girls in class talk like that," she chimed in a totally non-shocked tone of voice. A theater teacher (whose rehearsal, I later learned, hadn't been going well), mother of two, and a twenty-five year veteran of the classroom, I guess she'd seen her share of humiliated girls, since humiliating them was her specialty. I was well aware that parents and teachers never apologized after chewing you out, but her utter lack of remorse pissed me off even more, and if I could have moved one, I would have thrown a toilet at her.

When I didn't stop crying, she switched to her I'm-busy-and-late-for-class sugarcoated voice of exasperation, explaining that secrecy is vital during rehearsals to preserve a play's dramatic impact for opening night. That made sense and I was wrong. Give her credit, she didn't report me. I just had to finish a tainted term of world history and Greek mythology with the only teacher out of dozens over a lifetime, who I couldn't find it in my heart to like.

New Lincoln was an early pioneer in political correctness. Mrs. Oliver informed us first day of class, that American Indians would henceforth be known as the Indigenous Population.

"Indians," she felt, was demeaning. It connoted ignorant savages as portrayed in movies and television, so we were instructed to use a more respectful term that none of us had heard before.

Ours was a school that nurtured individuals and championed differences. Show business personalities and liberal New Yorkers sent their kids to New Lincoln because the school wasn't afraid of artists, intellectuals or progressive thinkers who, among other things, believed in integration and voting rights for black people. Several parents, including Zero Mostel, who had been subjected to the inquisitional McCarthy hearings, wanted their children shielded from the prejudice and anti-Communist madness still sweeping the country.

In Susan Loesser's biography of her father, *A Most Remarkable Fella*, she cites an example of how blacklisting affected another New Lincoln parent, Abe Burrows, whose daughter Laurie was the friend we consoled in the bathroom. During World War II, with help from Mr. Loesser, a young soldier named Stuart Ostrow, who would later win a Tony for *M Butterfly*, had pulled off a coup and gotten Abe Burrows to write the script for a play Ostrow was preparing for Air Force entertainment. Ostrow said:

> "I was in heaven... I went back to Washington and said, 'Yup. Got 'em.' And two days later was summoned to a senator's office, and they started asking me questions: What political groups did I belong to ... and so forth. And suddenly I realized what was going on. This was the McCarthy era, and Abe had been blacklisted. I also realized that Frank had agreed to do this show to help Abe—get him identified with the United States Government. I thought that was the most remarkable thing. It didn't happen, though, because the government said no. And I had to go back to Abe Burrows and tell him the government didn't want him."[3]

Among our diverse faculty and student body was one misfit named Ben. The school had several nonconforming, Bohemian, beatnik, odd-duck originals, but no one like Ben. I can only speculate that his parents made him come to New Lincoln because he needed to lighten up. The repressive political climate was improving and Senator McCarthy was about to be disgraced, but we still had this large, loud, conservative fifteen-year-old who, if I didn't know better I'd swear was the young Rush Limbaugh, although at age fifteen, Limbaugh probably wasn't the windbag he is now.

Ben wasn't there on scholarship, like I was. He was Mr. Money; a rich Park Avenue kid who knew exactly how the world should run. He noisily voiced his opinions on communists, liberal thinkers and teachers who didn't shave their legs. When we had a mock, all-school presidential election, we suspected that Ben cast the single nay vote against Adali Stevenson.

One day we were told by the Student Governance Committee that a Russian would be coming to the next all-school assembly. This was the sort of thing New Lincoln did so well. With the free world shunning Russia, New Lincoln used the close proximity of the Soviet Consulate to their advantage and invited a diplomat in for a chat. That was true progressive, experiential learning. Throughout high school, I thought kids who signed up for Governance were more intimidating than most of our teachers. They looked and acted like they were in charge of the school, or the world. I worked in the safe confines of the Display Committee, designing and decorating seven floors of bulletin boards. In the art room, instead of discussing NATO and SEATO, we debated whether to use burnt sienna or zinc orange.

The pending diplomat's visit may have been a joint effort by students, administrators and a diplomat-parent from another country on friendlier terms with the Soviets. At varying times, we had international students whose parents were in New York with the United Nations, or they worked with European or Asian corporations. At any rate, the Russian was coming and this was a very big deal. New Lincoln was a liberal school, interested in fostering academic honesty and modern teaching methods, but coddling Russians was not part of its agenda. No matter how young and politically naive any of us were about communism, we all knew that Russians were barbarians, capable of annihilating us at a moment's notice, and their mothers really did wear combat boots.

We were coached on the uniqueness of this event and told how to behave. No confrontational questions that might cause an international incident. In fact, the questions were planted and pre-approved. No smiling. Dress up. Be polite. "Use of the word 'comrade' is inappropriate sarcasm," Dick Miller told us. "Above all, don't refer to his country as Russia," Mrs. Oliver said. "Call it the Soviet Union." And put a muzzle on Ben, I silently added.

Tension in the auditorium was palpable. Nervousness caused all of us to softly murmur and fidget. During the introduction, David, our student moderator, his arms folded like Ed Sullivan's, displayed his usual frightening aplomb, sailing through all the appropriate clichés: "This is a special occasion and cultural exchange," he told us. "It is a great pleasure for us to have such an honored guest as we search for openness, information, educational opportunity and a better future."

When the Russian began talking, his chilly manner swept over us like a Siberian wind. More stunning was that this man, with an unpronounceable name, spoke flawless, unaccented English. With his clean-cut good looks and well-tailored suit, he contrasted sharply with Khrushchev, his portly, dough-faced boss. This man could have blended in with the Madison Avenue lunch crowd, and probably did. Although I remember him easing up a bit on the attitude, probably because David's courtesy and poise was making him look like a paranoid Soviet jackass, I no longer recall much of the strained exchange between students and guest. However, I don't think any of us in the room will ever forget this significant happening, including Ben, who like everyone else except assigned questioners, sat quietly, held their breath and listened.

Another New Lincoln-esque event occurred shortly afterwards. Perhaps for security reasons, there was no prelude to this one. After school one day, I walked into Dreamland luncheonette, our three o'clock hangout, and instantly recognized Minniejean Brown. She was one of the Little Rock Nine, a group of black students whose faces were continually plastered across America's newspapers and television screens. After weeks of violence and harassment from Arkansas segregationists and fellow students, the Nine, with considerable White House and 101st Airborne Army intervention, had been admitted to their city's formerly all-white Central High School. They were in, but it was a volatile situation because they were constantly being kicked, hit, harassed in the hallways and cafeteria. Their books were stolen and their lockers broken into.[4]

In a victory for the segregationists, Minniejean Brown got suspended. She apparently was the most emotional, least docile of the Nine and was punished for fighting back. Because of additional notoriety, her face was the one best known throughout the country. Everyone assumed she would return to Little Rock's black high school. Instead, Minniejean came North to complete eleventh and twelfth grades at New Lincoln.

Dreamland's proprietor was the same Snooky, of the warrior mentality, who owned the Sugar Bowl restaurant where I met Stan. At three o'clock on some days, Dreamland filled up with noisy New Lincoln kids, all of us except Snooky, feeling groovy because school was over. Even though we spent money, he was always kicking kids out for dripping chocolate on the table, or lingering too long over an egg cream. And the man had eyes in back of his head for spotting a sitter—anyone not spending money. Despite constant harassment, we kept going back, although I personally avoided the place when the only thing in my pocket was lint and a bus pass.

I must have been flush with quarters the day I went in to find an animated Minniejean, wearing a teen-tall pastel dress with bobby socks and brown loafers, surrounded by an instant following of upper school friends and supporters. She was also leaning considerable weight against Snooky's jukebox. Instead of his usual Nazi routine, I guess Snooky got swept into Minniejean's celebrity aura, because he gave her and the rabble a pass that time and kept his grumpy butt in the kitchen.

I could tell right off that this strapping, tall saucy black girl, who confidently fielded questions from admirers, would have been hard to push around. She had a cute crooked smile, but was blunt, looked strong enough to lay anyone flat and did not seem interested in ass-kissing all the kids who gathered around to welcome her. Two days later, she was up on the school stage leading assembly with her big voice rendition of *He's Got the Whole World in His Hands*, which became a kind of theme song for her.

In some ways, Minniejean reminded me of my friend Michele; both were fearless, hair-pulling, bust-your-chops kind of girls who conveyed toughness and attitude by sheer size and impatience, although Michele wasn't a fighter. And as far as I knew, the only altercation Minniejean ever had was the one that caused her to be put on a plane to New York City. Watching her that day, I could imagine some black-hearted prom queen in Central High's lunchroom, or maybe it was the Big Man On Campus, who recognized Minniejean was reaching her boiling point. He, or she, then zeroed-in and egged her on until she got suspended for dumping a bowl of food on one of her tormenters.[5]

Considering her unwillingness to suffer fools, it remains a puzzle to me why advisors put her through that desegregation experience. Though they appeared spontaneous, many civil rights cases and public showdowns were planned, well-thought-out encounters. Two years before the Little Rock uproar, Rosa Parks became a champion for civil rights when she declined to relinquish her seat to a white man on a Montgomery, Alabama bus.

Mrs. Parks was the first black Montgomery woman to challenge her arrest for defying segregated seating laws in public places, but she wasn't the first black female in the state to be arrested for this offense. Eight months earlier, a feisty high school girl, Claudette Colvin, was hauled off a Montgomery bus and jailed for refusing to yield her seat to a white man. A multiracial, civil rights group considered turning Claudette Colvin's defense into an attack on segregation. However, after learning she was immature, prone to cursing and worse, pregnant, they just bailed her out of jail[6] and wished her luck.

In part, Mrs. Parks became an American Civil Rights icon because she was the perfect dignified lady who photographed well. She also happened to be a well-spoken, religious woman who appeared on television and in newspapers wearing a style of rimless eyeglasses that made her appear intellectual. And although she was an intelligent woman, she was a seamstress and considered working class enough to lead the effort to desegregate the Montgomery, Alabama bus system.[7]

After Minniejean's suspension, she left Arkansas with help from influential members of the New Lincoln community, including Drs. Kenneth and Mamie Clark, whose research on the detrimental effects of segregation on black children was used as evidence in the landmark case, Brown vs. The Board of Education.

Enrolling her in our school fit the mission of this socially conscious institution. She could finish high school and in the process teach all of us well-intentioned, but naive black, white and yellow Northerners, about the "hard knocks" brand of civil rights. Despite the school's noble goal of fostering integration, when she arrived, New Lincoln received its share of "commie-yellow-pinko-bastard" hate mail.[8]

But every day was not always a happening, nor was a progressive approach to learning always a good fit for me. Mrs. Carpenter's American history textbook was Charles Beard's *Rise of American Civilization*, a continuous 800-page wall of tiny print with page-length paragraphs and no pictures or diagrams. Ben pompously applauded using a college level text, saying Beard's in-depth masterpiece was an intellectual epitome, or dichotomy, or some such SAT word I hadn't gotten the hang of.

My friends in public school, and even other private schools, used normal textbooks with subsections, a mixture of fonts, maps and occasional pictures to break up the onslaught of words. They also came away with letter or numeric grades that got to the heart of whether they were A, B or C students. Our core class grades were narratives. I received thoughtful comments; squishy treatises of encouragement that probably took an hour to compose, but led me to believe I was still a work in progress. When I inquired about my exact status, I heard, "You're doing just fine."

To overcome math phobia, the summer before junior year, I took Algebra II and Trigonometry in a public session, before taking it "for real." I kept it secret from friends and I don't know if George Washington High School sent my 100% grade and 95% Regents score to New Lincoln. I mastered problems and equations, and in September felt ready for whatever Mrs. Peller threw our way. Pre-preparation made little difference in an arena of laissez-faire sophistication. Math that year was full of smoke and fuzzy numbers, including mine, that were still in the 75% range.

Open, progressive learning wasn't proving to be as all-encompassing as it purported to be. I thrived on structure and remained out of step, afloat in a warm womb of solace, vaguely aware of another dimension. Chumminess and emphasis on self-esteem hid the fact I was in a sea of sharks. College was approaching, stakes were high and I did not know the rules of this highly competitive game. Why hadn't I realized Friday's informal chat was really a lecture? That sitting around laughing over Murray Kempton's column, in which he skewered some overarching politician, would result in a quiz? Or that working at my own speed was fine, but the power levels were set at a higher velocity?

275

As always, before I fell into a funk, something wonderful happened. On a three-day break from Charles Beard and algebraic equations, our chartered interstate bus headed down the Jersey Turnpike, towards Pennsylvania Dutch farm country. Riding the highway in a pre-iPod, filter-tipped cloud of Kool, we made our own music, singing *Turn, Turn, Turn* and *The Bells of Rhymney*. Having graduated from Sondheim and Loesser show tunes, to focus on social awareness, girls with sweet womanly voices now sang passionately for justice and peace, and for those, I sang along. Jimmy, our guitar man, helped the time pass by strumming *100 Bottles of Beer* and *A Hundred Miles*. New mantras were *Where Have all the Flowers Gone* and *We Shall Overcome*, protest music honed by many of us having volunteered at CORE and SNCC offices, helping prepare for the upcoming Youth March on Washington.

Sometimes we're lucky to emerge from the fog and catch the world in all its wonder. What had seemed tedious in American history, suddenly came alive on a sunny afternoon, in a small Pennsylvania town with a Shoshone-sounding name, inside a dairy barn that milked 1000 Holsteins every day, enabling me to pour milk over my Corn Flakes each morning. In the rolling Blue Mountains, bearded Amish men trotted up to our bus in open-sided carriages, before introducing us to their homespun life of simplicity. On the second day, the country's economic and industrial might stepped off the textbook pages at Bethlehem Steel's 200,000 acre plant, where white-hot liquid metal, miraculously hardened into steel beams, giving new meaning to the immensity of learning.

When we left on Sunday, it was one of the few times I wasn't in a hurry to get back home. Harlem had grounded me and given me a foundation. But after spending six years in an intellectually stimulating school environment and two short days riding a bus around small town America, I knew the possibilities in my life were endless. In a matter of months I would go off to college, which meant I would be leaving sweet Harlem and, like a wise woman, she was showing signs of letting me go.

Afterword

By the start of the next decade (1970s), when I end this story, the very soul of our community was unraveling. Guys who finished high school and should have gone to work, to City College or joined the service, instead became junkies. If they didn't die or do time, young men, women too, stayed under- or unemployed, further hurting themselves and the community; others resorted to drugs or crime.

Harlem has always been freewheeling and unpredictable. It isn't the same place today as the one I write about in this book. Now, tourists visit by the thousands. Refurbished parks, once the domains of undesirables, are filled with mommies and toddlers. Young people are keeping their parents' apartments, or moving in from faraway places; others are coming back home from the suburbs. They're techies, actors, physicians, housewives, doormen, investment bankers, entrepreneurs and hustlers who refurbish brownstones and open restaurants and businesses along Lenox and Seventh Avenue.

Harlem isn't perfect; it never was and never will be. But this new crop of survivors and strivers are willing to put their money on a horse named Harlem. Their determination and success is producing a trickle-down effect that has helped bring the *joie de vivre* back uptown.

Where Are They Now?

FAMILY
- Elder family members: deceased
- Houston: retired Naval Intelligence Specialist and Counselor for at-risk youth, Tacoma, WA
- Cousin Charles: retired Naval aviator and high school physics teacher, Philadelphia, PA
- Cousin George: deceased, 2008

THE EDGECOMBE AVENUE GANG
- Jackie Beverly: semi-retired teacher and administrator for NYC Public Schools
- Mary Jo: retired NYC Public Schools safety officer
- Ellen: still lives on Edgecombe
- Dedi: whereabouts unknown
- Jim Cummins (Jimmy in Chapter 3): photographer for *The New York Times, New York Newsday*, ESPN, NBA, Atlantic Records and other organizations
- Mark Wright (in Chapter 1): retired NYPD
- Billy and Ronald Goodwin: deceased
- Philip Goodwin: lives in the Bronx
- Wallace Goodwin: lives in Harlem, employed by Uptown Chamber of Harlem
- John B. Williams (Johnny in Chapter 14): lives in Los Angeles; bassist for numerous performers; 7 years with house band on *The Tonight Show with Johnny Carson*; 25-year musical association with singer Nancy Wilson
- Sonny Rollins: lived 4 houses away, but was not mentioned in book because he was too old to play with us. Sonny is the widely acclaimed jazz tenor saxophonist and a 2011 Kennedy Center Honoree.
- Albert Hawkins: deceased
- James Grisham: deceased

P.S. 46 CLASSMATES
- Michele: deceased, 1999
- Reginald E. Gilliam, Jr. (Reggie, in Chapter 15): Sodexo, Senior Vice President, Government Affairs

Notes

CHAPTER 1: THE NUMBER TWO BUS
1. Bolton, Reginald Pelham, *Washington Heights, Manhattan, Its Eventful Past* (New York: Dyckman Institute, 1924), p. 102.

CHAPTER 2: HARLEM VISTA: AN ICE AGE BEAUTY
1. Raymo, Chet, *The Crust of the Earth An Armchair Traveler's Guide to the New Geology* (New York: Prentice Hall Press, 1983), p 51.

CHAPTER 3: SIDEWALKS OF NEW YORK
1. Conversation with Ellen Jamieson at the National American Indian Museum, 2003.
2. Fairservis, Walter A. Jr., "Relocating the Indian Museum will be a Breach of All Trusts," *The New York Times*, Letter to the Editor, p. 32., 24, Feb. 1989.

CHAPTER 4: ON BEING RICH
1. Conversation with Paul Glassman, Director of the Morris-Jumel Museum, 1995.
2. Morris-Jumel Museum Visitor's Brochure.

CHAPTER 5: THE WAY IT WAS
1. www.NYLandmarks.org/programs_services/grants/city_ventures_fund/projects/345_edgecombe_avenue
2. Gray, Christopher, "1888 Mansion built by the Bailey of Barnum & Bailey," *The New York Times*, p. 7., 8, Apr. 2001.
3. Chernow, Ron, *Alexander Hamilton* (New York: The Penguin Press, 2004), p. 245.
4. Kennedy, Roger, G., *Burr, Hamilton, Jefferson A Study in Character* (Oxford University Press, 1999), p. 101.
5. Ibid, p. 102.
6. Ibid. p. 103.

CHAPTER 7: THE NUMBERS GAME AND TWELVE PLANETS
1. Konje, Uriah, Prof., *The H.P. Dream Book* (West Hempstead, NY: Parris Co., Inc., 1980), p. 88.
2. Ibid.

CHAPTER 8: ABOUT GOOD OL' BOYS, BIBLE THUMPERS, CHARLATANS AND NUNS

1. Lehmann-Haupt, Christopher, "Reverend Ike, Who Preached Riches, Dies at 74," www.nytimes.com/2009/07/30/nyregion/30ike.html

CHAPTER 9: THE CORNER

1. Conversation with Mr. Harold Thomas, 1996.

CHAPTER 11: A SPORTY KIND OF GUY

1. Schiffman, Jack, *A Pictorial History of Modern Black Show Business and the Apollo Theater* (Buffalo: Prometheus Books, 1984), p. 164.

CHAPTER 12: AN AMERICAN ORIGINAL

1. Undated clipping, *Norfolk Journal and Guide*.
2. de la Baume, MAIA, "A Feast of Innards Nourishes French Nostalgia," *The New York Times*, p. A6, 27, Oct. 2010.

CHAPTER 15: SIDDINESS AND BLACK SOCIETY

1. Anderson, Jervis, *This Was Harlem A Cultural Portrait 1900-1950* (New York: The Noonday Press, Farrar Straus Giroux, 1981), p. 139.
2. Ibid. p. 136.
3. Dolkart, Andrew and Sorin, Gretchen S., *Touring Historic Harlem Four Walks in Northern Manhattan* (New York Landmarks Conservancy, 1997), p. 89.

CHAPTER 16: NEW LINCOLN SCHOOL

1. Wolff, Tom, *Bonfire of the Vanities*, (New York: Bantam Books, 1987) p. 143.
2. Conversation with Verne Oliver, 1997.
3. Loesser, Susan, *A Most Remarkable Fella, Frank Loesser and the Guys and Dolls in His Life* (New York: Donald I. Fine, Inc. 1993), p. 231.
4. Halberstam, David, *The Fifties* (New York: Villard Books, 1993), p. 688.
5. Ibid. p. 689.
6. Branch, Taylor, *Parting the Waters in the King Years 1954-63* (New York: Simon and Schuster, 1988), p.123.
7. Ibid.
8. Conversation with Mrs. Oliver, 1997.

TERRY BAKER MULLIGAN

Terry Baker Mulligan was born and raised on Sugar Hill, in Harlem. Her short non-fiction work on the Sugar Hill area of Harlem (penned under the name Theresa Baker Mulligan) has received an award from the Heartland Writers Guild and was published in *Labor History*. She is married, has two grown sons and now lives in St. Louis, Missouri. This is her first book.

Acknowledgements

A wise person once said it takes a village to raise a child and without the inspiration of my dear Edgecombe Avenue friends, neighbors and my beloved family, many of whom have passed on, this book would not be possible. I will forever be thankful to them.

I'm especially grateful to Jackie Beverly for keeping me informed about our old friends and Jim Cummins for his enthusiasm, technical advice and wonderful photographs. Suzanne O'Keefe has consistently provided reference materials and architectural updates on Harlem and New York City, and Jackie Fischer, my New Lincoln classmate, generously opens her home to me. Mike Kelly reconnected just at the right time, and towards the end of the process, Sue Sylvia designed the book and Patrick Berzinski at Tranquility49.com provided invaluable media guidance.

Over the years, my friend and teacher, Rick Skwiot, not only urged me to not give up on the book, he provided sound advice after reading the manuscript.

I'm grateful to those who read and offered suggestions: Phyllis Bernstein, Juanita Jahn, Lyna Colombo, Peggy Crowe, CeCe Luecking, Colette Walsh, Kathi Crane, Joan Girard, Diana Drisko, Kathy Ratino, Zita Casey, Jackie Fisher, Charles Jones, Susan Gilbert and Steve Coleman. Judy Deutsch read, passed along resources and cheered me on. Thank you, Susan Loesser, for reading and editing an early version of the manuscript and Cheryl Whelan for doing likewise with a later copy.

As always, thank you Mike, Brennan, Colin and Houston for your love and support.

Index